T0330319

# Critical Perspectives on Leadership

NEW HORIZONS IN LEADERSHIP STUDIES

**Series Editor:** Joanne B. Ciulla, *Professor and Coston Family Chair in Leadership and Ethics, Jepson School of Leadership Studies, University of Richmond, USA*

This important series is designed to make a significant contribution to the development of leadership studies. This field has expanded dramatically in recent years and the series provides an invaluable forum for the publication of high quality works of scholarship and shows the diversity of leadership issues and practices around the world.

The main emphasis of the series is on the development and application of new and original ideas in leadership studies. It pays particular attention to leadership in business, economics and public policy and incorporates the wide range of disciplines which are now part of the field. Global in its approach, it includes some of the best theoretical and empirical work with contributions to fundamental principles, rigorous evaluations of existing concepts and competing theories, historical surveys and future visions.

Titles in the series include:

# Critical Perspectives on Leadership

Emotion, Toxicity, and Dysfunction

*Edited by*

Jeanette Lemmergaard

*Associate Professor of Human Resource Management and Internal Communication, Department of Marketing and Management, University of Southern Denmark*

Sara Louise Muhr

*Associate Professor of Organization Studies and Human Resource Management, Department of Organization, Copenhagen Business School, Denmark*

NEW HORIZONS IN LEADERSHIP STUDIES

**Edward Elgar**

Cheltenham, UK • Northampton, MA, USA

Published by
Edward Elgar Publishing Limited
The Lypiatts
15 Lansdown Road
Cheltenham
Glos GL50 2JA
UK

Edward Elgar Publishing, Inc.
William Pratt House
9 Dewey Court
Northampton
Massachusetts 01060
USA

A catalogue record for this book
is available from the British Library

Library of Congress Control Number: 2012955459

This book is available electronically in the ElgarOnline.com Business Subject Collection, E-ISBN 978 0 85793 113 9

ISBN 978 0 85793 112 2

Typeset by Columns Design XML Ltd, Reading
Printed and bound in Great Britain by T.J. International Ltd, Padstow

*To Josephine and Andreas*

*To Noël and Mathias*

# Contents

# Contributors

**Mats Alvesson** is a Professor of Business Administration at the University of Lund, Sweden and at the University of Queensland Business School, Australia. Research interests include critical theory, gender, power, management of professional service (knowledge intensive) organizations, leadership, identity, organizational image, organizational culture and symbolism, qualitative methods and philosophy of science. Recent books include *The Triumph of Emptiness* (Oxford University Press 2013), *Qualitative Research and Theory Development* (Sage 2011, with Dan Kärreman), *Constructing Research Questions* (Sage 2013, with J. Sandberg), *Interpreting Interviews* (Sage 2011), *Metaphors We Lead By: Understanding Leadership in the Real World* (Routledge 2011, edited with Andre Spicer), *Oxford Handbook of Critical Management Studies* (Oxford University Press, edited with Todd Bridgman and Hugh Willmott), *Understanding Gender and Organizations* (Sage 2009, 2nd edition with Yvonne Due Billing) and *Reflexive Methodology* (Sage 2009, 2nd edition, with Kaj Skoldberg).

**Yvonne Due Billing** works at the Department of Sociology, University of Copenhagen, Denmark and is Visiting Professor at the Department of Sociology, Lund University, Sweden. Billing holds a PhD in Sociology from University of Lund, Sweden, and a PhD in Business Administration from Copenhagen Business School, Denmark. She is associate editor of the journal *Gender, Work & Organization*, and an editorial member of the journals *Leadership* and *Organization*. Her research interests include gender, organizational cultures, leadership, power, identity and ethics. She is author of *Understanding Gender and Organizations* (Sage 2000, 2nd edition, with Mats Alvesson) and *Gender, Managers and Organizations* (de Gruyter 1994, with Mats Alvesson). Billing's work has been published in journals such as *Gender, Work & Organization*; *Organization Studies* and *Scandinavian Journal of Management*.

**Nathan Harter** had been practising law for several years when Purdue University, in Indiana, US, hired him to teach Organizational Leadership for its College of Technology. Twenty-two years later, after being tenured and eventually promoted to full Professor, he joined the Department of

Leadership and American Studies at Christopher Newport University, in Newport News, VA, where he also serves as Director of Interdisciplinary Studies. A former chair of the scholarship section of the International Leadership Association, Harter published *Clearings in the Forest*, which was named in Jackson and Parry (2011) as one of the ten books on leadership you should read before you die.

**Clare Howard** is a change and talent development consultant, trainer and performance coach with over 20 years' experience helping senior management, teams and individuals improve cross-cultural communications and their effectiveness to deliver required business results. With an expert understanding of corporate teams and political dynamics, she has worked with top organizations across Europe and globally to help them implement strategic plans for cross-cultural communications, talent development, change leadership, leadership skills, self-managed development, and organization-wide training programmes. She is President of London Type – a special interest group for those interested in furthering their understanding and the application of Jungian Type theory. She is the representative of the British Association of Psychological Type (BAPT) to the European Association of Psychological Type (EAPT). She is the special interest coordinator for Learning and Development for BAPT. She is a regular writer and speaker on issues relating to type and organizational development.

**Emma L. Jeanes** works at the University of Exeter, UK, and is affiliated to Lund University, Sweden. Emma's research explores experiences of work, focusing on gender, family cultures and the distinctions between work and life 'outside', the intersection of organizations and activism/ethics, and ethics in research and within the research community. Her research draws on philosophy and sociology and is empirically grounded. Jeanes edited the *Wiley Handbook of Gender, Work and Organization* (2011) with D. Knights and P.Y. Martin, *Men, Wage Work and Family* (Routledge, 2012) with P. McDonald, and is currently editing *Reflections from the Field* (Sage, forthcoming 2013) with T. Huzzard.

**Jeanette Lemmergaard** is Associate Professor of Human Resource Management and Internal Communication in the Department of Marketing and Management at the University of Southern Denmark in Odense. Her empirically grounded research explores experiences of work, focusing on the psychological and ethical climate of organizations at a micro-level, and at a macro-level focusing on strategic human resource management, dysfunctional leadership, diversity and corporate social responsibility (CSR). In 2011, Lemmergaard was in collaboration with

Sara Louise Muhr, guest editor on *European Journal of International Management*, with the special issue; 'Everybody hurts, sometimes: emotions and dysfunctional leadership'. Her work has appeared in journals such as *Scandinavian Journal of Management*, *Journal of Business Ethics*, *Organization*, *Service Industry Journal* and *Team Performance Management*. She is a frequent speaker at conferences and events.

**Sara Louise Muhr** works as an Associate Professor at Copenhagen Business School and is affiliated with Lund University, Sweden, as Docent. Her research focuses on critical perspectives on managerial identity and HRM, especially in relation to issues around coping with diversity and expectations in modern, flexible ways of working. Following this broader aim she has worked with various empirical settings such as management consultancy, prisons, pole dance studios and executive networks where she has engaged with issues such as emotional labour, gender, ethnicity, leadership and work–life balance. In 2011, Muhr collaborated with Jeanette Lemmergaard as guest editor on *European Journal of International Management* with the special issue; 'Everybody hurts, sometimes: emotions and dysfunctional leadership'. Her work has appeared in journals such as *Organization*, *Journal of Business Ethics*, *Scandinavian Journal of Management* and *Gender, Work & Organization*.

**Alexander Paulsson** is a doctoral candidate at the School of Economics and Management at Lund University, Sweden. His current research interests concern issues such as the political and economical relations within and beyond the organization, the hierarchical organization of human and animal relations, and the ontology of projects. His work has been published in ephemera and his dissertation is due to be published in 2013.

**Alf Rehn** is Chair of Management and Organization at Åbo Akademi University, Finland. His research has dealt with subjects as varied as creativity, haute cuisine, project management, popular culture, philosophy, boredom, innovation and luxury, and has, despite this, published a series of books and a large number of articles. He is a devoted fan of Ethel Merman and the divine Patsy Cline.

**Stephan Schaefer** is a doctoral researcher at the School of Economics and Management, Department of Business Administration, Lund University, Sweden. His doctoral research project investigates tensions and coping mechanisms of software managers in their efforts to organize creativity. Other research interests include the performativity of critical research, the concept of absurdity in work organizations and existentialism/phenomenology. His work has been published in the *Academy of Management Best Paper Proceedings* and his doctoral thesis is due to be published in 2013.

**André Spicer** is Professor of Organizational Behaviour at Cass Business School, City University, London. He holds a PhD from the University of Melbourne. His research focuses on political dynamics in and around organizations. He has published a number of books including *Contesting the Corporation* (with Peter Fleming), *Unmasking the Entrepreneur* (with Campbell Jones), and *Metaphors We Lead By: Understanding Leadership in the Real World* (with Mats Alvesson).

**Sverre Spoelstra** is a researcher at the Department of Business Administration, Lund University, Sweden. His present research interests include leadership studies, theological motives in management knowledge, and discourses of relevance and excellence. He is a member of the editorial collective of ephemera.

**Michael Walton** is a chartered psychologist and Director of 'People in Organisations Ltd' a small bespoke UK consultancy working with top and senior executives on personal and organizational change. His primary interest is in examining the bases of executive success and failure and the apparent 'stupidities' of organizational life. In November 2011 he was appointed Visiting Senior Research Fellow in the Department of Defence Studies at King's College London for a year, and between 2004 and 2011 Walton was connected with the Centre for Leadership Studies at the University of Exeter Business School, UK where he worked with postgraduate students and undertook consulting assignments. He is a member of the Associate Faculty of the Ashridge Business School, UK.

# Preface

Emotions at work – in the forms of, for example, mood swings, tantrums, belittling of others and the stark exercise of power – is one of the fastest-growing areas of research within the fields of leadership and organizational behaviour and with good reasons. With increasing stress levels and strained relationships at work, the field of emotions deserves our serious academic attention (Ashkanasy and Cooper 2008; Rehn and Lindahl 2011). However, answering the question of how emotions influence leadership is a complex undertaking that cuts across multiple disciplines. Tackling this question – and the related question of how leadership toxicity and dysfunctionality influence organizational life and work – demands a broadening of perspective well beyond our own discipline of leadership.

Contributing to the field of critical leadership studies, the chapters contained in this volume set out to explore the relationship between leadership and emotions within organizations discussing leadership toxicity and dysfunctionality. The chapters in this volume question the general assumption that rationality's antithesis per excellence is emotionality. We recognize emotionality as being ever-present and a critical dimension of organizational life just as rationality is – still – the hallmark of mainstream organizational discourse. Moreover, the volume takes the discussion of leadership emotions even further and discusses critically how toxicity and dysfunctionality are not simply negatively coercive or repressive connotations, but also potentially productive and enable connotations. Emotions can, as the chapters here demonstrate, both be seen as interference and as nurture of organizational life. As this volume sets out to explore, issues of rationality-emotionality are not dichotomies akin to good–bad for organizations just as well as toxicity and dysfunctionality are not exceptional 'bad apples', but rather institutionalized rules or manifestations of systemic functions.

This volume provides an entry point to work from a variety of perspectives and across a range of topics, sub-disciplines and themes. The volume is divided into three parts. Part I of this volume opens with an overview of traditional leadership thinking related to the topic of emotions by Jeanette Lemmergaard and Sara Louise Muhr. The opening chapter demonstrates how the complex dynamics of leaders' – and followers' – emotions make it impossible to distinguish between functional and dysfunctional emotional behaviour and between non-toxic and toxic behaviour. This chapter demonstrates the need for more nuanced theory and research which recognizes that leadership is mediated and shaped by emotions and it challenges current theorists, researchers and practitioners to develop more complex awareness about leadership. By critically exploring the dichotomy of emotionality-rationality, this chapter seeks to make an innovative and nuanced contribution to our understanding of leadership.

Part II, which follows the critical overview of the leadership theory in Part I, consists of five empirically based chapters critically exploring the grey zones of emotions, toxicity and dysfunction in leadership. The events and characters depicted in part two are unique, however, not uncommon. Each of the case studies represents positive as well as negative encounters of leadership principles and behaviours. They exhibit what characterizes the leaders as people; their personalities and their strengths and foibles in a decisive, evaluative and forceful manner. While the depth of the cases is important, they will all exhibit strong theoretical ties to the critical literature on leadership, emotion, toxicity and dysfunction laid out in Chapter 1.

The volume completes with a collection of theoretical reflections in Part III, which takes the introductory chapter and the case-based chapters in Part II as a reference point. These critical reflections all explore different phenomena – ignorance, authenticity, functional stupidity and vanity – and knit together the topics of leadership and emotion and open into further agendas of thinking and investigation. In these chapters the contributing authors philosophize in a pervasive and self-rectifying way, which question and provoke many of the mainstream debates we currently witness in leadership studies.

It is our hope that the book in its entirety will point to the future of leadership with particular emphasis on how best to advance the arguments, methods and effectiveness of leadership recognizing the mere fact that leaders are normal human beings with both ideal and flawed behaviours, habits and emotions. Recognizing that leaders, whom we expect to 'be themselves' and express personality authentically in all their uniqueness and difference (Fleming 2009; Fleming and Sturdy 2009) will fascinate and attract some while intimidate and corral others (Muhr 2010; Muhr 2011). This volume presents a fascinating challenge to our common-sense perceptions and judgements of leaders; and by bringing the competing perspectives into direct confrontation, we hope to contribute to a better understanding of the pros and cons of both.

Before stepping into the fields of leadership and emotions, we would like to give a tremendous thank you to all contributing authors for their enthusiastic support and dedication to providing new perspectives to the study of emotion and leadership. We feel privileged to have worked with such an outstanding group of co-authors, and we owe each a debt of gratitude. Without their efforts, dedication and insights to the field, this book would not have materialized. The quality of the book reflects their efforts and is to their credit. We are also grateful to all the staff at Edward Elgar Publishing, especially Francine O'Sullivan and Jennifer Wilcox, who have worked indefatigably to bring this book to completion. Their assistance and patience has been invaluable and much appreciated.

**Jeanette Lemmergaard** and **Sara Louise Muhr**
November 2012

# REFERENCES

Ashkanasy, N.M. and C.L. Cooper (2008), *Research Companion to Emotions in Organizations*, Cheltenham, UK, and Northampton, MA, USA: Edward Elgar.

Fleming, P. (2009), *Authenticity and the Cultural Politics of Work: New Forms of Informal Control*, Oxford: Oxford University Press.

Fleming, P. and A. Sturdy (2009), 'Just be yourself – towards neonormative control in organizations?', *Employee Relations*, 31 (6), 569–83.

Muhr, S.L. (2010), 'Leaders as cyborgs: leadership through mechanistic superiority', in M. Alvesson and A. Spicer (eds), *Metaphors We Lead By: Understanding Leadership in the Real World*, London: Routledge, pp. 138–61.

Muhr, S.L. (2011), 'Caught in the gendered machine: on the masculine and feminine in cyborg leadership', *Gender, Work and Organization*, 18 (3), 337–57.

Rehn, A. and M. Lindahl (2011), 'Leadership and the 'right to respect' – on honour and shame in emotionally charged management settings', *European Journal of International Management*, 5 (1), 62–79.

# PART I

# Leadership moments

I say there is no darkness but ignorance.
William Shakespeare

# 1. Broadening the critical leadership repertoire: emotions, toxicity and dysfunctionality

## Jeanette Lemmergaard and Sara Louise Muhr

### INTRODUCTION

The conventional literature on leadership and emotions is complex and multifaceted, focusing on norms and techniques, correct–incorrect and/or desirable–undesirable (see Lemmergaard and Muhr 2011). The underlying assumption is that leadership is a self-evident force for good that represents an (imperfectly) rational instrument for achieving shared goals. We challenge this mainstream understanding of leadership by focusing primarily on leadership toxicity and dysfuntionality, however recognizing that leaders' emotions are contagious and create affective events (Brief and Weiss 2002; Lockyer and McCabe 2011) that trigger both positive and negative emotional reactions. Since leaders socially constitute and construct emotional boundaries of appropriate emotional display, they also strongly influence the way employees interpret and respond emotionally to a given situation (Rehn and Lindahl 2011). It is traditionally assumed as a given fact that employees watch the leaders and take their emotional quest from the leaders. We do not question this assumption per se, but argue that the dilemma raised by this assumption is far more complex. We argue that behind the face of efficiency, equity and humanity – which surrounds formal organizations – lie distinct concentrations of emotions, which cannot be understood as specific understandings of toxic–nontoxic or functional–dysfunctional. Not only is it restrictive to rely on the traditional distinction between good and bad, also the leader–subordinate relationship is far more complex than is depictured in the traditional literature on leadership (for example, Cluley 2008). Not only do the leaders' emotions rub off on the employees, also the opposite occurs as employees' emotions rub off on the leaders. We therefore question the understanding that leaders by for example recognizing employees can increase excitement and pride (Dasborough 2006; Grandey et al. 2002), and by mishandling employee discipline automatically foster strong negative emotions (Ball et al. 1992). Instead we argue that emotions are mostly overlapping and difficult – sometimes even impossible – to distinguish from one another. Supposedly toxic and dysfunctional as well as assumed non-toxic and functional emotions can be positive as well as negative, and can be creative as well as repressive (Lemmergaard and Muhr 2011).

Throughout this introductory chapter we draw on these perspectives in constructing a basic understanding of the field of leadership and emotions. Before, however, going into a critical discussion, the traditional literature of leadership, emotions, toxicity and dysfunctionality will be reviewed individually. The aim of this general overview is to provide an outline of the development and basic ideas of emotions, toxicity and dysfunctionality with regard to leadership. This is important as it provides the context to which our critical approach is responding. With this overview we also offer a collection of comparatively accessible points of entry to non-specialists and practitioners as well as academics. Realizing this objective requires a focus on the concepts such as broad-ranging intellectual movements and practices geared to developing a better understanding of the broader framework. After the critical lens and the closing remarks that draws the analyses together and discusses their implications and limitations, the chapter closes with an introduction of the three parts of the book.

## TRADITIONAL LEADERSHIP THINKING

The amount of theory and empirical studies relevant to the practice of leadership is impressive. Theories like the 'great man' theory (Carlyle 1841) and trait or quality theories (for example, McCall and Lombardo 1983) have focused on the behaviour and qualities of successful leaders. Later theories like the participative theory (Wright 1996) and the relationship theory (Turnley et al. 2003) have given more importance to followers. Recently, scholars have employed a variety of terms to describe new kinds of leadership (for example, charismatic leadership, visionary leadership and distributed leadership), which appear to be accompanied by an acceptance of the distinction between transactional and transformational leadership, with an emphasis on the latter (Meindl 1990). Yet, a different line of research on leadership has explored the ideal image of the heroic and charismatic leader and discussed this as an instinct provoked by crisis situations (Muhr and Lemmergaard 2009).

It is incontestable that the concept of leadership has been studied from a number of different approaches. Yet, most of these approaches and theories tend to favour the positive over the negative (Heller et al. 1988; Miller and Monge 1986). Over the past decade, however, research on the darker side of leadership in organizations has emerged. Research on derailed, incompetent, toxic, tyrannical or failed leaders is about not only the pathology of individuals but also about how leaders hypnotize followers and abuse situations to bring about chaos (Furnham 2010). This avenue of leadership research has mainly focused on capturing the 'other side' of leadership.

## A Plethora of Typologies and Conceptualizations

The concept of leadership has a long history in research in psychology and organizational behaviour. The key issue in this research has mainly been the question of what set of qualities constitutes a great (effective) leader and what makes leaders effective in influencing and mobilizing followers so as to achieve high levels of performance and goal attainment. This discussion is almost as old as recorded history and can be found in the Greek and Latin classics, the Old and New Testaments of the Bible, the writings of the ancient Chinese philosophers and in the early Icelandic Sagas (Bass 1990). The number of theories explaining the personality traits and behaviours distinguishing 'effective' from 'ineffective' leaders and 'leaders' from 'non-leaders' are rather small compared to the number of empirical studies concerned with these issues.

Carlyle (1841) being considered the father of the 'great man' theory has also been regarded as one of the pioneers of the 'trait' theory, using a trait approach to identify the talents, skills and physical characteristics of powerful male (as opposed to female) leaders. The main aim of these theories has been to detect the defining characteristics of great leaders building on the implicit belief that leaders are born rather than made. Surveys of early trait research by Stogdill (1948) and Mann (1959) reported that many studies identified personality characteristics that appear to differentiate leaders from followers according to for example age, height, weight, appearance, intelligence and social skills. However, as Wright (1996, p. 34) has commented, 'others found no differences between leaders and followers with respect to these characteristics, or even found people who possessed them were less likely to become leaders'.

The trait theories are not definitive and there is rarely solid empirical evidence in support of each as the findings are seldom replicated in multiple studies (House and Aditya 1997). This has led to scepticism about personality and leadership, not least following Stodgill's (1950) authoritative review. Even then Stodgill concluded that 'leadership is not a matter of passive status or of the mere possession of some combinations of traits' (p. 66). Combined with the growing number of inconsistent findings regarding which skills, competences and other special qualities make great leaders, this has led to the conclusion that leaders are not fundamentally different from followers (Fineman 2000). Leaders are people like the rest of us, human beings with fears and desires.

The simplicity of the trait theory has for a large part reduced its attractiveness for scholars. For approximately 50 years following Stodgill's review, situational theories of leadership dominated the field. In recent years, however, a revival of trait-based views of leadership has re-emerged leading to interesting findings with regard to the relations between personality characteristics and leadership perceptions, leadership emergence, leadership effectiveness and overall job success of leaders (House and Aditya 1997; Judge et al. 2002).

As the early researchers ran out of steam in their search for traits, they turned to what leaders did and how they behaved (especially towards followers). They moved from leaders to leadership – and this became the dominant way of approaching leadership within organizations in the 1950s and early 1960s. More recently, a study by Morgan et al. (2005) concluded that supportive coaching by leaders and leader preparedness were positively associated with followers' perceptions concerning leader effectiveness. From an LMX (such as leader–member exchange) perspective, research indicates that factors such as followers' levels of effort and their attitudes toward their job and their leader can promote functional leadership behaviours that help foster high quality relationships (for example, Dienesch and Liden 1986). Similarly, Paul et al. (2002) highlight the role of followers' attitudes and Harvey et al. (2006) developed a conceptual model predicting the influence of biased causal explanations for follower behaviours and outcomes on a leader's functionality and the quality of leader–follower relationships.

Situational leadership theories followed the research on leaders' behaviours. In the period between the trait approach and the new leadership approach, leadership researchers focused on leadership style and how a given leadership style is contingent on the situation, implying that certain leadership behaviours will be effective in some situations but not in others. This theory grew out of impatience with classical management approaches, which seemed to prescribe universal solutions to all leadership problems, irrespective of different local circumstances. One of the more well-known thinkers within contingency leadership research is Fiedler (1967) who developed the controversial and often debated least preferred co-worker scale, which purports to measure the leadership orientation of the person completing it. Within this line of thought, Fiedler (1967) predicted sets of leadership styles, which are most likely to prove effective in different contexts. Hersey and Blanchard's (1999) situational leadership theory is another well-known theory taking the context into consideration. In 1986, Lord et al. identified factors (such as, for example, fit between leader behaviours and situational norms) that can promote leadership behaviours that are perceived as being functional by followers.

Yet a different line of leadership theory is linked to Burns' (1978) argument that it is possible to distinguish between transactional and transformational leaders. Whereas transactional leadership is based on exchange, transformational leadership is based on leaders' awareness of followers' needs. According to Bass (1985), transformational leaders inspire ideal and emotional influence. Their assumed inspirational vision, values and norms transform their followers always keeping the focus on consideration for the individual and always paying attention to the intellectual stimulation of the followers. Transformational leadership hereby contrasts transactional leadership, which includes contingent reward, management-by-exception, negative feedback and contingent aversive reinforcement. Transformational leaders are argued to have a considerable influence on organizations; although, these influences are not automatically considered valuable (Conger 1990; Yukl 1998).

Participative leadership, defined as joint decision-making or at least shared influence in decision-making by a superior and his or her followers (Wagner and Gooding 1987), is still a central theme within leadership research. This approach to leadership is often categorized under the label 'new leadership approaches' which from the early 1980s and onwards has described and categorized a number of approaches to leadership that seemed to exhibit common or at least similar themes, although they are undoubtedly different (Bryman 1992). Examples of dynamic leadership approaches can be found in Alvesson and Spicer (2010b) and Hatch et al. (2005) who emphasize leadership as metaphors. Most recently, focus has been on post-charismatic and post-transformational leadership including for example spirituality of leadership and the art of leadership (Chakraborty and Chakraborty 2004; Fry and Kriger 2009). The movement away from the behaviours and styles of leadership has led to an interest in the spirituality of leadership, including a theological angle to the discussion (Dunne and Spoelstra 2010; Hicks 2002).

## The Ideal Leader of the 21st Century

Irrespectively of approach, conventional leadership theories and models generally assume that cause-and-effect relationships among key variables can be identified. Hereby it is assumed that it is possible to increase desired outcomes by manipulating the causes associated with the outcomes (Van Fleet and Griffin 2006) and consequently, leaders can create the 'right' employee behaviour. Moreover, the conventional literature generally expects, albeit idealistically, that leaders will do the right thing. The hype about transformational leadership has built upon the assumption that transformational leaders are able to motivate and inspire followers to perform beyond expectations (Bass 1985). Ideally, leaders are expected to act honourably, in accordance with organizational and institutional values as well as acting ethically. They are said to excite, arouse and inspire their followers acting as role models and as communicators of a vision or a mission. Their consideration is for the individual and for intellectual stimulation. Hereby, followers are coached and are mentored to achieve their fullest potential (Yammerion and Bass 1990) and stimulated to rethink (Bass and Avolio 1990).

Judging from the popular press as well as leading mainstream business writers, a consensus seems to be growing that the ideal leader of the 21st century is supposed to integrate all the necessary followers and know how to build a team while making themselves dispensable (Bass and Steidlmeier 1999; Storey 2004). They know how to lead a diverse workforce, possess strategic skills, have a learning focus as well as an international orientation. They offer constructive criticism when things go wrong. They resolve conflicts diplomatically and they respect followers' expectations and ambitions. In addition, ideal leaders are expected to be passionate about their jobs. They are supposed to show emotional commitment and devotion and are expected to involve their personal lives in the organization, thereby integrating their own 'selves' into the life of the organization (Alvesson and Spicer 2010b). They are one with the organization; a symbol of its being.

However, this scenario is problematic as such leaders are mostly mythical creatures (Gemmill and Oakley 1992) creating a corporate cultism around them (Tourish and Pinnington 2002). In reality most leaders gain their position due to technical expertise rather than an ability to develop human resources (Sveningsson and Larsson 2006), and consequently tend to be strong in operational and technical skills, but less so with regard to people and relation-building skills (Muhr 2010). In-depth empirical studies of leaders have in fact shown that leadership often disappears in much more mundane activities such as listening and chatting (Alvesson and Sveningsson 2003a, 2003b). Moreover, leaders' performance tends to be measured on a cost-efficiency basis, and when pursuing functional objectives, leaders can often be dysfunctional for the well-being of those who are charged with delivering this functionality. Leaders' incompetence manifests itself in various ways, such as indecisiveness and over-controlling behaviour or an overriding concern for production and efficiency at the expense of the human resources (Muhr 2010; Spicer 2010). As such, opinions on leadership and leaders are thus often constructed on the basis of diverse rather than shared meanings. Moreover, many 'successful' leaders may have psychopathic, narcissistic and histrionic personality disorders (Kets de Vries 1985; Rosenthal and Pittinsky 2006), which, although such disorders may sometimes help leaders in climbing the ladder of success, eventually will result in a dysfunctional workplace for others (Maccoby 2004; Padilla et al. 2007; Pullen and Rhodes 2008; Rosenthal and Pittinsky 2006).

Leaders make mistakes, their actions have different consequences to those that were intended, and sometimes they do not act at all. The behaviours and attitudes of leaders are often a main source of pain in organizations, not least because there is no such thing as unambiguous intentions, styles or acts in everyday life. Leadership is difficult and leaders are often caught in ambiguities, confusion and incoherencies (Sveningsson and Alvesson 2003). Even competent leaders have their 'off days', and otherwise competent leaders ascribe different meanings to specific behaviours and communicate both mixed and incoherent messages (Alvesson and Spicer 2010b). Alternatively as expressed by Whicker (1996, p. 17) 'leaders are regarded as the source of all good, and the root of all evil'. Leaders (and followers) invariably experience highs and lows in their emotional states on a day-to-day and moment-by-moment basis which brings about non-toxic as well as toxic and functional as well as dysfunctional leadership. If, however, we want to understand and explain why and how emotions, toxicity and dysfunctionality influence leadership and exert the effects that they do, then we must also understand the concepts of emotions, toxicity and dysfunctionality. Those concepts will now be introduced and discussed in relation to leadership.

# LEADERSHIP EMOTIONS

Practitioners and mainstream researchers have now recognized that emotions do not simply switch off when organizational members enter the organization; emotions tick, quietly signalling how things are and how we are doing – and what we want to do next (Fineman 2000). In this way, organizations are emotional arenas where emotions shape events, and events shape emotions (Fineman 2007). The study of emotions in organizations stems from the acknowledgement that our experience of work is often essentially about moods and emotions, such as of joy, pride, fear, anger, guilt, embarrassment, compassion and love (Bramming and Johnsen 2011; Lockyer and McCabe 2011; Rehn and Lindahl 2011). Emotions are central to just about everything humans do and as such emotions inject meaning into working moments – positive, negative, mixed, conflicting or ambivalent.

Practitioners as well as organizational researchers have historically ignored the complexity of emotions, particularly in organizational contexts, and organizational members have been pictured as cognitive stick figures whose behaviour is unaffected by emotions (Mowday and Sutton 1993). However, Hochschild's (1983) book *The Managed Heart* seems to have initiated the more recent interest in emotions at work by suggesting that some employees are required to manage emotions as part of their work role. This 'emotional labour' – being employed to smile, enthuse, be sincere – is in the mainstream literature believed to be an onerous, identity-disturbing form of role playing (Hochschild 1983; Wouters 1989). Others argue that this organizational control of emotional performance can be seen to be relatively benign, even fun. The enthusiasm, smile, and 'have a nice day' can be split off from private emotions – in order to sustain the organizational act or social game. Others, mostly from a social psychological and work psychology angle, have revealed a great deal about specific workplace emotions, including frustration (Fox and Spector 1999), anger (Fitness 2000), love (Bramming and Johnsen 2011), shame (Rehn and Lindahl 2011) and toxicity (Frost 2003). Generally speaking, from the mid-1990s, researchers gave emotions in organizations new life emphasizing that the employees are the very centre of organizations and revealing that emotions are the prime medium through which organizational members act and interact. While this might seem obvious, research has focused not on emotions per se but more on attitudes towards work, such as for example job satisfaction, or extreme negative states related to impaired performance such as, for example, occupational stress, strong internal competition and time pressure. A comprehensible introduction to these areas can be found in Fineman (2000, 2007), whereas more in-depth discussions on emotions and their effects in the workplace are covered by, for example, Ashforth and Humphrey (1995) and by Ashkanasy and Cooper (2008). However, despite an increasing interest there is still much to learn and extract from those on the front lines to uncover the complicated nature of emotions in organizations, not least from a critical perspective.

## Moods, Feelings and Emotions are Distinct Phenomena

We commonly talk about emotions, feelings and moods interchangeably, and although there is no strong consensus on the definitions of the terms, some useful distinctions can be drawn as the three concepts represent distinct phenomena. Moods are not as specific as emotions and they are not linked to any particular object or event. Moods, which are often hard to disguise, are either positive or negative, and moods both linger and undulate gradually over time. The cause or trigger is often obscure and can be created by stimuli of relatively low intensity, or can be left behind by emotions that fade so that the initial antecedent is no longer salient (Cropanzano and Mitchell 2005; Elfenbein 2007). You may wake up in a particular mood – lethargic, pleasant, irritated, annoyed, excited or distressed – without knowing why you feel that way. A feeling is essentially a subjective, private experience. It is a personal awareness of some bodily state, which can change on personal reflection, discussion and through argument. Some work-related feelings have a special status, a flow-related experience where the self is absorbed – such as getting 'lost' in one's work. What is felt is subjective elements of emotions such as for example fear, sadness, compassion, or joy, whereas what is shown is the displayed feature of emotions (Fineman 2007). Emotion episodes and private feeling do not always correspond – one can act angry without feeling angry. With dramatic skill, emotion display can be used strategically or politically in organizations to attract attention or influence decisions or relationships. This line of self-presentation thinking – also called impression management – has increasingly been recognized as an explanatory model for a broad range of organizational phenomena.

Emotions are responses to identified causes or targets arising from the interaction of events. As such emotions are also believed to be situationally or normatively defined. The correct or appropriate emotional displays are social constitutions that often have been tacitly negotiated. However, emotion generation is not only based on stimuli from the outside world, it is also heavily intertwined with the disposition of the individual which enables motivational, behavioural, physiological and (sub)consciously felt response components (Frijda 2006). Denzin (1983) forwards the idea of emotion as self-feeling and defines emotions as temporally embodied self-feelings which arise from emotional social acts people direct to themselves or have directed towards them by others (p. 404). This definition stresses the symbolic interaction tradition where social interaction with others provides the self with a context that is required to experience emotion. Hereby, the significance of society and culture for understanding emotions is emphasized. Collins (1990) extends the definition of emotions arguing for emotion also being important for societal cohesion. He holds that society is held together by values, which are cognitions infused with emotions. Emotions are immediate reactions to specific targets or events (Ortony et al. 1988) based on a pleasure-pain valence scale (Elster 1998). But in understanding emotional reactions it is important to note that emotions are likely clouded by the potential conflict in our interpretations of the emotion-eliciting event and as such emotions are anything but single discrete reactions (Frijda 2006).

Traditionally, emotional processes have been deemphasized or even separated from cognitive thinking and it has been claimed that rationality in organizations is achievable if interfering emotions can be controlled or obliterated. Others, however, have suggested that optimal rationality is unattainable as emotions will unlock a problem or change the course of events. Emotions will steer us down some paths and guide us away from others. According to Darwin (1872) many of our emotional reactions are rooted in prehistoric patterns of survival, the genetic residue of which is still with us. These include dealing with sexual infidelity, fighting, falling in love, finding food and responding to the death of a family member. This primitive programming is believed to be part of our work settings and shapes the emphasis on hierarchies, male patterns of dominance, alliances and aggression (Nicholson 2000). For example rage is considered a powerful emotion that motivates '… animals of all kinds, and their progenitors before them, when attacked or threatened by an enemy' to fight and defend themselves (Darwin 1872, p. 74). Consistent with Darwin's evolutionary perspective, Freud's 'danger signal' theory emphasized the adaptive utility of anxiety for motivating behaviours that helped a person cope more effectively with potentially harmful situations (Freud 1933). Moreover, it was studied, for example, how anxiety, stemming from primitive, unconscious, vulnerability, is enacted in work-life and how anxiety hinders effective leadership and group processes. Here it is found that employees coping with anxiety produce protective individual and social defences that prevent rational thought and action (Kets de Vries 1985,1990). It is within this line of thinking that, for example, snarling which is believed to have developed from the action of biting, now simply shows displeasure.

According to Elfenbein (2007) five basic families of emotions exist; approach (for example, interest, hope and participation), achievement (for example, relief, satisfaction, contentment, pride and joy), deterrence (for example, anxiety, fear and distress), withdrawal (for example, sadness, shame and resignation), and antagonism (for example, irritation, anger and hate). But mostly what, how and why we feel at work is paved with a complex picture of ambivalence, or as expressed by Moore and Hope-Hailey (2004), 'emotions are messy' (p. 3). The complexity behind our emotional experience is rooted in our subjective sense-making and construction of reality. However, in an organizational context this messiness is often set aside by the persistent attempt to quantify and operationalize emotions as discrete phenomena or as Fineman (2004) concludes: many in organization studies seek to 'make inchoate tangible through quantification' (p. 721) while ignoring the subjective, interpretive nature of how we define emotions. Scholars such as, for example, Fong and Tiedens (2002) admit that the ambivalence of everyday work-life is underexplored and that identifying when and why emotional conflict is necessary to uncover what contributes to the specific type of ambivalence. As Weiss et al. (1999) argued, it is necessary to explore what meaning individuals attach to their ambivalence and its consequences for behaviour.

When not viewed as undesirable phenomena that should be prevented by institutionalizing norms of rationality, emotions have been viewed as outcomes of cognitive evaluation processes. Starting in the 1980s, however, the literature has experienced what could be called an affective exploration of both short-term fluctuation in affective states and stable individual differences in emotions at work (Fox and Spector 1999; George 1990; Weiss and Cropanzano 1996). An important part of this growth has been attention to specific emotions, as encouraged by authors like Lazarus and Cohen-Charash (2001) and the positive psychology movement (Fredrickson 2003).

Besides being biological, emotions can also be seen as social, whereby the focus is moved towards the cultural setting in which emotions are learned and expressed. Social learning is seen to transform, or overwrite, evolutionary impulses (Fineman 2007). The social rules of emotional display will vary according to the specific situation, and how the specific situation is interpreted by the individual person, who mostly will conform to conventional rules of emotional behaviour because of special, learned, social-control emotions. Interestingly, research shows that if we are persuaded to, for example, put on a happy face in a situation where happiness is expected then we may actually begin to feel happy (Fineman 2007). Barsade (2002) found that emotional reactions played a significant role in work–group dynamics, influencing not only group members' emotions but their individual cognitions, attitudes and behaviours as well. As such, emotions motivate behaviour and have a significant impact not only for the individual employee, but also for the organization at large. Emotions are not solely individual states of mind; emotions are also part of someone's social relational role, implying scripts and rules about how to feel and express emotions in relation to others, not least when performing the leadership role.

**Leaders' Emotions**

The very idea of leadership is imbued with emotion and is central to organizing processes. In most of the leadership literature, the primary role of leaders is to influence others to achieve group or organizational goals, and in this context respect for – or fear of – the leader is assumed to reduce the likelihood of chaos in the organization. Emotions spread through organizations by creating chains of events, such that organizational members who witness emotion-generated pro-social behaviours are likely to engage in pro-social acts themselves (Fredrickson 2003). In the traditional literature leadership is believed to bring with it special normative expectations about the importance of pursuing collective goals in a complex emotional web. Combined with the fact that leaders transfer emotions – both positive and negative – to followers (Bono and Ilies 2006; Cherulnik et al. 2001; Lewis 2000; Sy et al. 2005), leaders need both social and emotional competences in order to handle both their own and others' emotions and to drive these emotions in the right direction in accordance with the collective goals. This is particularly important as emotion-generated behaviours tend to produce similar emotional reactions in others (Hatfield et al. 1993). For example, when comparing negative events with positive events, Miner et al. (2005) found that the effect on employees' emotions was five times stronger for negative events, in spite of positive events occurring three to five times as often. In a similar vein, employees are better at recalling negative events and negative events have a greater impact than positive events (Dasborough 2006). Negative emotion is more likely to spill across the work–private boundary than positive (Williams and Alliger 1994) and co-workers converge more strongly in their negative versus positive emotions (Bartel and Saavedra 2000). Adding to this picture, the emotions of organizational leaders are more likely to produce similar reactions in others, as leaders in the conventional way of thinking are typically perceived as role models by other organizational members.

Functioning as role models, leaders' personal power is important. Whereas position power relates to the formal authority and is related to the position in the hierarchy, the personal power – based for example on expertise, friendship and loyalty – derives from the leader's relationship with others. Research (for example, Yukl and Falbe 1991) has shown that these two types of power are relatively independent. A leader's personal power and influence tactics are important when for example leaders act as toxic handlers (Frost and Robinson 1999) as they translate, soothe and absorb emotions. For example using inspirational appeals, the leader makes a request or proposes something that arouses the follower's interest and enthusiasm by appealing to his or her values, ideals and aspirations or by increasing the followers' self-confidence. A leader might alternatively use the influence tactic of ingratiation whereby the leader uses flattery, praise or friendly behaviour to put the follower in a good mood or think favourably of the leader before making a request. Alternatively a leader can use personal appeals to the follower's feelings of friendship and loyalty when asking for something. Yukl and Falbe (1991) identified nine proactive tactics, which besides inspirational, ingratiation and personal appeals included pressure, exchange, coalition, legitimating, rational persuasion and consultation appeals. These tactics are of course not only used by leaders when trying to influence subordinates, they are also used to influence peers. Performing the leadership role therefore implies constraints with regard to the emotional mask. Not only do leaders transfer emotions – both positive and negative – to followers, if the emotional mask slips, the leadership encounter is threatened.

## TOXICITY AND DYSFUNCTIONALITY

Inspired by the media's focus on what seemed to be an 'epidemic' of workplace violence and aggression, researchers seem to have renewed the interest in organizational toxicity and dysfunctionality (Lindgren et al. 2011; von Groddeck 2011). Following the thoughts of the classical organizational theorists like Cyert and March (1963) and Katz and Kahn (1978), toxicity and dysfunctionality are simply normal by-products of organizational life that can have serious negative effects on individuals and their organizations. Organizational members are simply from time-to-time prone to act in ways that undermine efficiency, or conflict with the desires of the organization's dominant coalition. Building on this line

of thinking several researchers by the mid-1990s conceptually investigated the phenomenon of dysfunctional or toxic workplace behaviour.
The body of literature is large and a myriad of constructs and operation-
alizations exist. The lines, however, are often blurred between one
construct and the next (Robinson 2008). For example, Robinson and
Bennett (1995) developed the 'workplace deviance' construct, O'Leary-
Kelly et al. (1996) theorized about 'organizationally-directed aggression'
and Vardi and Weiner (1996) developed a theory of 'organizational
misbehaviour'. Constructs such as bullying and harassment (Einarsen et
al. 2007; Kärreman 2010), workplace victimization (Aquino 2000) and
social undermining (Duffy et al. 2002) have also been studied. Despite
the myriad of studies, the findings are relatively similar. They point to the
disruptive or harmful impact that toxic and dysfunctional workplace
behaviour has upon individual organizational members. Research has
even shown that individuals can be harmed by merely being exposed to,
hearing about, or witnessing toxic and dysfunctional workplace behaviour (Robinson 2008).

Many of these studies also demonstrate the impact of ineffective
leadership in predicting toxic and dysfunctional workplace behaviour.
Traditional literature in general concludes that ineffective leadership
predicts various types of toxic and dysfunctional behaviour. Influence
over the followers is, in the conventional literature, the essence of
leadership. Moreover, it is the underlying assumption of most mainstream
literature that followers internalize norms and comply even when it is
against their interests to do so. Nevertheless, the literature also builds
upon the belief that theory is about providing leaders with 'better' ways
of managing their organizations (Willmott 1995). As such leadership is,
in modern management studies, assumed to be a legitimate existence
with the purpose of negotiating a reconciliation of conflicting interest.
For some leaders evil wins out, leading to organizational toxicity and
dysfunctionality. Organizational toxicity and dysfunctionality includes for
example physical violence, harassment and bullying, which can be seen
as repeated and persistent attempts by one person to torment, wear down,
frustrate or get a reaction from another (Bast-Pettersen et al. 1995). As
such violence includes also intimidation, interrogation, surveillance,
subjugation, discrimination and exclusion. While leadership systems
might not be intended to generate directly harmful or violating effects,
they may contribute to organizational cultures that in turn increase
tension and/or vulnerabilities, which may facilitate intentionally harmful
behaviours in the workplace (Lewis and Simpson 2007). At the individual

level, such behaviour is believed to leave people in a constant flight-or-fight response, making it difficult to function productively in the long term (Frost 2003). At the organizational level for example Analoui (1995) found that 65 per cent of all acts of sabotage stemmed from discontent with leaders and their perceived unfair behaviour towards workers. Crino and Leap (1989) found that dissatisfaction with leaders leads to reduced loyalty, and once loyalty is destroyed sabotage is more likely. It is the response of the individual that determines whether it is negative.

Whether investigating the heroic or the tyrannical leader, leadership research in general implicitly categorizes functionality and dysfunctionality, almost neglecting the mere fact that leaders are human beings with both strengths and weaknesses, and with basic emotional needs expressed as positive or negative feelings. Focusing on weaknesses while ignoring strengths can be a course of failure, and glorifying strengths while ignoring weaknesses can be equally unproductive. As shall be elaborated in the next section and discussed in the following chapters of this volume, leaders are not one-dimensional, but a blend of good and evil. A blend which cannot per se be categorized as functional and dysfunctional or as non-toxic and toxic.

## THE CRITICAL LENS

In general there is a tendency in the leadership literature to argue for the inherent goodness of positive emotion and the inherent badness of negative emotions (Elfenbein 2007). This volume, however, leans on the social functional theorists, who have argued that even unpleasant emotions have valuable roles for social and work-life (Friedlund 1994; Keltner and Haidt 1999). Whereas positive emotions are rewards, negative emotions are warnings and punishments, and whereas positive emotions are crucial for daily functioning and cooperation, negative emotions are critical for responses to survival situations (Elfenbein 2007). Therefore it is impossible to distinguish between functional and dysfunctional emotional leadership behaviour, and as such it is relevant to investigate the blurry area between leadership and emotionality, between non-toxicity and toxicity and between functionality and dysfunctionality.

Leaders' ability to manage their own emotions and to influence the emotions of others usually has a dramatic impact on organizational results. History is full of examples of leaders who others have looked to for assurance, clarity and approval. This applies both to great leaders and morally questionable leaders. Both to leaders who have inspired, ignited others' passion and brought out the best in their followers; and to leaders who have appealed to others' feelings of insecurity and fear and induced their followers to commit the cruellest and most barbarian acts. An excellent example of the latter is described in Kets de Vries book *Lessons on Leadership by Terror* (Kets de Vries 2004). Through the tale of Shaka Zulu, Kets de Vries introduces his readers to the despotic tendencies of human nature and thus familiarizes the reader with the human side, however horribly oppressive and destructive, of leadership by terror. Shaka Zulu is an excellent example of the impossibility of distinguishing between functional and dysfunctional leadership. He was a warrior-king of epic proportions who brought the Zulu nation to greatness by being a ruthless psychopath and despot in the manner of Hitler, Stalin, Pol Port and Saddam Hussein. In spite of all his human frailties, Shaka Zulu was an unusual and visionary leader who despite being a barbaric tyrant was also a true nation-builder who managed to gather many dispersed and warring tribes and built them into a single cohesive entity – the Zulu nation. The tale depicts both an elitist and a participationist approach to leadership depending on the lens through which the tale is viewed. In addition, the tale depicts the emotional arena of pride, fear, guilt, revenge and compassion. The tale demonstrates how an organization – in this case represented in the form of an army – can be an arena where emotions shape events and events shape emotions.

Leadership cannot primarily be considered as an obvious, rational and unproblematic phenomenon. It is equally possible to view leadership as intimately associated with dominance, special interests and dependence (Alvesson and Sveningsson 2003a; Alvesson and Sveningsson 2003b). Historically, leadership researchers have tended to present leaders in an overly rational and determined way (for example, Barker 1993; Delbridge et al. 1992; Sewell and Wilkinson 1992) ascribing 'to decision-makers a high level of purposiveness and intentionality' (Bryman 1984, p. 401). In this literature leadership (dys)functionality and emotions are often hidden or ignored. This literature simply neglects the humiliation, desire, insecurity, pride and fear; in short, the emotions that inform everyday life (Fineman 2000; Fineman 2007; Hochschild 1983).

The mere exercise of leadership lays the foundation of functionality as well as dysfunctionality. Leadership equals taking risks, bending and sometimes breaking rules (Spicer 2010), and more often than not pushing, persuading and even manipulating others to accomplish things whose end result they may not yet – if ever – understand (Frost 2003). Consciously or not, leaders might create conditions of discomfort and even pain for those who are led. For example, Frost (2003) identified that organizational dysfunctional events fall into one or more of seven major categories (such as intention, insensitivity, incompetence, infidelity, institutional forces, intrusion and inevitability) generated by either leaders' behaviours or structural processes and policies within organizations. These events generate emotions that prove to be destructive to both the psychological and physiological health of individuals within an organization, and the goals the organization is trying to achieve.

Summing up on the leadership literature, most studies assume that leadership 'exists' as a rather rational phenomenon consisting of traits, styles and forms. While the expanding post-charismatic and post-heroic leadership literature has challenged this (Collinson 2005; Heuy, 1994), much of this work still adheres to the belief that it is possible to grasp some kind of 'essence-like' quality of what a leader does and what leadership is about (Alvesson and Spicer 2010a). Already in 1977, Pfeffer argued for the ambiguity in definition and measurement of leadership and concluded that leadership is primarily 'phenomenological'. Nevertheless, research still seems to demonstrate a 'comparative lack of recognition of the possibility that "leadership" can encapsulate a diverse range of meanings or multiple frames of reference' (Bresnen 1995, p. 496). Ambiguity and incoherence are still neglected aspects in the studies on leadership leading to functionality as well as dysfunctionality.

## CLOSING REMARKS

It is our hope that this opening overview will point to the future of leadership with particular emphasis on how best to advance the arguments, method, and effectiveness of leadership recognizing the mere fact that leaders are normal human beings with both ideal and flawed behaviours, habits and emotions. Recognizing that leaders, whom we expect to 'be themselves' and express their personality authentically in all its uniqueness and difference (Fleming and Sturdy 2009), will fascinate and attract some while intimidating and corralling others (Muhr 2010; Muhr 2011). We hope to inspire our academic and professional colleagues to (re)investigate the complex nature of leadership and emotions in organizations from a more reflexive approach accepting that leadership is not just a 'technology' that can increase the desirable outcomes of functionality and reduce the undesirable outcomes of dysfunctionality. Negative emotions are generally considered an overly disruptive state to be regulated and are rarely put to productive use. We hope to nurture a more nuanced picture on emotions in line with authors like Dilorio and Nusbaumer (1993) and Morris and Keltner (2000), who showed that negative emotions in the workplace can be beneficial when used within their intended role: such as an emotion of moral justice that provokes us to confront an obstacle or offender to change the behaviour of another. Moreover, if we are happy all the time we will lose the evolutionary value of negative emotions (Elfenbein 2007). Emotions help improve organizations to make them safer, fairer, more rewarding and generally more emotionally fulfilling.

# REFERENCES

Alvesson, M. and A. Spicer (2010a), 'Introduction', in M. Alvesson and A. Spicer (eds) *Metaphors We Lead By: Understanding Leadership in the Real World*, London: Routledge, pp. 1–7.

Alvesson, M. and A. Spicer (2010b), *Metaphors We Lead By: Understanding Leadership in the Real World*, London: Routledge.

Alvesson, M. and S. Sveningsson (2003a), 'The great disappearing act: difficulties in doing "leadership"', *The Leadership Quarterly*, **14** (3), 359–81.

Alvesson, M. and S. Sveningsson (2003b), 'Managers doing leadership: the extraordination of the mundane', *Human Relations*, **56** (12), 1435–59.

Analoui, F. (1995), 'Work place sabotage: its styles, motives and management', *Journal of Management Development*, **14** (7), 48–65.

Aquino, K. (2000), 'Structural and individual determinants of workplace victimization: the effects of hierarchical status and conflict management', *Journal of Management*, **26** 171–93.

Ashforth, B.E. and R.H. Humphrey (1995), 'Emotion in the workplace: a reappraisal', *Human Relations*, **48** (2), 97–125.

Ashkanasy, N.M. and C.L. Cooper (2008), *Research Companion to Emotions in Organizations*, Cheltenham: Edward Elgar.

Ball, G.A., L.K. Trevino and H.P.J. Sims (1992), 'Understanding subordinate reactions to punishment incidents: perspectives from justice and social affect', *The Leadership Quarterly*, **3** (4), 307–33.

Barker, J.R. (1993), 'Tightening the iron cage: concertive control in self-managing teams', *Administrative Science Quarterly*, **38** (3), 408–37.

Barsade, S.G. (2002), 'The ripple effect: emotional contagion and its influence on group behavior', *Administrative Science Quarterly*, **47** (4), 644–75.

Bartel, C.A. and R. Saavedra (2000), 'The collective construction of work group moods', *Administrative Science Quarterly*, **45** (2), 197–231.

Bass, B.M. (1985), *Leadership and Performance Beyond Expectations*, New York: Free Press.

Bass, B.M. (1990), 'From transactional to transformational leadership: learning to share the vision', *Organizational Dynamics*, **18** (3), 19–31.

Bass, B.M. and B.J. Avolio (1990), *Transformational Leadership Development: Manual for the Multifactor Leadership Questionnaire*, Palo Alto, CA: Consulting Psychologist Press.

Bass, B.M. and P. Steidlmeier (1999), 'Ethics, character and authentic transformational leadership behavior', *The Leadership Quarterly*, **10** (2), 181–217.

Bast-Pettersen, R., E. Bach, K. Lindström, A. Toomingas and J. Kiviranta (1995), *Research on Violence, Threats and Bullying as Health Risks among Health Care Personel*, Copenhagen: Tema Nord.

Bono, J.E. and R. Ilies (2006), 'Charisma, positive emotions, and mood contagion', *The Leadership Quarterly*, **17** (4), 317–34.

Bramming, P. and R. Johnsen (2011), 'Love will tear us apart: transformational leadership and love in a call centre', *European Journal of International Management*, **5** (1), 80–95.

Bresnen, M.J. (1995), 'All things to all people? Perceptions, attributions, and constructs of leadership', *The Leadership Quarterly*, **6** (4), 495–513.

Brief, A.P. and H.M. Weiss (2002), 'Organizational behavior: affect in the workplace', *Annual Review of Psychology*, **53** (February), 279–307.

Bryman, A. (1984), 'Leadership and corporate culture: harmony and disharmony', *Personnel Review*, **13** (2), 19–23.

Bryman, A. (1992), *Charisma and Leadership in Organizations*, London: Sage.

Burns, J.M. (1978), *Leadership*, New York, NY: Harper & Row.

Carlyle, T. (1841), *On Heros, Hero Worship and the Heroic in History*, Boston, MA: Adams.

Chakraborty, S.K. and D. Chakraborty (2004), 'The transformational leader and spiritual psychology: a few insights', *Journal of Organizational Change Management*, **17** (2), 194–210.

Cherulnik, P.D., K.A. Donley, T.S.R. Wiewel and S.R. Miller (2001), 'Charisma is contagious: the effect of leaders' charisma on observers' affect', *Journal of Applied Social Psychology*, **31** (10), 2149–59.

Cluley, R. (2008), 'The psychoanalytic relationship between leaders and followers', *Leadership*, **4** (2), 201–12.

Collins, R. (1990), 'Stratification, emotional energy, and the transient emotions', in T.D. Kemper (eds), *Research Agendas in the Sociology of Emotions*, New York: State University of New York Press, pp. 145–79.

Collinson, D. (2005), 'Dialectics of leadership', *Human Relations*, **58** (11), 1419–42.

Conger, J.A. (1990), 'The dark side of leadership', *Organizational Dynamics*, **19** (2), 44–55.

Crino, M.D. and T.L. Leap (1989), 'What HR managers must know about employee sabotage', *Personnel*, **5** (May), 31–8.

Cropanzano, R. and M.S. Mitchell (2005), 'Social exchange theory: an interdisciplinary review', *Journal of Management*, **31** (6), 874–900.

Cyert, R. and J. March (1963), *A Behavioral Theory of the Firm*, Englewood Cliffs, NJ: Prentice Hall.

Darwin, C. (1872), *The Expression of the Emotions in Man and Animals*, London, UK: Murray.

Dasborough, M.T. (2006), 'Cognitive asymmetry in employee emotional reactions to leadership behaviors', *The Leadership Quarterly*, **17** (2), 163–78.

Delbridge, R., P. Turnbull and B. Wilkenson (1992), 'Pushing back the frontiers: management control and work intensification under JIT/TQM factory regime', *New Technology, Work and Employment*, **7** (2), 97–106.

Denzin, N. (1983), 'A note on emotionality, self, and interaction', *American Journal of Sociology*, **89** (2), 402–9.

Dienesch, R.M. and R.C. Liden (1986), 'Leader–member exchange model of leadership: a critique and further development', *Academy of Management Review*, **11** (3), 618–34.

22 *Critical perspectives on leadership*

Dilorio, J.A. and M.R. Nusbaumer (1993), 'Securing our sanity: anger management among abortion escorts', *Journal of Contemporary Ethnography*, **21** (4), 411–38.

Duffy, M.K., D.C. Ganster and M. Pagon (2002), 'Social undermining in the workplace', *Academy of Management Journal*, **45** (2), 331–51.

Dunne, S. and S. Spoelstra (2010), 'The gift of leadership', *Philosophy Today*, **54** (1), 66–77.

Einarsen, S., M.S. Aasland and A. Skogstad (2007), 'Destructive leadership behavior: a definition and conceptual model', *The Leadership Quarterly*, **18** (3), 207–16.

Elfenbein, H.A. (2007), 'Emotion in organizations: a review and theoretical integration', *The Academy of Management Annals*, **1**, 315–86.

Elster, J. (1998), 'Emotions and economic theory', *Journal of Economic Literature*, **36**, (1), 47-74.

Fiedler, F.E. (1967), *A Theory of Leadership Effectiveness*, New York: McGraw-Hill.

Fineman, S. (2000), *Emotion in Organizations*, London: SAGE.

Fineman, S. (2004), 'Getting the measure of emotion – and the cautionary tale of emotional intelligence', *Human Relations*, **57** (6), 719–40.

Fineman, S. (2007), *Understanding Emotions at Work*, Thousand Oaks, CA: SAGE.

Fitness, J. (2000), 'Anger in the workplace: an emotion script approach to anger episodes between workers and their superiors, co-workers and subordinates', *Journal of Organizational Behavior*, **21**, 147–62.

Fleming, P. and A. Sturdy (2009), 'Just be yourself – towards neonormative control in organizations?', *Employee Relations*, **31** (6), 569–83.

Fong, C.T. and L.Z. Tiedens (2002), 'Dueling experiences and dual ambivalences: emotional and motivational ambivalence of women in high status positions', *Motivation and Emotions*, **26** (1), 105–21.

Fox, S. and P.E. Spector (1999), 'A model of work frustration-aggression', *Journal of Organizational Behavior*, **20** (6), 915–31.

Fredrickson, B.L. (2003), 'Positive emotions and upward spirals in organizations', in K.S. Cameron, J.E. Dutton and R.E. Quinn (eds), *Positive Organizational Scholarship*, San Francisco, CA: BK Publishers, pp. 163–75.

Freud, S. (1933), *New Introductory Lectures on Psychoanalysis*, New York: W.W. Norton & Co.

Friedlund, A.J. (1994), *Facial Expressions: An Evolutionary View*, San Diego, CA: Academic Press.

Frijda, N.H. (2006), *The Laws of Emotion*, Mahwah, NJ: Lawrence Erlbaum.

Frost, P. (2003), *Toxic Emotions at Work*, Boston, MA: Harvard Business School Press.

Frost, P. and S. Robinson (1999), 'The toxic handler: organizational hero – and causality', *Harvard Business Review*, **77** (4), 96–106.

Fry, L. and M. Kriger (2009), 'Towards a theory of being-centered leadership: multiple levels of being as context for effective leadership', *Human Relations*, **62** (11), 1667–96.

Furnham, A. (2010), *The Elephant in the Boardroom: The Causes of Leadership Derailment*, Basingstoke: Palgrave MacMillan.

Gemmill, G. and J. Oakley (1992), 'Leadership: an alienating social myth?', *Human Relations*, **45** (2), 113–29.

George, W.R. (1990), 'Internal marketing and organizational behavior: a partnership in developing customer-conscious employees at every level', *Journal of Business Research*, **20** (1), 63–70.

Grandey, A., A. Tam and A. Brauburger (2002), 'Affective states and traits in the workplace: diary and survey data from young workers', *Motivation and Emotions*, **26** (1), 31–55.

Harvey, P., M.J. Martinko and W.L. Gardner (2006), 'Promoting authentic behavior in organizations: an attributional perspective', *Journal of Leadership and Organizational Studies*, **12** (3), 1–11.

Hatch, M.J., M. Kostera and A.K. Kozminski (2005), *The Three Faces of Leadership: Manager, Artist, Priest*, Malden, MA: Blackwell.

Hatfield, E., J.L. Cacioppo and R.L. Rapson (1993), 'Emotional contagion', *Current Directions in Psychological Science*, **2** (3), 96–99.

Heller, F., P. Drenth, P. Koopman and Z. Rus (1988), *Decisions in Organizations*, Newbury Park, CA: SAGE.

Hersey, P. and K. Blanchard (1999), *Leadership and the One-Minute Manager*, New York: William Morrow.

Hicks, D.A. (2002), 'Spiritual and religious diversity in the workplace: implications for leadership', *The Leadership Quarterly*, **13** (2), 379–96.

Hochschild, A.R. (1983), *The Managed Heart: Commercialization of Human Feeling*, Berkeley, CA: University of California Press.

House, R.J. and R.N. Aditya (1997), 'The social scientific study of leadership: quo vadis?', *Journal of Management*, **23** (3), 409–73.

Judge, T.A., D. Heller and M.K. Mount (2002), 'Five-factor model of personality and job satisfaction: a meta-analysis', *Journal of Applied Psychology*, **87** (3), 530–41.

Kärreman, D. (2010), 'The leader as bully', in M. Alvesson and A. Spicer (eds), *Metaphors We Lead By: Understanding Leadership in the Real World*, London: Routledge, pp. 162–79.

Katz, D. and R.L. Kahn (1978), *The Social Psychology of Organizations*, New York: John Wiley and Sons.

Keltner, D. and J. Haidt (1999), 'Social functions of emotions at four levels of analysis', *Cognition and Emotion*, **13** (5), 505–21.

Kets de Vries, M.F.R. (1985), 'Narcissism and leadership: an object relations perspective', *Human Relations*, **38** (6), 583–601.

Kets de Vries, M.F.R. (1990), 'The organization fool', *Human Relations*, **43** (8), 751–70.

Kets de Vries, M.F.R. (2004), *Lessons on Leadership by Terror. Finding Shaka Zulu in the Attic*, Cheltenham, UK and Northampton, MA, USA: Edward Elgar.

Lemmergaard, J. and S.L. Muhr (2011), 'Everybody hurts, sometimes – emotions and dysfunctional leadership', *European Journal of International Management*, **5** (1), 1–12.

Lewis, K.M. (2000), 'When leaders display emotion: how followers respond to negative emotional expression of male and female leaders', *Journal of Organizational Behavior*, **21** (2), 221–34.

Lewis, P. and R. Simpson (2007), *Gendering Emotions in Organizations*, New York, NY: MacMillan.

Lindgren, M., J. Packendorff and H. Tham (2011), 'Relational dysfunctionality: leadership interactions in a Sarbanes-Oxley Act implementation project', *European Journal of International Management*, **5** (11), 13–29.

Lockyer, J. and D. McCabe (2011), 'Leading through fear: emotion, rationality and innovation in a UK manufacturing company', *European Journal of International Management*, **5** (1), 48–61.

24        *Critical perspectives on leadership*

Lord, R.G., C.L. De Vader and G.M. Alliger (1986), 'A meta-analysis of the relation between personality traits and leadership perceptions: an application of validity generalization procedures', *Journal of Applied Psychology*, **71** (3), 402–10.

Maccoby, M. (2004), 'Narcissistic leaders: the incredible pros, the inevitable cons', *Harvard Business Review*, **82** (1), 92–101.

Mann, R.D. (1959), 'A review of the relationship between personality and perform-ance in small groups', *Psychological Bulletin*, **56** (4), 241–70.

McCall, M.W.J. and M.M. Lombardo (1983), *Off the Track: Why and How Successful Executives Get Derailed*, Greensboro, NC: Centre for Creative Leadership.

Meindl, J.R. (1990), 'On leadership: an alternative to the conventional wisdom', *Research on Organizational Behavior*, **12**, 159–203.

Miller, K.I. and P.R. Monge (1986), 'Participation, satisfaction and productivity: a meta-analytical review', *Academy of Management Journal*, **29** (4), 727–53.

Miner, A.G., T.M. Glomb and C. Hulin (2005), 'Experience sampling mood and its correlates at work', *Journal of Occupational and Organizational Psychology*, **78** (2), 171–93.

Moore, C. and V. Hope-Hailey (2004), 'Anything else is just one-sided myopia: researching emotion at work – dabbing some color on the emotional canvas', paper presented at the Fourth International Conference on Emotions in Organizational Life, London.

Morgan, H., P. Harkins and M. Goldsmith (2005), *The Art and Practice of Leadership Coaching*, Hoboken, NJ: John Wiley & Sons.

Morris, M. and D. Keltner (2000), 'How emotions work: the social functions of emotional expression in negotiation', *Research in Organizational Behavior*, **22**, 1–50.

Mowday, R.T. and R.I. Sutton (1993), 'Organizational behavior: linking individuals and groups to organizational contexts', *Annual Review of Psychology*, **44** (February), 195–229.

Muhr, S.L. (2010), 'Caught in the gendered machine – on the masculine and feminine in cyborg leadership', *Gender, Work and Organization*, **18** (3), 337–57.

Muhr, S.L. (2011), 'The leader as cyborg – leadership through mechanistic superior-ity', in M. Alvesson and A. Spicer (eds), *Metaphors We Lead By: Understanding Leadership in the Real World*, London: Routledge, pp. 138–61.

Muhr, S.L. and J. Lemmergaard (2009), 'Crisis, responsibility, death – sacrifice and leadership in school shootings', *Philosophy of Management*, **8** (2), 21–30.

Nicholson, N. (2000), *Executive Instinct*, New York: Crown Business.

O'Leary-Kelly, A., R.W. Griffin and D.J. Glew (1996), 'Organization-motivated aggression: a research framework', *Academy of Management Review*, **21** (1), 225–572.

Ortony, A., G.L. Clore and A. Collins (1988), *The Cognitive Structure of Emotions*, Cambridge: Cambridge University Press.

Padilla, A., R. Hogan and R.B. Kaiser (2007), 'The toxic triangle: destructive leaders, susceptible followers, and conductive environments', *The Leadership Quarterly*, **18** (3), 176–94.

Paul, J., D.L. Coastley, J.P. Howelly and P.W. Dorfman (2002), 'The mutability of charisma in leadership research', *Management Decision*, **40** (1), 192–200.

Pfeffer, J. (1977), 'The ambiguity of leadership', *Academy of Management Review*, **2** (1), 104–12.

Pullen, A. and C. Rhodes (2008), '"It's all about me!": gendered narcissism and leaders' identity work', *Leadership*, **4** (1), 5–25.

Rehn, A. and M. Lindahl (2011), 'Leadership and the 'right to respect' – on honour and shame in emotionally charged management settings', *European Journal of International Management*, **5** (1), 62–79.

Robinson, S. and R. Bennett (1995), 'A typology of deviant workplace behaviors: a multi-dimensional scaling study', *Academy of Management Journal*, **38** (2), 555–72.

Robinson, V.M.J. (2008), 'Forging the link between distributed leadership and educational outcomes', *Journal of Educational Administration*, **46** (2), 555–72.

Rosenthal, S. and T.L. Pittinsky (2006), 'Narcissistic leadership', *The Leadership Quarterly*, **17** (6), 617–33.

Sewell, G. and B. Wilkinson (1992), 'Empowerment or emasculation? Shop floor surveillance in a Total Quality Organization', in P. Blyton and P. Turnbull (eds), *Reassessing Human Resource Management*, London: Sage, pp. 97–115.

Spicer, A. (2010), 'Leaders as commanders: leadership through creating clear direction', in M. Alvesson and A. Spicer (eds), *Metaphors We Lead By: Understanding Leadership in the Real World*, London: Routledge, pp. 118–37.

Stogdill, R.M. (1948), 'Personal factors associated with leadership: a survey of the literature', *Journal of Applied Psychology*, **25** (1), 35–71.

Stogdill, R.M. (1950), 'Leadership, membership and organization', *Psychological Bulletin*, **47** (1), 1–14.

Storey, J. (2004), 'Changing theories of leadership and leadership development', in J. Storey (eds), *Leadership in Organizations: Current Issues and Key Trends*, London: Routledge, pp. 11–38.

Sveningsson, S. and M. Larsson (2006), 'Fantasies of leadership: identity work', *Leadership*, **2** (2), 203–24.

Sveningsson, S. and M. Alvesson (2003), 'Managing managerial identities: organizational fragmentation, discourse and identity struggle', *Human Relations*, **56** (10), 1163–93.

Sy, T., S. Côte and R. Saavedra (2005), 'The contagious leader: impact of the leader's mood on the mood of group members, group affective tone, and group processes', *Journal of Applied Psychology*, **90** (2), 295–6.

Tourish, D. and A. Pinnington (2002), 'Transformational leadership, corporate cultism and the spirituality paradigm: an unholy trinity in the workplace?', *Human Relations*, **55** (2), 147–72.

Turnley, W.H., M.C. Bolino, S.W. Lester and J.M. Bloodgood (2003), 'The impact of psychological contract fulfillment on the performance of in-role and organizational citizenship behaviors', *Journal of Management*, **29** (2), 187–206.

Van Fleet, D.D. and R.W. Griffin (2006), 'Dysfunctional organizational culture: the role of leadership in motivating dysfunctional work behaviours', *Journal of Managerial Psychology*, **21** (8), 698–708.

Vardi, Y. and Y. Weiner (1996), 'Misbehavior in organizations: a motivational framework', *Organization Science*, **7** (2), 151–65.

von Groddeck, V. (2011), 'The function of dysfunctions: the paradox of value-based leadership communication', *European Journal of International Management*, **5** (1), 30–47.

Wagner, J.A. and R.Z. Gooding (1987), 'Shared influence and organizational behavior: a meta-analysis of situational variables expected to moderate participation-outcome relationships', *Academy of Management Journal*, **30** (3), 524–41.

Weiss, H.M. and R. Cropanzano (1996), 'Affective events theory: a theoretical discussion of the structure, causes and consequences or affective experiences at work', *Research in Organizational Behavior*, **18**, 1–74.
Weiss, H.M., K. Suckow and R. Cropanzano (1999), 'Effects of justice conditions on discrete emotions', *Journal of Applied Psychology*, **84** (5), 786–94.
Whicker, M.L. (1996), *Toxic Leaders: When Organizations Go Bad*, Westport, CT: Quorum Books.
Williams, K.J. and G.M. Alliger (1994), 'Role stressors, mood spillover, and perceptions of work-family conflict in parents', *Academy of Management Journal*, **37** (4), 837–69.
Willmott, H. (1995), 'The odd couple? Reengineering business process, managing human resources', *New Technology, Work and Employment*, **10** (2), 89–8.
Wouters, C. (1989), 'The sociology of emotions and flight attendants: Hochschild's 'managed heart'', *Theory, Culture & Society*, **6** (1), 95–123.
Wright, P.L. (1996), *Managerial Leadership*, London: Routledge.
Yammerion, F.J. and B.M. Bass (1990), 'Transformational leadership and multiple levels of analysis', *Human Relations*, **43** (10), 975–95.
Yukl, G. (1998), *Leadership in Organizations*, Upper Saddle River, NJ: Prentice-Hall.
Yukl, G. and C.M. Falbe (1991), 'Importance of different power sources in downward and lateral relations', *Journal of Applied Psychology*, **76** (3), 416–23.

# PART II

# Leadership behaviour in practice

Anyone can hold the helm when the sea is calm.

Publius Syrus

# 2.   Introduction to Part II

## Jeanette Lemmergaard and Sara Louise Muhr

This part consists of five empirically based chapters critically exploring positive as well as negative encounters with leadership principles and behaviours as they occur in a variety of settings. The chapters exhibit what characterizes leaders as people: their personalities and their strengths and foibles in a decisive, evaluative and forceful manner.

In Chapter 3, Michael Walton discusses how leaders are vulnerable to the influence of their own emotions and how emotional power-plays can backfire and result in leader toxicity and dysfunction. Walton walks the readers through the emotional experiences of leaders from two different organizations demonstrating that leadership is not 'emotional neutral'. One of the leaders in Walton's case study exhibits increasingly arrogant and counter-productive behaviour and is eventually removed from office pending criminal charges. The other believes he is entitled to a seat on the Board and when denied this possibility becomes increasingly self-serving and insensitive to others. Both cases are about the seduction of power and privilege in the workplace and about how emotive motivations can, seemingly, blind leaders to their own dysfunctional behaviour and to the corrosive impact such behaviour exerts within the organization as a whole.

Walton also illustrates how leadership is an intensely personal and idiosyncratic matter and not something that can be examined as a static, universally defined and discrete entity. One leader's sense of perceived injustice and the other leader's unconstrained authoritative behaviour emerged as Achilles' heels to their ambitions and ultimately derailed their careers and damaged their organizations. To study the emotional con-comitant of leadership from a positivistic perspective is to risk missing the essential humanness of leadership behaviour in practice and to neglect the emotional constraints of leadership.

In Chapter 4, Jeanette Lemmergaard and Clare Howard empirically examine different leadership styles, behaviours and emotions; and shows how the tendency to polarize around archetypes of leadership undermines the complexity of leadership. Two leaders are studied, who hold the same position at different points in time. After the first leader leaves the organization, suddenly, angrily and with no warning signs; the succeeding leader is recruited internally overnight to fill in the open position. Whereas the first leader was action-oriented, extraverted and self-decisive, the succeeding leader is reflective, introvert and consensus-seeking. Going from sheer energy and visionary leadership, the organization changes overnight to an organization where reflective thinking and considered opinions are valued and expected.

Lemmergaard and Howard demonstrate how leadership is not a one-size-fits-all proposition, which works well in all sets of circumstances. Rather, what their case study demonstrates is that it is impossible to predetermine which leadership style and behaviour is most valuable as it depends on the specific context of the situation and on the relations. Despite representing two different type preferences, the two leaders studied were victims and perpetrators of the blind side of leading in their own image. They both demonstrated intolerance, albeit they demonstrated this very differently. Moreover, both leaders were intensely social beings, who needed interaction with followers, although their styles were very different.

Emma L. Jeanes, in Chapter 5, locates the nature of leadership in the relations rather than in the individual, when she empirically examines the leadership roles performed in a family business. Jeanes compares the principal of a family business to the patriarch of the family who plays many roles from 'the man-in-charge', to the cuckolded husband, the doted upon and teased father, and the man at risk of the Oedipal drive to take the place of the father. Using the family metaphor, Jeanes reveals the ambiguities in different leadership identities, and shows how leadership is a process that one dips in and out of. Jeanes also demonstrates how leaders rely on a range of relational devices to enact their leadership roles; roles that are complex and uncertain, and which must constantly be negotiated.

Jeanes examines the complexity of management in a medium-sized family-owned firm. Building on the family analogy, Jeanes demonstrates that families – and family businesses – comprise a set of co-determined and co-produced emotional relations that are simultaneously functional and dysfunctional. This duality is demonstrated at multiple levels. The managing director is for example portrayed both as the archetype of a strong father-figure and as a manager lacking confidence especially when faced with difficult decisions. Consequently, he often does not play the expected role of the 'man-in-charge'. The managing director's wife and her both official and unofficial leadership roles are also portrayed in this chapter. Officially she is in charge of the administration of the firm, but in practice her role in the firm is rather unclear which leads to both emotional and functional ambiguities. Especially because she is attending when she pleases and is generally blamed for the 'bad atmosphere' in the office.

In Chapter 6, Stephan Schaefer and Alexander Paulsson focus is shifted from the leaders *per se*, to the consequences of different leadership behaviours and emotions. Schaefer and Paulsson investigate the organizational outcome measured as levels of innovation. Schaefer and Paulsson question the assumption that only positive emotions (such as excitement, relatedness and optimism) lead to successful leadership of innovation and suggest that negative emotions (such as anger, fear and anxiety) can play a constructive role as well. They argue that in the interaction between leaders and followers an interdependent dialectic relationship between negative and positive emotions develops which impacts innovation. The interconnectedness between emotions – whether positive or negative – complicates the separation of leadership styles and accordingly also the separation between functional and dysfunctional leadership for innovation. Following this line of thinking, Schaefer and Paulsson revisit Schumpeter's oxymoronic notion of 'creative destruction'.

Interviewing engineers and managers of a recently established joint venture in the high-tech sector, Schaefer and Paulsson demonstrates how the innovation process can be compared to a rollercoaster ride in which fear and frustration emerge alongside joy and optimism, and in which developments look bright and possibly gloomy at the same time. As such the case study illustrates the co-existence of negative and positive emotions and their conjoint effect on innovation outcomes; and – of equal importance – the case study challenges the authentic leadership literature on the dimensions of possibility, desirability and ambiguity.

The final chapter in Part II of this volume by Yvonne Due Billing maintains the focus on the consequences of different leadership behaviours and emotions as she focuses specifically on followers. More precisely, Billing highlights the importance of leaders' ability to 'read' and understand the emotional state of their followers. Billing demonstrates this by discussing distributed leadership, which is the way leaders grant their followers autonomy to make strategic decisions on their own. Here she argues that instead of leading to more freedom, autonomy may lead to over-commitment and entrapment, which in turn may lead to stress and burnout. Billing studies knowledge workers and their managers in a well-reputed Scandinavian IT organization characterized as caring, friendly, informal and with a high level of cohesion.

Despite being a reputable workplace and having a well-functioning work climate, the organization is facing severe problems in terms of retaining a healthy work culture as followers seem to be 'working till they drop'. Billing discusses the need for a balance between stress and fun and is directing our attention to the importance of leaders dealing with the unfortunate consequences of workaholic attitudes. An attitude that – sometimes unconsciously – is fostered by leaders themselves.

# 3. The Rottweiler and the flying penguin: 'peacock power' in the workplace

**Michael Walton**

## INTRODUCTION

It is interesting to note, in spite of the publicity generated by the dysfunctional and criminal behaviour of high profile leaders in recent years (Byron 2004; Gray et al. 2005; Hamilton and Micklethwait 2006; McLean and Elkind 2004; Mitchell 2001; Newton 2006) how much of the leadership literature has focused on the constructive and *positive* aspects of 'leadership'. This is not too surprising perhaps as an emphasis on leadership as grandiose, beautiful, transformational, charismatic and heroic may reflect a basic human desire to retreat from engaging with the less positive and appealing – yet complementary – toxic, duplicitous, destructive, criminal and dysfunctional dimensions of leadership. While there have been exceptions (Conger 1990; Goldman 2009a; Kets de Vries 2006; Lindgren et al. 2011; Padilla et al. 2007; Walton 2007; 2008a; Whicker 1996; Yukl 1998) the prevalence of counter-productive leadership behaviour makes a mockery of this seeming oversight by many of those concerned with examining leadership and management.

The workplace triggers behaviour, which can result in personally and organizationally damaging dysfunctional, disruptive and destructive behaviour from leaders (Dotlich and Cairo 2003; Furnham 2010; Lubit 2004a; McCall and Lombardo 1983; McCall 1998; Schell 1999). Yet from much of the leadership literature it can appear as if emotions at work do not exist. As Goldman (2009a) comments '… the absence or denial of emotions in the workplace is reason for concern' (p. 13). Business organizations *are* hot-houses of emotionally charged labour; they are cauldrons of activity capable of generating intense feelings, dynamic interactions and highly charged emotional exchanges (Ashkanasy and Cooper 2008; Fineman 2000; Fitness 2010; Gabriel 1999;

Hirschhorn 1988; Hochschild 1983; Langan-Fox et al. 2007; Levinson 1978; Walton 2008b; Zaleznik 1970). At the heart of workplace dynamics are the everyday emotive interplays of issues concerning personal identity, reputation, survival, envy, jealousy, fear, love, betrayal and pride (Ashforth 1995; Aasland et al. 2008; Bramming and Johnson 2011; Einarsen et al. 2007; Hogan 2007; Kets de Vries 1989a; 2009; Lockyer and McCabe 2011; Rehn and Lindahl 2011; Stein 1997; Zaleznik and Kets de Vries 1985).

Insufficient attention given to such matters would seem at best ill-advised and at worst a recipe for potential personal and organizational disaster (Fineman 2003; Frost and Robinson 1999; Kupers and Weibler 2008; Payne and Cooper 2001). Although it may seem obvious – as Lord and Harvey (2002) observe – 'Emotions occur in context, and the relevant context establishes the intensity of emotions and the time parameters in which events and processes must occur in order to have meaning' (p. 116). Now while the behaviour of many leaders will oscillate between being predominantly functional and marginally dysfunctional – depending on context, situation and character – more profound leadership dysfunctionality remains an unavoidable possibility (Frost 2003; Furnham 2007; Gallos 2008; Goldman 2009b; Hogan 2007; Kaplan 1990; Kaplan and Kaiser 2006; Lubit 2004b; Zaleznik 2008)

The chapter describes workplace behaviour, which unseated two hitherto well-regarded senior managers who, through persistent counterproductive behaviour, became the architects of their own downfall. These 'close-to-practice' cases illustrate how two competent leaders became 'bad' (Kellerman 2004) and 'toxic' (Lipman-Blumen 2005; 2008) and highlights how (i) those in positions of organizational power remain vulnerable to the influence of their own emotions and (ii) how emotional power-plays can backfire and result in leader toxicity and dysfunction. In each case increasingly excessive, demanding and dysfunctional behaviour ultimately derailed their careers and damaged their organizations. Both executives failed primarily through a mismanagement of their behaviour, which became emotionally toxic, destructive and dysfunctional and in each case the contexts of their organizations – the Alpha Business Unit and Beta Corp. – was a significant factor in their decline and failure.

My interest is in leadership behaviour-in-context (Walton 2005), which I approach from a psychological perspective in my work as an external consultant, coach and advisor to senior executives. I am intrigued and interested in the ebbs and flows of business life and the ways in which my clients – and I – engage with the dynamic uncertainties of leadership behaviour. A behaviour which is often in the grey zone between what is clearly dysfunctional and criminal on the one side, and what is clearly constructive and positive on the other side.

# THE CASE MATERIAL: RULA AND FREDERICK

## Considerations about the Method

The cases outlined are based on my notes and experiences of working as an external advisor with two leaders – in-situ – over a protracted period. From my perspective as a participant observer their psychometric profiles, 360-degree assessments, third-party observations, reporting officer feedback, coaching sessions, personal disclosures together with my observations from a period of over two years provide the foundations for this chapter (Gill and Johnson 2005; May 2006; McCall and Simmons 1969; Richardson 1997).

The 'close' nature of my involvement enabled me to integrate what they told me with how I saw them operate in practice and I could also consider the predictive validity of their psychometric profiles – and of my interpretations – as they went about their work. I saw them in a variety of corporate and non-corporate settings and was able, over time, to build up a rounded picture of both executives and of the contexts within which they found themselves. This high level of access and long-term involvement enabled me to build up a 'rich-picture' (Checkland 1981) of my clients' working environments and cultures from the inside (Coffey and Atkinson 1996; Coffey 1999); and while not an ethnographic study *per se* (Watson 1994) it nevertheless has some similarities with such studies. While fully aware that my commentary reflects post-hoc interpretations the substantial amount of contact time – observing and discussing their behaviour – leads me to have confidence in the pertinence, for leadership research, of the four 'key features' which emerged from my post-assignment reflections.

The cases, which follow, describe the behaviour of 'Rula' and 'Frederick' both senior executives who were operationally and professionally competent, ambitious and high achievers. They worked in prestigious, successful, profitable organizations; both were articulate, smart and experienced – and appropriately qualified for the roles they occupied. In each case their behaviour – which was initially constructive, valued, rewarded and welcomed – came, over time, to be undermined through their own toxic and dysfunctional behaviour.

The first case describes how Rula when promoted to director exhibited increasingly arrogant and counter-productive behaviour and was ultimately removed from office pending criminal charges. In the second case Frederick – a senior professional advisor – believed he was entitled to a seat on the Board. Denied this possibility his behaviour became so self-serving that his remit was marginalized by his managing director as a means of constraining and avoiding contact with him.

### Case 1: Rula 'Alpha BU' – Fear and Trepidation at Work

'Alpha BU' is a profitable business unit within a global FTSE 100 Corporation. The corporation had ambitious plans and diversified its product range accordingly to maximize its global market potential. It failed, however, to put into place sufficient internal checks for one of its products and the Alpha BU was established to manage growing adverse consumer reactions, recover the position and protect the corporate brand.

The poor performance of this business unit, however, was generating additional adverse press publicity and this reached the stage where the image, and the share price of the parent corporation was coming under threat. As a consequence, the corporate panic button was pressed and a replacement managing director and head of operations were drafted in to sort it out, turn things around and rescue the position. Unlimited resources were provided to get the job done and the Alpha BU was allowed increased operational independence in an attempt to avoid an impending 'doom' scenario, which could have profoundly compromised the reputation and standing of the parent corporation.

My work was in support of the newly appointed managing director and his head of operations (Rula) – on whom this case is focused – in facilitating constructive review and change. Prior to my involvement I had just begun an executive coaching assignment with Rula and I was subsequently invited to support her in her new role, which I did, sporadically, for over two years.

Rula's appointment was based on her reputation for getting things done and holding colleagues to their commitments. She was known for having a low tolerance for non-performance and a brusque manner. A determined, high-profile, attention-seeking, dynamic and strongly extroverted person she expected to have her own way and pushed things through in a tough manner when required.

Many changes were initiated during her reign. While her managing director primarily managed key external stakeholder relationships, Rula concentrated on the internal organization and managed its day-to-day performance. Her quick tongue and bright manner contrasted sharply with the dull, bureaucratic predecessors she had replaced and she was seen as a ray of bright – if at times startling – light. She made a positive difference and, based on her early successes, was given more latitude and freedom of action.

The appointment of friends into senior roles created an inner circle which began to insulate itself from the wider business and fed a growing sense of personal entitlement, which showed itself in her change of office, accumulation of furnishings and off-site activities. She acquired and then showed off the latest version of whatever device was 'cool' – even fabricating loss or theft to enable the latest version to be purchased for her. She bucked the corporate car policy and got away with it. She referred to 'my boys' as if she were the leader of a street gang each of whom would, unquestioningly, do her bidding. Her 'in-group' of friends and colleagues reinforced her grandiosity, showed allegiance and deferred to her mercurial ups and downs – 'Oh ... that's just Rula, that's just how she is ... '

Over time an intimidating and bullying climate took hold combined with – almost childlike – emotional outbursts when her plans were challenged, thwarted or diluted. On one occasion, bursting out of her corner office during a meeting with me, shouting – to the astounded ranks of staff busy at their desks – 'He's disagreeing with me!'. In another instance the cover of a promotional booklet had to be reprinted because she had designed it to depict herself in too prominent a position, obscuring the line drawing of a more senior colleague.

It became apparent that those who satisfied the head of operations got on well, while those who challenged or queried decisions were penalized or exorcized from the organization – often with a damaged reputation. With the exception of her three 'friends', tenure on Alpha's management team was generally short-lived and a high churn rate resulted. Subordinates who failed to please were discarded – 'Oh 'X'? ... He's gone!' or demeaned as 'He was just not good enough'. She began to use staff to run errands, collect clothes, book private appointments and increasingly behaved 'as if' she owned the organization.

She was so skilful in managing upwards that she was singled out as an exemplary ethical leader whose attributes others were recommended to replicate. Noticed, and championed, by the group managing director, there seemed little to impede her rise to prominence within the corporation's senior executive group. In due course Rula was appointed director of Alpha BU and given full rein and responsibility for the allocation and use of resources together with authority for outsourcing work.

Following her promotion, and the absence of the hitherto moderating influence of her previous managing director, a more casual and diffident approach to attending meetings and other time-tabled responsibilities ensued. She showed an inability to countenance personal error and her harassing behaviour appeared closer to that of an imperious 'Lady of the Manor' than as a mature and focused business leader. She came to be described by staff as 'The Rottweiler' because of her no-nonsense and, at times, savage 'JFDI' behaviour (see Chapter 4 for further elaboration on personality typologies). Impatient, difficult to influence and uncompromising in her behaviour, she would over-talk or interrupt others and had a tendency to discount the contributions of others unless they were supporting her views. She threw her weight around and intimidated, demeaned and harassed those who displeased her.

Her personal assistant reported unexpected – and unexplained – periods away from the office. She would 'swan around' at conferences bestowing grace and favour and on one occasion feeding food to some male colleagues. Not exactly a 'cyborg leader' as hypothesized by Muhr, (2011, p. 154) but definitely an attention demanding '... shining and intimidating man-machine' highly skilled at self-promotion, image and impression management. The regular progress review meetings with the group managing director were increasingly stage managed – Rula muted her management team who were told 'You only answer direct questions if I ask you to!'

Pleasing the boss became the primary work priority – 'good' news was wanted; 'bad' news was not (Wright and Smye 1996). An illusion of successful accomplishment was created and bad news was withheld and underlying problems were disguised as unexpected 'blips'. Distracting high energy 'change interventions' were energetically enacted when work flow problems surfaced. Prizes for top team performance were promised – even though this was contrary to company policy. A gap began to open up between how the unit was presented as performing and what was actually happening on the ground.

Rula utilized emotional displays as a means of social control and intimidation, and her high status had enabled her to behave badly far longer than would otherwise have been tolerated (Sloan 2008) especially as she kept a tight veil over the details of Alpha's operations. Unable to safely vent their emotions a sense of powerlessness and hopelessness developed. Staff learned to disguise and sanitize their reactions and emotions to avoid incurring her displeasure. People, however, talked in corridors, in the lift-wells and on the stairs about her behaviour and commented that she could never admit she could be wrong about anything. Such emotional repression and suppression generated anger, a sense of being exploited and a fear of retribution for speaking out of turn. It was not exactly a 'reign of terror' as described by Duchon and Drake

(2008), but nevertheless was an unfriendly and intimidating place within which to work. Bies and Tripp (1998) accurately describe the type of abusive characteristics exhibited – including mood swings, tantrums, belittling of others and the stark exercise of power – seen during this period of Alpha's history.

Through persistent self-promotion, dynamic and energetic posturing, successful impression management and force of character she had maneuvered herself into an unassailable position of trust from above and abject fear from below. I was told by her PA that '… they will line the lift shaft and kick it when she goes down!' The tight 'in-group' pretty much did as they wished and created tight controls over what was presented as happening in the business. The lid only came off the conformity (Hewlin 2003), and the pretence of accomplishment and effective working, when whistle-blower letters to a newly appointed group managing director prompted an investigation into Rula's behaviour. She was subsequently removed from office pending inquiries into suspected malpractice.

This case illustrates how (i) a leader's increasing boldness and directness can morph into arrogance, and (ii) how explosive volatility can come to replace constructive energy and enthusiasm and generate a climate of uncertainty and fear throughout the unit. This case highlights how – under certain circumstances – good intentions can become toxic and how a preoccupation with style and seductive emotional displays can replace substance and common sense.

## Case 2: Frederick 'Beta Corp' – Self-isolation

'Beta' Corp is a well-regarded and prestigious organization weighed down by its history, traditions, conservatism and a culture of complacency. For more than two years I was involved in an advisory and coaching capacity with the board, its senior managers and other professionals. Aware that its market position was being eroded, it nevertheless maintained an overly conservative approach to competitor activity; and any desire for urgent change was hampered from the top by a complacent, and largely unresponsive, self-satisfied workforce.

The organization avoided managing poor performance in anticipation of adverse publicity and the critical political comments such an action would generate and because employment legislation made such action difficult to take. A waiting strategy was usually adopted and performance issues were resolved through inaction, internal transfer, re-allocation of responsibilities, over-staffing or denial. A stultified internal structure resulted in which those out of favour were, as far as possible, ignored and left to fester or to resign.

This case focuses on the behaviour of 'Frederick' – a bright, well-qualified professional who was responsible to the board for his group of professionally qualified specialists. The culture in which he had succeeded for several years was ultra conservative, heavily logical-rational and ponderous in manner, slow-moving and overly consensual in approach. The staff enjoyed a protected and privileged 'time-served' and risk-averse existence. As group head of function, he was the most senior advisor to whom the board looked for advice on confidential and sensitive business problems and initiatives. Reporting to the managing director, he was in a position of privilege and had to be trusted – and trustworthy – in order to execute his professional guidance in an unimpeachable manner. He delivered sound, competent and well-considered work. The conservative, respectful of time-served, indulgent organization suited him and he had been appointed to an additional role as secretary to the chairman on a significant external body. This gave him more status, enhanced political visibility and access to sensitive sector information beyond what would have normally been available to him at his level in the organizational hierarchy. He had clout, and political privilege. He did well, had flair, was charming and good company – while somewhat earnest and pretentious – and was never slow in offering to take on responsibilities that would help portray him in a good light. He was an ambitious and somewhat officious gentleman, who loved, enjoyed, encouraged and respected the formalities of business life.

When two board appointments became open Frederick applied – and expected to be appointed – and was astounded, bemused and amazed when this did not happen. He could not understand why he was not successful and in discussion with me considered that progression to the top level was primarily a cognitive matter (of choosing the 'right' ways of behaving, of providing 'the' right answer, etc., of knowing 'what' to do).

He took himself *very* seriously and his high opinion of himself, and his increasing self-promotion and stubbornly held logic about his entitlement for promotion, began to backfire as his arrogant disposition and self-serving behaviour took hold. Although this began to alienate key colleagues he seemed unaware of the counter-productive impact his behaviour was having on those around him. In spite of consistent evidence-based feedback from me, he seemed unable to see or manage the emotional impact of his behaviour as it became increasingly dysfunctional and counter-productive. Increasingly he seemed to only have eyes for himself and stalked around in an imperious manner. His actions came to be seen as transparently manipulative and 'on the make'. Tolerance for his selfishness began to wane and he was progressively marginalized as his grandiosity was increasingly seen to be without merit. It seemed as if he genuinely believed that the organization should revolve around his needs. He told me of his aggravation that the managing director – his boss – would neither champion his cause nor continue to discuss such matters as his status or promotion prospects and how he felt dishonoured, demeaned and dismayed by this.

He seemed susceptible to delusion of heroic proportions and consequently the denial of the status he pined for hit him hard and resulted in him trying even harder to push his case for special treatment, privilege and attention. His attempts at securing greater prominence and increased power, status and standing were to no avail however and merely served to alienate him further from his boss and other key colleagues (de Botton 2004).

I was told how he invariably tried to be photographed next to influential people only to then be maneuvered to the periphery of such group photographs. He demanded invitations to high-profile civic events insisting that he 'must' have been on the VIP invitation list and therefore that his name had been omitted by mistake. He bought tickets to prestigious high-profile social events – and ensured colleagues knew about it. He was rude to peers and more junior colleagues and, conversely, sought to curry favour with those of influence. His violations of socio-moral codes of behaviour – in this traditional and conservative organization – did not go unnoticed and contributed to feelings of repulsion towards him (Rozin et al. 1999).

He began to be described by colleagues as lazy, slow, passive and resistant in his behaviour and a poor man-manager. He alienated well-regarded and competent professional staff, who subsequently left the business. It was reported that he took the credit for the work of his professionally trained colleagues and that he cherry-picked high profile assignments that would show him in a good light. He was prone to blame others for poor work, and for work he had failed to deliver on time. Problems were never his fault and the blame was always laid on his staff. Others came to be suspicious of his motives and were more guarded when he was around; increasingly less trusted, his professional authenticity was significantly undermined. Externally there were adverse comments about his behaviour following long hospitality lunches, and afternoons did not seem to be the most productive period of his working day. Politically ambitious he sought to exploit his political connections to reinforce his image and sense of importance within the organization. It was common practice for him to declare in meetings that he had a 'special' meeting to go to, or that he may not be able to deliver on a promise because 'the Chairman may require … ' and these were rebuffed and became the source of overt humorous comments in meetings.

Frederick demonstrated each of the four disgust-eliciting behaviours identified by Cunningham et al. (1997) namely *intrusions and dominance displays* (for example, giving commands or giving criticism without having legitimate authority thus implying the other is of lower status); *insensitivity and non-reciprocity* (for example, asking inappropriate questions, engaging in monologues, and constantly interrupting and talking over colleagues); *norm violations and discrepant behaviours* (for example, avoiding work, cheating, being indiscrete, giving misleading information or telling lies and half-truths) and *physical violations* (for example, invading personal space, body odours, unkempt appearance; see Fitness 2008, p. 65).

A case, perhaps, of catastrophic 'emotional blindness' combined with an inability to engage with the constructive feedback available to him. While Frederick was smart, able, bright, quick and alert he seemed unable to comprehend how his behaviour was self-destructive. He seemed immune to constructive discussions about such matters that, for example, through exploration of relevant psychometric profiles and of the stark negative 360-degree feedback (on two occasions), which indicated how colleagues experienced his narcissism, rampant selfishness, falsehoods and lazy self-serving behaviour. Commenting on a lack of discernible changes since an earlier 360-degree 12 months previously, one respondent concluded it unlikely that Frederick would be able to change, or as they put it, 'Can you teach a penguin to fly?'

From initially being viewed as bright, yet somewhat pedantic and pompous, his arrogant behaviour increasingly alienated colleagues and he came to be despised. He became a marginalized and isolated figure who few wanted to work with, and a figure of contempt and loathing. He continued to see himself as 'special' and entitled to special treatment and status. Far from heeding Schein's advice, he was not able to '… be deceptive both with regard to intentions and the means used to achieve personal ends' (1979, p. 291). From being viewed as a valued and respected corporate citizen with solid professional skills he slowly became a person whose behaviour became a focus for adverse comment, ridicule and an annoying irrelevance. Beta Corp. decided to reorganize the provision of the professional services rather than deal head-on with the performance issues Frederick was presenting.

## COMPARISON OF THE CASES

These cases are about the corrupting corrosive effects of the drive for power and privilege in the workplace – both expressed feelings of envy, jealousy and unfairness and felt they deserved and were entitled to more status, money and privileges – and about how such motivations can, seemingly, blind executives to their own dysfunctional behaviour (Conger 1990; Kets de Vries 1989b; 1995; 2001; Levinson 1978; Maccoby 2003; Sankowsky 1995; Stein 2005; Zaleznik 2008). As Kets de Vries (1989a) noted 'If leaders get too much uncritical admiration ... they may begin to believe that they really are as perfect, intelligent, or powerful as others think' (p. 10). It is a dangerous belief, given the power of leaders to enact delusions of grandeur.

Rula and Frederick transited from being valued, constructive and well-regarded contributors to become impediments to constructive organizational performance. They came to crave too much success and enhanced status – and to be accorded special treatment. Both feared loss of face, loss of status and recognition, and of being excluded from power yet that is precisely what transpired. In spite of the evidenced-based constructive feedback they received about the negative impact on their behaviour they remained unable – or unwilling – to change.

The case of Rula illustrates how, in building on initial success in her new role, she was able to redefine her unit's operating procedures and success criteria to reinforce her position as *primus inter pares*. Initially this degree of unequivocal control and command was both needed and valued, but it led to a despotic and dysfunctional situation in which the primary needs being served revolved around Rula and her acolytes. One is reminded of the saying attributed to Lord Acton, a British historian and moralist, in whose opinion 'Power tends to corrupt, and absolute power corrupts absolutely ... ' (Lee-Chai and Bargh 2001, p. 264).

Working within a more highly structured and conservative organization, Frederick had little opportunity to influence how he would be assessed. He also had little influence on the freedom of action to generate favourable false impressions, which had been enjoyed by Rula. He was initially viewed as a competent and shrewd specialist, albeit somewhat self-important and opinionated, who delivered commendable work. Paradoxically, however, what may well have turned Frederick's head, and blinded him to his counter-productive behaviour, was the absolute lack of power he craved through which to carve out the preeminent position to which he believed he was entitled. Rula generated feelings of fear, humiliation, tension and uncertainty as well as grudging admiration at her assertiveness. Where they could, however, colleagues avoided contact with Rula through fear, as she was perceived as dangerous, penalistic and unpredictable. Frederick, however, generated feelings of mistrust, loathing, exasperation and disdain and was also avoided whenever possible.

At first sight the course of events these two executives followed – each seemingly the architect of their own downfall – is baffling. Unless they had become fixated on self-destruction why might they have failed to deviate from patterns of behaviour that would derail them and which had been brought to their attention? In examining these cases, four key factors emerged which seem to illuminate the transitions described.

**Four Key Features**

What was going on? The following 'key features' help illuminate this question:

- Key feature 1: Impaired awareness – in spite of feedback to the contrary about the damage their behaviour was doing to their reputation and standing, they failed to address the negative implications of their counter-productive conduct.
- Key feature 2: Dysfunctional context – the contextual conditions rewarded, facilitated, legitimized or ignored their counter-productive behaviour – and thus they perceived no reason to change.
- Key feature 3: Identity over all – their conduct suggested a significant misalignment between their sense of identity and their reputation contributing to a continuation of their self-destructive patterns of behaviour.
- Key feature 4: In the grip of Festinger and Janis – their perspectives may have become clouded and confused because of cognitive dissonance (in the case of Frederick) and 'groupthink' dynamics (in the case of Rula).

**Key feature 1: impaired awareness**

It is difficult to sustain a view that Rula was unaware of the damage her behaviour was having on colleagues but entirely possible that she failed to appreciate the damage to her reputation and organizational well-being which her high profile JFDI approach (see Chapter 4 for elaboration on expression of type in leadership) was having. Her ability to get her own way in debate, combined with the reticence of colleagues to challenge her, may well have diluted the impact of the feedback she received about her confrontational ways of working. Her behaviour towards those who opposed her – who were verbally assaulted, ridiculed or dismissed – generated a culture, which denied her accurate information about how she was really viewed by staff.

Frederick was less able psychologically to comprehend the emotional impact that his behaviour was generating in spite of feedback about this. While he could logically compute what he saw happening – that is for example his organizational marginalization, avoidance by others, lack of contact from his managing director and the reduction of his portfolio – he seemed emotionally disconnected from the negative consequences, which his behaviour was generating (Kets de Vries 1995). Protracted discussions with me about such matters – and over an extended period of time – failed to enable Frederick to connect his feelings with his overt behaviour (Goffman 1959; Goleman 1996; 1998; Walton 2011). His conviction about his entitlement to higher status may have blocked his capacity to consider the feedback about his counter-productive behaviour and enabled him to deny its validity.

A second possibility for the two leaders failing to take remedial action is that they both came to feel that they were invulnerable and consequently felt there was no need to pay attention to the personal feedback – and the growing dissent around them – because they believed that they could not be touched (Babiak and Hare, 2006; Furnham 2010; Hogan 2007; Kets de Vries 1989b; Lubit 2004a; Maccoby 2003; Price 2006; Zaleznik 2008).

For example Rula had the support of the group managing director (that is her boss' boss) and had become a figurehead for no-nonsense macho leadership. Furthermore, her grip within her business unit was complete and her inner-circle generated 'groupthink' dynamics (Janis 1982) which (i) reinforced her growing feeling of omnipotence and (ii) insulated her from many of the dysfunctional impacts which her behaviour was having. She may have convinced herself that there was no need to moderate her behaviour (Banks 2008; Hayward 2007; Kets de Vries 1993; Lee-Chai and Bargh 2001; McFarlin and Sweeney 2000; Wright and Smye 1996).

Frederick was aware that colleagues were beginning to avoid him, disregard his advice, challenge his motives and fail to show him the 'respect' and deference in meetings he believed his position merited. The politically significant and high-profile role he occupied may have deluded him into a sense of false security believing that his privileged position – and political contacts – would safeguard him from harm however he behaved (Gialcalone and Greenberg 1997; Lemert and Branaman 1997; Thomas and Hersen 2004).

**Key feature 2: dysfunctional context**

The contexts within which leaders function exert a critical influence on a leader's behaviour and shape how constructive, or not, that behaviour is seen to be (Kusy and Holloway 2009; Padilla et al. 2007). The Alpha BU was a failing, fragmented organization, internally disorganized, poorly led and disspirited. Morale and output was low and it was ripe for a major reorganization – and it was into this scenario that Rula was parachuted with a reputation for assertively getting things done.

Prior to her appointment, Rula had been one of a number of senior managers within a successfully managed unit where her assertive behaviour had been carefully directed and her predilection for attention seeking and aggressive behaviour managed and muted. The constraints of a more stable, conservative organizational context – as in Frederick's organization – would have curtailed her grandiose *prima donna* excesses and lessened the likelihood of her subsequent failure.

Frederick's organization was quite different, however, as in his case the context tolerated and sustained his dysfunctional behaviour for far too long through complacency, cowardice, lack of senior leadership, a strategy of containment and the onset of organizational atrophy. Those out of favour were, as far as possible, ignored in the hope they would find alternative employment. Poor performance was rarely directly addressed and in this case Beta Corp. decided to reorganize the provision of the professional services rather than deal head-on with the performance issues Frederick was posing. Perversely had Frederick been in the Alpha BU such a situation would not have been tolerated and he would have been asked to shape-up – and been told what he had to do to realize his promotional aspirations – or ship-out.

Albeit in different ways, the Alpha BU and Beta Corp. provided a breeding ground for leadership toxicity and drew Rula and Frederick away from the middle ground of competent leadership practice onto the rocks of excess and despair. Kupers and Weibler (2008) suggest that '... organizations probably become dysfunctional and unhealthy when they refuse to acknowledge and integrate feelings and emotions adequately' (p. 272). This offers a further perspective in examining our two cases. Rula dominated the emotional airspace to such an extent that only 'her' emotions prevailed – and her ego took over the place until she was replaced. In Frederick's organization no credence was given to the relevance of emotions or feelings in leadership and thus they were denied, dismissed as irrelevant or viewed as an impediment to a person's suitability for leadership. In such an organization Frederick had nowhere to go other than into his own personal world of increasing frustration (Hayward 2007; Kets de Vries 1989b; 1995; 2001).

## Key feature 3: identity over all

A prominent feature in both cases was a profound mismatch between each executive's perceptions of their 'self' (such as their identity) and how others perceived them (such as their reputation), which contributed to the continuation of their self-destructive patterns of behaviour. Workplace emotional displays reflect: (i) *who* we feel ourselves to be; (ii) *how* we believe we should be treated; (iii) *what* we believe in; and (iv) *reciprocal* workplace dynamics. Significant differences between such emotionally charged expectations are likely to generate tension. Hogan (2007), for example, notes how each of us will have a view about who we believe our self to be – our sense of identity – and that this will be the story we will tell ourselves and others about us. He contrasts this with the views, which other people will have about us – our reputation – which form the basis for the stories others tell about us. Reputation thus becomes a type of condensed summary evaluation of our past interactions as recalled by others. A mismatch between these two sets of perceptions and expectations will generate confusion, disharmony, interpersonal conflict and angst.

Rula was well attuned to the emotional dynamics she generated and may have deliberately manipulated – and staged – them for her own advantage (Gardner and Avolio 1998). This may have contributed to her over-playing her strengths too much (Dotlich and Cairo 2003; Downs 1997; Hayward 2007; Hogan 2007; Kaiser and Hogan 2010; Kaplan and Kaiser 2006; Rosenthal and Pittinsky 2006) whereas with Frederick it was his inability to address or 'see' the profound gap between his view of himself and how others perceived him that contributed to his problems. 'Identity' and 'reputational' incongruence was a factor in the emergence of dysfunctional behaviour in both cases.

Mangham (1986, p. 98) for example notes how: '... our upbringing and experience provide us with a structure of emotions and thoughts with regard to status and power ...'. The striving to achieve internally held idealized images may well drive a leader to try to become the person they have been socialized into seeking to be, rather than the person they are capable of being (Knights and Willmott 1999; Kets de Vries 1995). Such strivings – if unrealistic and unfounded – are likely to be psychologically damaging to the individual and may be costly to the organization as would seem to have been the case with Frederick.

**Key feature 4: in the grip of Festinger and Janis**

The two leaders' perspectives may also have become clouded and confused because of 'groupthink' dynamics (Janis 1982; Harvey 1988) in the case of Rula and cognitive dissonance (Festinger 1957) in the case of Frederick.

Janis describes three types of groupthink: (i) *Type I: overestimations of the group's power and morality*, which generates an illusion of invulnerability, creates excessive optimism and encourages more extreme risk-taking combined with an unquestioned belief in the group's inherent morality which, in turn, then inclines the group to ignore or rationalize the moral consequences of their decisions; (ii) *Type II: closed-mindedness* where the group discounts contradictory information through reasserting 'what we have decided to do ...' and through negatively stereotyping those outside the in-group as a further basis for the action proposed; and (iii) *Type III: pressure towards uniformity* involving conformity pressure on members who show doubt and the blocking of information contrary to the illusion of unanimity that has developed.

This concept primarily applies to Rula's behaviour where the tight in-group she dominated became consumed with their self-importance and omnipotence. The isolated and cohesive workings of Rula's inner group – combined with evidence of the personal damage inflicted on those who challenged this group – created a phoney and superficial impression of organizational cohesion. While contrary views were invited, they were unwelcome and those who raised them were invariably penalized; consequently, opinions contrary to Rula's were muted, constrained, outlawed or ridiculed. The concentration of positional and emotional power within her closed circle created a false sense of openness as whatever they decided to do was 'right' – and was invariably acted upon at breakneck speed. The pressure towards uniformity and compliance within the organization was high and casualties littered the building of those who raised questions deemed to be inconvenient or seen to challenge the veneer of uniformity. It is highly likely that '... An illusion of invulnerability ...' inclined them '... to ignore the ethical and moral consequences of their decisions' (Janis 1982, p. 174; Price 2006; 2008). This would seem to have been the case here as, following her departure, proceedings were initiated into possible court action for misdemeanours.

The notion of cognitive dissonance (Festinger 1957) introduced by Festinger hypothesized that when a person held cognitions that were at odds with each other (what could be labelled dissonant) internal psychological discomfort was generated which the person would then seek to remove or ameliorate and that such psychological dissonance is a normally occurring phenomena. Frederick was experiencing intense psychological discomfort because the treatment he was receiving from his boss and his colleagues was inconsistent with his belief about his high status and position of indispensability within the organization. As such he held two conflicting cognitions: (i) his view of his self as a high status and worthy person in the organization; and (ii) his cognitions about how he was being treated within that organization. The discomfort was further intensified because the personal coaching and feedback he was being offered also challenged the high opinion he held about himself.

In order to reduce – or ideally perhaps remove – this tension he was confronted with a stark choice. Revise the view he had of his worth and of his identity, or discount or discredit the contrary information he was receiving. I believe he chose to maintain his strong sense of identity, and the belief that he was special and entitled to privileged treatment. Thus, feedback dissonant to his preferred view of the world – and of his position within it – was consequently discounted, ignored, reconstrued as an anomalous blip, or explained away in some other manner. He described feeling that he was being discriminated against and increasingly cast himself as a victim who was losing out in sharp contrast to the favoured few who got all the 'goodies'. He maintained his unwavering beliefs about personal entitlement and his status as a VIP, which contributed to his persistent, puzzling and baffling, dysfunctional behaviour. However, it may well be that to have revised his view of himself would have been too damaging and problematic a matter for his ego to contemplate, and to explain socially.

The consistency with which both Frederick and Rula negated pertinent feedback about the emotional impact of their behaviour on others was startling and is likely to have reflected personal beliefs that may have become deeply entrenched and too traumatic, in psychological terms, to unpick, review or revise.

These four 'key features', in combination, highlight the significance which individual discretion, cognition and choice play in determining and shaping a leader's functional or dysfunctional behaviour. While insight about the emotional impact of one's behaviour as a leader is necessary to avoid becoming dysfunctional it is *how* such awareness is interpreted and applied that makes the difference – as these cases illustrate. The cases also illustrate the utility and potency of concepts such as groupthink (Janis 1982) and cognitive dissonance (Festinger 1957) in examining the determinants of executive behaviour and the role such concepts can play in resisting as well as encouraging toxic and dysfunctional excess.

## 'PEACOCK POWER' AND WORKPLACE BEHAVIOUR: EMOTION, TOXICITY AND DYSFUNCTION IN LEADERSHIP

At their core, these cases are about the seduction of power and privilege in the workplace and about how such emotive motivations can, seemingly, blind executives to their own dysfunctional behaviour and to the corrosive impact such behaviour exerts within the organization as a whole. As Zaleznik (1970) observes 'the competition for power is characteristic of all political structures. And, whatever else they may be, business organizations are political structures ...' (p. 48). These cases suggest that how a leader manages their emotions-in-context will be a significant factor in a leader's continuing success (Lord et al. 2002). The cases also suggest that leaders (i) without sufficient personal insight and (ii) who fail to exercise self-control may well be more likely to exhibit toxic and dysfunctional behaviour.

So how then does this chapter contribute to a fuller discussion about leadership emotion, toxicity and dysfunction? To begin with the material demonstrates that leadership is not 'emotion neutral'. There is a children's game played in the UK called 'follow the leader' in which every player has to copy the behaviour of the designated 'leader'. This type of copying applies to the adult world too and in business a leader's behaviour carries with it an emotional tag and invitation to comply with what the leader says and does. So how a leader behaves will – if not copied exactly – be noticed, decoded and variously acted upon.

While this may appear obvious, the business of leadership is an intensely personal and idiosyncratic matter and not something to be examined 'as if' it were a stable, universally defined and discrete entity that can be prodded, poked, segmented and tested for its inherent qualities. Essentially phenomenological the emotional attributes of leadership emerge through the variable relational and contextual interactions in any one place at any one time. Thus, to construe and examine the emotional concomitants of leadership primarily from a logical positivistic perspective is to risk missing the fundamental humanness of leadership *behaviour-in-practice* and to choose to disregard the emotional imperatives of leadership (Bedeian 1995; Goffman 1959; Goldman 2008; Goleman 1998; Roberts and Hogan 2002; Stein 2005).

Maintaining and defending their status and position was a major motivation for both Rula and Frederick (Price 2008). Indeed it could be argued that the primary motivations, which underpinned much of their dysfunctional behaviour, were deeply felt emotive concerns about the protection and exercise of their status, entitlement and power. These concerns may have evoked ontological anxiety and triggered overt defensive fight (from Rula) and flight (from Frederick), which subsequently led to excessive display of dysfunctional behaviour (van Deurzen 2002; Spinelli 1989). Furthermore, both needed to be respected – and craved to be honoured and held in high esteem – yet Frederick's sense of perceived injustice, and Rula's unconstrained authoritative behaviour emerged as Achilles heels to their ambitions. Their desire to better their position perhaps may have reflected Adam Smith's assertion that '... the better off men appear, the more likely they are to get the attention, approval, and praise of others' (Gray et al. 2005, p. 242). Rula, *groomed to survive*, had far exceeded modest familial expectations and, at times, could not quite believe the trappings of power and privilege she had attained even though she still wanted 'more'. In contrast Frederick, *groomed to excel*, had been conditioned to be the best within his family, and he behaved accordingly and expected to be treated as such within Beta Corp.

In reflecting on such narcissistic tendencies among high flyers, McCall (1998) quotes Harry Levinson on the grandiose self-image which can develop as executives become more senior: 'They think they have the right to be condescending and contemptuous to people who serve them. They (executives) think they are entitled to privilege and the royal treatment'. McCall concludes: 'In summary, the development of arrogance is one of the most insidious of the derailment dynamics. It is a negative that grows from a positive, deriving as it does from actual talent and success (1998, p. 46)' (see also Conger 1990; Lubit 2002; Lundeman and Erlandson 2004; Maccoby 2003; 2007; Kets de Vries 1989a; 2001; 2009). Both of these cases were infused with hubris born of success, personal grandiosity and entitlement derived, just as McCall observed '... from actual talent and success' but where, without self-management ego and narcissistic needs came to overwhelm them both (Collins 2009; Gardner and Avolio 1998; Goffman 1959; Kets de Vries 1993; Lubit 2002; Maccoby 2003; McCall 1998; Owen 2007).

Next was how the freedom of expression of emotions and behaviour reflected, and was conditioned by, organizational status (Lively and Powell 2006; Sloan 2004). Recent research has highlighted how those in positions of high status are less bound by norms governing the display of negative emotions (for example, anger) that constrain lower status workers. Whereas the expression of powerful negative emotions by high status individuals is more socially acceptable (Hochschild 1983; Erickson and Ritter 2001), the same emotions when expressed from low(er) status individuals will be seen as deviant or anomic (Tiedens 2001). Consequently, those at the top of the workplace hierarchy are likely to be freer in their emotional expression than those in more junior positions. In accordance with this, Rula became increasingly unconstrained and dismissive in her behaviour towards 'them'. One consequence was that staff held their tongues, maintained a safe psychological distance and became 'silent' (Perlow and Williams 2003), or told the boss just enough to avoid trouble (Bies and Tripp 1998b, p. 212).

In their research on the derailment and burnout of high-flyers Casserley and Megginson (2009) note how 'attempts to get them to change self-damaging behaviour will be frustrated by a lack of awareness of their condition or the consequent decline in their performance' (p. 49). The senior organizational status of Rula and Frederick enabled both to behave badly far longer than would have been tolerated had they occupied more junior posts (Sankowsky 1995; Sloan 2008).

Finally, maintaining self-control and developing self-insight emerged as key factors in the inability of Rula and Frederick to arrest their slide into dysfunction. This is in line with the research of Marcus and Schuler (2004) who highlight 'the importance of self-control as a key underlying factor in the likely incidence of general counterproductive behaviour (GCB) ... ' interestingly however they also note that much '... appear[s] to depend on the absence of effective internal constraints inhibiting GCB. In consequence our results point to the conclusion that developing a workforce consisting of sufficiently self-controlled individuals would be a highly effective countermeasure for problems associated with acts of GCB' (p. 656). The work of Marcus and Schuler (2004) highlights not only aspects of individual behaviour but also the importance of the operational context as a key mediating variable in facilitating or resisting leadership toxicity and the onset of what I term 'peacock power'. Instances where high-flyers come to believe their own publicity too much and egotistically succumb to a deluded belief of indispensability, omnipotence or invincibility.

Leadership, while necessary, is not necessarily a force for good and thus a broader exploration of this tortuous and ill-defined concept should be welcomed. Leaders remain susceptible to human vulnerabilities and therefore will be good *and* bad, rather than good *or* bad; ethical *and* immoral rather than ethical *or* immoral; competent *and* incompetent rather than competent *or* incompetent. Rula and Frederick had many positive points and had reached senior executive positions on merit. At the same time emotional mismanagement caused their human failings to become career limiting failings. Cases such as these enhance our understanding of leadership at work and contribute to leadership as theory, as planned research and as dynamic academic discourse.

## REFERENCES

Aasland, M., A. Skogstad and S. Einarsen (2008), 'The dark side: defining destructive leadership behaviour', *Organisations and People*, **15** (3), 20–8.
Ashforth, B. (1995), 'Emotion in the workplace: a reappraisal', *Human Relations*, **48** (2), 97–125.
Ashkanasy, N and C. Cooper (eds) (2008), *Research Companion to Emotion in Organizations*, Cheltenham, UK, and Northampton, MA, USA: Edward Elgar.
Babiak, P. and R. Hare (2006), *Snakes in Suits: When Psychopaths Go to Work*, New York: HarperCollins.
Banks, S. (2008), *Dissent and the Failure of Leadership*, Cheltenham, UK, and Northampton, MA, USA: Edward Elgar.
Bedeian, A. (1995), 'Workplace envy', *Organizational Dynamics*, **23** (4), 49–56.
Bies, R. and T. Tripp (1998a), 'Revenge in organizations: the good, the bad and the ugly', in C. Cooper and D. Rousseau (eds), *Trends in Organizational Behaviour*, Chichester: John Wiley & Sons, pp. 49–67.
Bies, R. and T. Tripp (1998b), 'Two faces of the powerless: coping with tyranny in organizations', in R.M. Kramer and M.A. Neale (eds), *Power and Influence in Organizations*, Thousand Oaks, CA: SAGE, pp. 203–20.
Bramming, P. and R. Johnsen (2011), 'Love will tear us apart – transformational leadership and love in a call centre', *European Journal of International management*, **5** (1), 80–95.
Byron, C. (2004), *Testosterone Inc.: Tales of CEOs Gone Wild*, Hoboken, NJ: John Wiley & Sons Inc.
Casserley, T. and D. Megginson (2009), *Learning from Burnout*, Oxford: Butterworth-Heinemann.
Checkland, P. (1981), *Systems Thinking, Systems Practice*, Chichester: John Wiley & Sons.
Coffey, A. (1999), *The Ethnographic Self: Fieldwork and the Representation of Reality*, London: SAGE.
Coffey, A. and P. Atkinson (1996), *Making sense of Qualitative Data: Complementary Research Strategies*, Thousand Oaks, CA: SAGE.
Collins, J. (2009), *How the Mighty Fall: And Why Some Companies Never Give In*, London: Random House Group Ltd.
Conger, J. (1990), 'The dark side of leadership', *Organizational Dynamics*, **19** (2), 44–55.
Cunningham, M., A. Barbee and P. Druen (1997), 'Social allergens and the reactions they produce', in R. Kowalski, *Aversive Interpersonal Behaviours*, New York: Plenum, pp. 189–214.
de Botton, A. (2004), *Status Anxiety*, London: Hamish Hamilton.
Dotlich, D. and P. Cairo (2003), *Why CEOs Fail: The 11 Behaviors That Can Derail Your Climb to the Top – And How to Manage Them*, San Francisco, CA: Jossey-Bass.
Downs, A. (1997), *Beyond the Looking Glass: Overcoming the Seductive Culture of Corporate Narcissism*, New York: American Management Association.

Duchon, D. and B. Drake (2008), 'Organizational narcissism and virtuous behavior', *Journal of Business Ethics*, **85** (3), 301–8.

Einarsen, S., M. Aasland and A. Skogstad (2007), 'Destructive leadership behaviour: a definition and a conceptual model', *The Leadership Quarterly*, **18** (3), 207–16.

Erickson, R. and C. Ritter (2001), 'Emotional labor, burnout, and inauthenticity: does gender matter?', *Social Psychology Quarterly*, **64** (2), 146–63.

Festinger, L. (1957), *A Theory of Cognitive Dissonance*, Stanford, CA: Stanford University Press.

Fineman, S. (2000), *Emotion in Organizations*, London: SAGE.

Fineman, S. (2003), *Understanding Emotions at Work*, London: SAGE.

Fineman, S. and Y. Gabriel (1996), *Experiencing Organizations*, London: SAGE.

Fitness, J. (2008), 'Fear and loathing in the workplace', in N. Ashkanasy and C. Cooper (eds), *Research Companion to Emotion in Organizations*, Cheltenham, UK, and Northampton, MA, USA: Edward Elgar, pp. 61–72.

Frost, P. (2003), *Toxic Emotions at Work*, Boston, MA: Harvard Business School Press.

Frost, P. and S. Robinson (1999), 'The toxic handler', *Harvard Business Review*, **77** (4), 96–107.

Furnham, A. (2007), 'Personality disorders and derailment at work', in C. Langan-Fox, R. Cooper and R. Klimoski (eds), *Research Companion to the Dysfunctional Workplace*, Cheltenham, UK, and Northampton, MA, USA: Edward Elgar, pp. 22–39.

Furnham, A. (2010), *The Elephant in the Boardroom: The Causes of Leadership Derailment*, Basingstoke: Palgrave Macmillan.

Gabriel, Y. (1999), *Organizations in Depth: The Psychoanalysis of Organizations*, Thousand Oaks, CA: SAGE.

Gallos, J. (2008), 'Learning from the toxic trenches', *Journal of Management Inquiry*, **17** (4), 354–67.

Gardner, W. and B. Avolio (1998), 'The charismatic relationship: a dramaturgical perspective', *Academy of Management Review*, **23** (1), 32–58.

Giacalone, R. and J. Greenberg (1997), *Antisocial Behavior in Organizations*, Thousand Oaks, CA: SAGE.

Gill, J. and P. Johnson (2005), *Research Methods for Managers*, London: SAGE.

Goffman, I. (1959), *The Presentation of Self in Everyday Life*, New York: Anchor Books.

Goldman, A. (2008), 'The enigma of the unintentionally toxic leader', *Organisations and People*, **15** (3), 55–62.

Goldman, A. (2009a), *Destructive Leaders and Dysfunctional Organizations: A Therapeutic Approach*, Cambridge: Cambridge University Press.

Goldman, A. (2009b), *Transforming Toxic Leaders*, Stanford, CA: Stanford Business Books.

Goleman, D. (1996), *Emotional Intelligence: Why It Can Matter More than IQ*, London: Bloomsbury.

Goleman, D. (1998), *Working with Emotional Intelligence*, London: Bloomsbury.

Gray, K., L. Frieder and G. Clark (2005), *Corporate Scandals: The Many Faces of Greed*, St Paul, MN: Paragon House.

Hamilton, S. and A. Micklethwait (2006), *Greed and Corporate Failure: The Lessons from Recent Disasters*, Basingstoke: Palgrave Macmillan.

Harvey, J. (1988), *The Abilene Paradox: And Other Meditations on Management*, Lanham, MD: Lexington Books

Hayward, M. (2007), *Ego Check: Why Executive Hubris is Wrecking Companies*, Chicago, IL: Kaplan Publishing.

Hewlin, P. (2003), 'And the award for the best actor goes to…: facades of conformity in organizational settings', *Academy of Management Review*, **28** (4) 633–42.

Hirschhorn, L. (1988), *The Workplace Within: Psychodynamics of Organizational Life*, Cambridge, MA: MIT Press.

Hochschild, A. (1983), *The Managed Heart: The Commercialization of Human Feeling*, Berkeley, CA: University of California Press.

Hogan, R. (2007), *Personality and the Fate of Organizations*, Mahwah, NJ: Lawrence Erlbaum Associates Publishers.

Janis, I. (1982), *Victims of Groupthink*, Boston, MA: Houghton Mifflin Co.

Kaiser, R. and R. Hogan (2010), 'How to (and how not to) assess the integrity of managers', *Consulting Psychology Journal: Practice and Research*, **62** (4), 216–34.

Kaplan, R. (1990), 'Introduction: why character and leadership?', *The Journal of Applied Behavioral Science*, **26** (4), 417–22.

Kaplan, B. and R. Kaiser (2006), *The Versatile Leader: Make the Most of Your Strengths Without Overdoing It*, San Francisco, CA: Pfeiffer.

Kellerman, B. (2004), *Bad Leadership*, Boston, MA: Harvard Business School Press.

Kets de Vries, M. (1989a), 'Leaders who self-destruct: the causes and cures', *Organizational Dynamics*, **17** (4), 5–17.

Kets de Vries, M. (1989b), *Prisoners of Leadership*, New York: John Wiley & Sons.

Kets de Vries, M. (1993), *Leaders, Fools, and Imposters: Essays on the Psychology of Leadership*, San Francisco, CA: Jossey-Bass.

Kets de Vries, M. (1995), *Life and Death in the Executive Fast Lane: Essays on Irrational Organizations and Their Leaders*, San Francisco, CA: Jossey-Bass.

Kets de Vries, M. (2001), *Struggling with the Demon: Perspectives on Individual and Organizational Irrationality*, Madison, WI: Psychosocial Press.

Kets de Vries, M. (2006), *The Leadership Mystique*, London: Prentice Hall.

Kets de Vries, M. (2009), *Reflections on Character and Leadership*, San Francisco, CA: Jossey-Bass.

Knights, D. and H. Willmott (1999), *Management Lives: Power and Identity in Work Organizations*, London: SAGE.

Kupers, W. and J. Weibler (2008), 'Emotions in organisation: an integral perspective', *International Journal of Work Organisation and Emotion*, **2** (3), 256–87.

Kusy, M. and E. Holloway (2009), *Toxic Workplace: Managing Toxic Personalities and Their Systems of Power*, San Francisco, CA: Jossey-Bass.

Langan-Fox, J., C. Cooper and R. Klimoski (eds) (2007), *Research Companion to the Dysfunctional Workplace*, Cheltenham, UK, and Northampton, MA, USA: Edward Elgar.

Lee-Chai, A. and J. Bargh (2001), *The Use and Abuse of Power: Multiple Perspectives on the Causes of Corruption*, Philadelphia, PA: Psychology Press.

Lemert, C. and A. Branaman (1997), *The Goffman Reader*, Malden, MA: Blackwell.

Levinson, H. (1978), 'The abrasive personality', *Harvard Business Review*, **56** (3), 86–94.

Lindgren, M., J. Packendorff and H. Tham (2011), 'Relational dysfunctionality: leadership interactions in a Sarbanes-Oxley Act implementation project', *European Journal of International Management*, **5** (1), 13–29.

Lipman-Blumen, J. (2005), *The Allure of Toxic Leaders*, New York: Oxford University Press.

Lipman-Blumen, J. (2008), 'Control myths: how followers unwittingly keep toxic leaders in power', *Organisations and People*, **15** (3), 111–20.

Lively, K. and B. Powell (2006), 'Emotional expression at work and at home: domain, status, or individual characteristics?' *Social Psychology Quarterly*, **69** (1), 17–38.

Lockyer, J. and D. McCabe (2011), 'Leading through fear: emotion, rationality and innovation in a UK manufacturing company', *European Journal of International Management*, **5** (1), 48–61.

Lord, R. and Harvey, J. (2002), 'An information processing framework for emotional regulation', in R. Lord, R. Klimoski and R. Kramer (eds), *Emotions in the Workplace: Understanding the Structure and Role of Emotions in Organizational Behavior*, San Francisco, CA: Jossey-Bass, pp. 115–46.

Lord, R., R. Klimoski and R. Kramer (eds) (2002), *Emotions in the Workplace: Understanding the Structure and Role of Emotions in Organizational Behavior*, San Francisco, CA: Jossey-Bass.

Lubit, R. (2002), 'The long-term organizational impact of destructively narcissistic managers', *Academy of Management Executive*, **16** (1), 127–38.

Lubit, R. (2004a), *Coping with Toxic Managers, Subordinates and other Difficult People*, Upper Saddle River, NJ: Pearson Education.

Lubit, R. (2004b), 'The tyranny of toxic managers: applying emotional intelligence to deal with difficult personalities', *Ivey Business Journal*, **68** (4), 1–7.

Ludeman, K. and E. Erlandson (2004), 'Coaching the alpha male', *Harvard Business Review*, **82** (5) 58–67.

Maccoby, M. (2003), *Narcissistic Leaders: Who Succeeds and Who Fails*, Boston, MA: Harvard Business School Press.

Maccoby, M. (2007), *The Leaders We Need and What Makes Us Follow*, Boston, MA: Harvard Business School Press.

Mangham, I. (1986), *Power and Performance in Organizations*, Oxford: Basil Blackwell.

Marcus, B. and H. Schuler (2004), 'Antecedents of counterproductive behaviour at work: a general perspective', *Journal of Applied Psychology*, **89** (4), 647–60.

May, T. (2006), *Social Research: Issues, Methods and Process*, Buckingham: Open University Press.

McCall, G. and J. Simmons (1969), *Issues in Participant Observation: A Text and Reader*, Reading, MA: Addison-Wesley.

McCall, M. (1998), *High Flyers: Developing the Next Generation of Leaders*, Boston, MA: Harvard Business School Press.

McCall, M. and M. Lombardo (1983), *Off the Track: Why and How Successful Executives Get Derailed*, Greensboro, NC: Center for Creative Leadership.

McFarlin, D. and P. Sweeney (2000), *Where Egos Dare*, London: Kogan Page.

McLean, B. and P. Elkind (2004). *The Smartest Guys in the Room: The Amazing Rise and the Scandalous Fall of Enron*, London: Penguin Books.

Mitchell, L. (2001), *Corporate Irresponsibility: America's Newest Export*, New Haven, CT: Yale University Press.

Muhr, S. (2011), 'Leaders as cyborgs: leadership through mechanistic superiority', in M. Alvesson and A. Spicer (eds), *Methaphors We Lead By*, London, UK: Routledge, pp. 138–61.

Newton, L. (2006), *Permission to Steal*, Malden, MA: Blackwell Publishing.

Owen, D. (2007), *The Hubris Syndrome: Bush, Blair and the Intoxication of Power*, London: Politico's Publishing.

Padilla, A., R. Hogan and R. Kaiser (2007), 'The toxic triangle: destructive leaders, susceptible followers, and conducive environments', *The Leadership Quarterly*, **18** (3), 176–94.

Payne, R. and C. Cooper (eds) (2001), *Emotions at Work: Theory, Research and Applications for Management*, Chichester: John Wiley & Sons.

Perlow, L. and S. Williams (2003), 'Is silence killing your company?', *Harvard Business Review*, **81** (5), 52–8.

Price, T. (2006), *Understanding Ethical Failures in Leadership*, New York: Cambridge University Press.

Price, T. (2008), *Leadership Ethics: An Introduction*, New York: Cambridge University Press.

Rehn, A. and M. Lindahl (2011), 'Leadership and the 'right to respect' – on honour and shame in emotionally charged management settings', *European Journal of International Management*, **5** (1), 62–79.

Richardson, J. (1997), *Handbook of Qualitative Research Methods*, Leicester: The British Psychological Society.

Roberts, B. and R. Hogan (eds) (2002), *Personality Psychology in the Workplace*, Washington, DC: American Psychological Association.

Rosenthal, S. and T. Pittinsky (2006), 'Narcissistic leadership', *The Leadership Quarterly*, **17** (6), 617–33.

Rozin, P., L. Lowery., S. Imada and J. Haidt (1999), 'The CAD triad hypothesis: a mapping between three moral emotions (contempt, anger, disgust) and three moral codes (community, autonomy, and divinity)', *Journal of Personality and Social Psychology*, **76** (4), 574–86.

Sankowsky, D. (1995), 'The charismatic leader as narcissist: understanding the abuse of power', *Organizational Dynamics*, **23** (4), 57–71.

Schein, V. (1979), 'Examining an illusion: the role of deceptive behaviors in organizations', *Human Relations*, **32** (4), 287–95.

Schell, B. (1999), *Management in the Mirror: Stress and Emotional Dysfunction in Lives at the Top*, Westport, CT: Quorum Books.

Sloan, M. (2004), 'The effects of occupational characteristics on the experience and expression of anger in the workplace', *Work and Occupations*, **31** (1), 38–72.

Sloan, M. (2008), 'Emotional management and workplace status: consequences for well-being', *International Journal of Work Organisation and Emotion*, **2** (3), 236–55.

Spinelli, E. (1989), *The Interpreted World: An Introduction to Phenomenological Psychology*, London: SAGE.

Stein, M. (1997), 'Envy and leadership', *European Journal of Work and Organisation Psychology*, **6** (4), 453–65.

Stein, M. (2005), 'The Othello conundrum: the inner contagion of leadership', *Organization Studies*, **26** (9), 1405–19.

Thomas, J. and M. Hersen (eds) (2004), *Psychopathology in the Workplace*, New York: Brunner-Routledge.

Tiedens, L. (2001), 'Anger and advancement versus sadness and subjugation: the effect of negative emotion on status conferral', *Journal of Personality and Social Psychology*, **80** (1), 86–94.

van Deurzen, E. (2002), *Existential Counselling*, London: SAGE.

Walton, M. (2005), *Executive Behaviour-in-Context*, Bradford: University of Bradford.

Walton, M. (2007), 'Leadership toxicity – an inevitable affliction of organisations?', *Organisations and People*, **14** (1), 19–27.

Walton, M. (2008a), 'Toxic leadership', in A. Marturano and J. Gosling, *Leadership: The Key Concepts*, Abingdon: Routledge, pp. 160–63.

Walton, M. (2008b), 'In consideration of a toxic workplace: a suitable place for treatment', in A. Kinder. R. Hughes and C. Cooper (eds), *Employee Well-Being Support: A Workplace Resource*, Chichester: John Wiley & Sons, pp. 9–24.

Walton, M. (2011), 'The self-awareness myth', *Organisations and People*, **18** (1), 42–51.

Watson, T. (1994), *In Search of Management: Culture, Chaos and Control in Managerial Work*, London: Routledge.

Whicker, M. (1996), *Toxic Leaders: When Organizations Go Bad*, Westport, CT: Quorum Books.

Wright, L. and M. Smye (1996), *Corporate Abuse: How 'Lean and Mean' Robs People and Profits*, New York: Simon and Schuster.

Yukl, G. (1998), *Leadership in Organizations*, Upper Saddle River, NJ: Prentice-Hall.

Zaleznik, A. (1970), 'Power and politics in organizational life', *Harvard Business Review*, **48** (3), 47–60.

Zaleznik, A. (2008), *Hedges and Foxes: Character, Leadership, and Command in Organizations*, New York: Palgrave Macmillan.

Zaleznik, A. and M. Kets de Vries (1985), *Power and the Corporate Mind*, Chicago, IL: Bonus Books.

# 4. Do it my way: a study on type, leadership and emotions

## Jeanette Lemmergaard and Clare Howard

## INTRODUCTION

Research continues to confirm that the model of management and leadership prevalent across Western organizations is heavily biased towards individuals who show personal preferences for logical, solution-centred and goal-driven achievement (Kroeger et al. 2002; Blass and Hackston 2008). Despite the fact that there is a growing interest in, for example, work–life balance, emotional intelligence and spirituality in the workplace (Fineman 2000; Adams 2005; Ashkanasy and Cooper 2008; Case and Gosling 2010) the vast majority of research is still missing voices on alternative decision-making preferences, for example, those concerned with making decisions based on people-centred values and emotions. The literature on values and emotions that do exist seems mainly to revolve around aggression, violence and 'warfare', rather than on care, cooperation and empathy, despite the fact that empathy, for example, is part of our primate heritage (Rehn 2010).

Arguing from a socio-historic and psychological perspective, this chapter contributes to and extends the leadership literature by discussing how different leadership repertoires are influenced by personality and how such repertoires influence behaviour and emotions. Building on a combination of quantitative findings on leadership typology and a reconstructed narrative case study, the chapter discusses what is missing, when for example a strong leadership style does not allow other voices to be heard and acted upon, and when the emotional aspect of leadership is not accounted for. The chapter also shows why organizations should resist the temptation to simply clone themselves in hiring and nurturing new personnel. While defending a reflexive position, this chapter draws inspiration from the rather functionalistic Myers–Briggs Type Indicator (MBTI®) that identifies leadership type as a moderator of the effects of leaders' emotional displays on follower perceptions and behaviour. The

MBTI® analysis should, in this study, be seen as a comparative frame into which we place the leadership phenomena. Not for the purpose of stating law-like generalizations, but for the purpose of outlining an analytical bridgehead. The chapter shows how leadership is sometimes oversimplified through uncritical usage of typology measures with the risk of underestimating emotional fluctuations and individual differences with regard to emotional interpretations and reactions. The chapter compares leadership to the uneasy resemblance of Dr Jekyll and Mr Hyde and shows the inseparability of either the dark or the compassionate side of leadership by demonstrating how different types of leaders can be equally successful and ineffectual depending on the interpretations and reactions of followers. Based on a case study presented as a reconstructed narrative, the chapter questions the understanding of leaders as isolated heroes and instead considers how the psychologies of leaders are shaped and transformed by interaction between the individual leaders and their followers, and how different types of leaders are best suited to lead in particular situations, albeit recognizing that all situations are in constant flux and nothing is static.

To explore this, the chapter is structured as follows. First, the chapter explores the topics of type. This is done from the perspective of a practical application of Jungian theory and experience in a context of leadership and emotions. The goal is not to question the validity of the instrument, but rather to raise awareness about the use and misuse of the instrument relative to its intended use in relation to leadership. Thus, this chapter follows a more humble approach to leadership than is usually entertained among scholars on type theories. Following this, a reconstructed narrative case study is presented. The chapter concludes with a discussion on the intentional and unintentional consequences of relying too strongly on leadership archetypes as leaders' – and followers' – personalities and behaviour is context-sensitive. Not only do different contexts demand different forms of leadership, leadership is also a dynamic interaction between leaders' and followers' personalities and behaviours.

## THEORIES OF TYPE

Numerous theories, books, workshops and tests have been developed to help leaders understand their own and others' personality, behaviour and character. In fact, so many personality concepts, and so many different psychometric instruments have been developed to measure an individual's capabilities and to learn about preferences that the characterization of a '... Babel of concepts and scales...' seems appropriate for the personality domain (John and Srivastava 1999, p. 102).

The idea of classifying individuals in accordance to universal characteristics is not new. The first attempt to divide individuals into types took its departure in the classical thought of the four elements; earth, air, fire and water. Empedocles, a Greek pre-Socratic philosopher living in the fifth century BC, believed that all matter is comprised of the four 'roots' or elements of earth, air, fire and water, which are not only physical manifestations or material substances, but also spiritual essences. According to Empedocles, the nature of the universe is based on the interaction of two dynamic twin forces of 'love' and 'strife', which are determined by these four primary elements (such as earth, air, fire and water), and which could bring about the mixture and development of life (Kirk et al. 1983).

Another ancient Greek philosopher and scientist who subscribed to the idea of four personality types was the physician Hippocrates of Cos, often referred to as the 'Father of Medicine'. Rather than considering 'roots' or elements, he subdivided personalities in accordance with four bodily fluids each representing a temperament (choleric, melancholy, sanguine and phlegmatic). Fire is akin to his conceptualization of blood (active, enthusiastic), earth to phlegm (apathetic, sluggish), air to yellow bile (irritable, changeable) and water to black bile (sad, brooding) (Jastrow 1915; Wilson 2006).

Similarly, these four elements also play an important part in, for example, astrology where they are important features of the delineation when translated as personality traits or temperaments. Later attempts to subdivide human beings into types took as a point of departure the body form, and tried to determine the correlation between body form and psychological characteristics (Greenbaum 2005). However, as with the old Greek theories these later theories have found little scientific support.

Nevertheless, the idea that human beings can be divided in accordance to type has remained. With the rise of science and the use of mathematics in the nineteenth century, hope was raised that mathematical models could be harnessed to understand and explain human behaviour and motivation and to make predictions about this. The hope remains that, through the use of mathematics, psychological tests can be developed that will use a small sample of an individual's behaviour (as exhibited on the test) to reveal a great deal more about that specific individual. The psychological test is an attempt to diagnose some broad and significant aspects of an individual's behaviour in order to reveal something about him or her or to predict how that particular individual will perform in the future.

## Myers–Briggs Type Indicator (MBTI®)

In 1921, Jung, one of the founders of modern psychology, published a theory on personality types based on the assumption that human behaviour is not random, but is in fact predictable and therefore classifiable. Jung claimed that differences in behaviour are a result of preferences related to the basic functions our personalities perform (Kroeger et al. 2002). These preferences emerge early in life, forming the foundation of our personalities, and such preferences become the core of our attractions and aversions to others, tasks and events (Jung 1923). As Jung studied mystical literature and alchemy, it is close at hand to assume that his conceptualization of intuition, sensation, thinking and feeling as the four basic archetypes or components of personality is clearly a derivation of Empedocles' ancient theories about fire, earth, air and water. Jung focused initially on the polarities of introversion (directing one's attention inward toward thoughts, feelings and awareness) and extraversion (directing one's energy outward toward people, actions and external objects), combining each polarity with predominance in thinking, feeling, sensing and intuiting, to develop eight basic personality types.

In 1940, Briggs and Myers began developing a tool, the Myers–Briggs Type Indicator (MBTI®) that suggested a correlation between different types of success and failure in relationships and careers. Following Jung's proposal, Briggs and Myers' tool shares the idea that style is one part of the observable expression of a relatively stable personality type. The tool is now one of the most widely used tools to describe personality (Myers and McCaulley 1985; Myers et al. 1998). It does not measure ability or intelligence and does not predict performance. Instead the profiles measure preferences, which tend to be relatively stable, although life experiences can gradually affect them. As well as being an indicator of likely communication, team working and leadership behaviours, Jungian theories can also be used to explore what happens in times of change and of stress (Quenk 2002).

MBTI® is a self-assessment instrument which has a series of questions associated with four pairs of dichotomies. The dichotomies distinguish between various preferences on bipolar discontinuous scales: extravert or introvert (for energy); sensing or iNtuition (for perception and content); thinking or feeling (for judgement and decision-making); and judging or perceiving (for structure and organization). The terms extravert and introvert (E or I) are referred to as attitudes. The terms describe where an individual is focusing his or her attention and getting his or her energy. Some individuals are stimuli hungry and energized by action and interaction with the outer world (the extraverts). Others (the introverts) get their energy – and charge their batteries – by their inner world of ideas, internal processing and reflection. Words frequently associated with the extravert attitude are gregarious, sociability, interaction and extensive. Words often said about introverts are reflective, territoriality, concentration and intense. Extraverts usually want to process their perceptions and thoughts out loud in interaction and may find it difficult to clarify their thinking without such interaction with others. Introverts, on the other hand, typically think their ideas through before communicating them with others or acting on them. When they do share their ideas with others, they usually manifest as a finished product, a conclusion that has been carefully considered and decided upon (Kroeger et al. 2002).

The second dynamic (sensing and iNtuition) describes an individual's preference for content and information gathering. The way information is gathered is the starting point for almost all human interaction. If, however, two individuals pay attention to information differently, it becomes readily apparent that all further communication is at risk, whereas sensors are literal and want facts and details of situations and experience, iNtuitives are attracted by ideas, patterns and connections, wanting to explore and move towards future possibilities. Words typically associated with sensors are specific, direct, perspiration and detailed, and words associated with iNtuitives are general, random, inspiration and visionary. Sensors search for specific information and they expect facts and details, in contrast to iNtuitives that tend to have disdain for details and prefer to look for possibilities, meanings and relationships between and among various things. Sensors trust what is immediate and real and are frustrated and act with disbelief if information is provided that is not based on facts. iNtuitives trust the subconscious and prefer to look at the grand scheme, the holistic aspect of things, and try to understand input in a theoretical framework (Kroeger et al. 2002).

The third dynamic describes how individuals prefer to take in information and approach decision-making. It is the route to the decision, not the decision itself that characterizes an individual. Thinkers arrive at decisions through a solution-focused, analytical and achievement-oriented process. Thinkers tend to base their decisions on logic 'true or false, if-then' connections and on objective analysis of cause and effect. Feelers base their decision-making on values and on people-centred issues. Feelers use 'more or less, better–worse' evaluations. This is often seen as the tension between truth and fact; critique and appreciation; logic and empathy. Words frequently associated with thinkers are fairness, they are analytical and determined. Feelers are characterized by compassion, heart, sympathy and devotion. Often thinkers think that feelers are fuzzy-headed, and feelers feel that thinkers are cold-hearted jerks (Kroeger et al. 2002).

The final dynamic is often referred to as the lifestyle or decision-making dynamic. This dynamic is related to the preference for structure and organization and in type terminology, this is the difference between judging and perceiving. Judgers follow the rules, are on time and plan work carefully. Perceivers go with the flow and keep their options open. They have great faith that, during the process, a plan will develop spontaneously and, with the burst of last minute energy, they will complete it on time. Words associated with judgers are scheduled, decided and controlled, whereas perceivers are spontaneous, pending and adaptive. At their respective extremes, perceivers are virtually incapable of making decisions, whereas judgers find it almost impossible to change theirs (Kroeger et al. 2002).

On the basis of scores on the four bipolar scales, the MBTI® instrument gives 16 type personalities. The instrument suggests that each style has its strengths and weaknesses and none is universally better than the rest. In addition, there are no absolutes and it is all relative as each type encompasses a wide range of behaviour, styles, values and tastes. Understanding and appreciating the different types may help individuals and organizations in many ways. It may make interpersonal relationships less confusing and frustrating and as such it may enhance communication. Understanding the differences may help leaders to identify potential sources of conflict. It may help individuals identify careers that match their preferences, optimize the use of the respective individual preferences in an organizational setting, and help leaders and colleagues to understand how different personalities react to different situations, like crisis or stress (Petersen 2006).

## Good Reasons to Cast a Critical Eye

The commercial success of the tool has been extensive over at least the past 50 years (Gardner and Martinko 1996; Bayne 2003), but considerable criticism has also been raised primarily from academic psychologists (Paul 2004; Petersen 2006). A major criticism has been related to the mere origin of the MBTI® stemming from astrology and alchemy (Case and Phillipson 2004). Among the concerns raised has been the use of a typology to describe personality (Mendelsohn et al. 1982), the use of dichotomous sources that force a choice (Cohen 1983; Gardner and Martinko 1996), and the fact that the data are self-reported (Podsakoff and Organ 1986; Walck 1992; Fleenor et al. 1996). The MBTI® does not measure how well the preferred functions are performed. For example, scoring high on a strong preference for thinking does not necessarily mean that the person is logical (Coe 1991). In addition, a tool does not measure how well the shadow functions are performed (Ramaprasad and Mitroff 1984). All in all, in the descriptions of the different types, there seems to be something in there that seems to fit any individual as one just has to focus on the parts that one recognizes as fitting (also known as the Forer effect (Forer 1949)). Adding to this, the instrument gives no indication of pathology, and Hitler conceivably had the same psychological type as Mother Teresa (Coe 1991).

The almost type-mania tendency might cause people to exert excessive effort to belong to the more illustrious personality types specified by the MBTI®. This is something which is claimed to be easily possible as the MBTI® is one of the more easily manipulated instruments as it focuses narrowly upon a discrete moment in time rather than on actual pathogenesis. More general construct validity issues have been raised as a critical point of attention (McCrae and Costa 1989; Gardner and Martinko 1996). Adding to this is the point of criticism that feeling types on the MBTI® are providing more congruent self-ratings than thinking types, as feeling types are sensitive to the feelings of others and are more likely to be attentive to feedback (Roush and Atwater 1992). In addition, MBTI® is concerned with self-descriptions of thinking and decision-making preferences as opposed to actual decision-making (Lewis and Jacobs 1992), which is much more difficult to measure.

Despite the limitations of the MBTI®, in this chapter we follow McCaulley (1990) who asserts that from a type perspective; one would not ask the question 'what type is the best leader?' Rather, one would ask, 'how does each type of leader show leadership?' As good leadership is not a one-size-fits-all proposition. Leadership is about making things happen, but all too often leaders subconsciously rely on common leadership approaches that work well in one set of circumstances, but fall short in others (Snowden and Boone 2007). Simple contexts, properly assessed, require straightforward leadership. In such contexts businesses are successfully led by conclusions that are derived from analysis and logic, and decisions are implemented across a structured and organized environment. Here leadership is intentional and is about influencing followers in a chosen direction. Making sure that followers efficiently implement a structured plan towards a desired goal characterizes the command and control style of leadership, the basis of much classical leadership thinking and application throughout the 19th and 20th centuries. As Frederick the Great is credited with saying: 'Soldiers should fear their officers more than all the dangers to which they are exposed ... Good will can never induce the common soldier to stand up to such dangers; he will only do so through fear'. But often contexts are complicated and disordered. Consequently, multiple options must be investigated before decisions can be made. This imbalance requires novel thinking which might be a managerial challenge as different personality types have different preferences for taking in information, making decisions, and dealing with the outer world. Individual differences do not necessarily dictate behaviour. They do however establish zones of comfort for certain behaviours and actions. Therefore understanding types, using for example the MBTI® lens, is only a door-opener not gospel.

## The Expression of Type in Leadership

Recognizing the limitations – and the strengths – of the MBTI® tool and especially recognizing the tendency of leaders to see any personality test as an easy answer to organizational problems, this section links the conventional management and leadership thinking to the personality types represented in the MBTI® type indicator. Research continues to confirm that the model of management and leadership prevalent across Western organizations is heavily biased towards individuals who show personal preferences for logical, solution-centred and goal-driven achievement (Kroeger et al. 2002; Blass and Hackston 2008). This is the comfort zone of extraverts, thinkers and judgers. The question now is how these rather functionalistic preferences extraversion/introversion, judging/perceiving, iNtuition/sensing and thinking/feeling are expressed in the organizational world in accordance to the Myers–Briggs type indicator (MBTI®).

### Impact of energy: extraversion versus introversion

First, what is the impact of preferences for energy (extraversion/introversion) in the organization according to the MBTI®? If the energy is about taking action and talking about something to reach consensus or an understanding (extraversion), organizational leaders as well as followers are assumed to communicate enthusiastically, and be active. A typical extravert leader tends to have meetings, and lots of them, one-to-ones and in small and large groups. If not meeting face-to-face they will be on the phone or in conference calls. Emails are likely to bounce around, with large distribution lists, and gathering comments and momentum as they sally forth. Such leaders seem to like to have their say, and they like the stimulus of working with others. Energy is in action, which means that there is lots of travelling, locally, nationally and globally. The extraverted leader is comfortable with getting out and about, being busy and active.

Networking is seen as a good way of making contact and keeping in touch. However, without thinking time, the extraverted leader can find themselves consistently jumping into action, over-committing themselves and their resources, and not thinking through what is actually the best action to take.

On the other hand, if focus of the organizational energy is more about reflection (introversion), it will be the norm to think things through before acting. Introvert leaders will probably spend a lot of time thinking deeply about the business to understand what is needed in terms of action. Such leaders might well enjoy constructing business plans, as it gives the chance to reflect on what the business is about. However, a business lives (or dies) on its activities in the outer world. Most crucially, interpersonal relationships – both with clients and staff – depend on strong and active communication. Do the organizational members know what leaders are thinking? Do the leaders sometimes think about something for so long that opportunities are missed?

**Impact of structure: judging versus perceiving**
If there is a structured and organized (judging) approach to business life, the leaders as well as followers prefer to have a clear view of what lies ahead in order to plan for the week, the month or the year. An organization dominated by this type of leader is thus likely to have plans, structure charts, clear policies, protocols and procedures. There will be targets, and reviews of achievement against targets. It is a great strength to have a plan and work the plan – especially if the business has learnt the flexibility and adaptability to make the most of the unexpected. But what happens when the business does not achieve those targets? What happens when something gets in the way of the business achieving what it has planned to do? And what if the organizational members do not follow through, or are not as focused as the leaders expect?

Other organizations are led by leaders who are better at 'going with the flow' (perceiving). They enjoy and remain open to change, and are always willing to adapt to new information. They prefer to explore new trains of thought and activities, rather than conforming to others' schedules and systems. They often leave things till the last minute (or even later!), needing the pressure of a real deadline to get things finished. This is a useful approach to start-up businesses, but as an implementation strategy – this approach can be stressful for leaders as well as for customers, suppliers and staff. When running a business, especially as the company develops and grows, systems and structures are essential.

**Head in the clouds, or feet on the ground? iNtuition versus sensing**
Intuitive leaders tend to be dreamers who focus on the future and the possibilities. They read between the lines, trust their subconscious and are abstract thinkers. They are often good at spotting patterns and taking a high-level view. Nevertheless the intuitive leader often needs a sensing partner to stay focused. Sensing leaders are practical and focus on the 'here and now'. They tend to be factual, process information through the five senses and trust their own direct experiences. They will happily dig into the fine detail of the situation and value organization and practicality as ends in themselves. Because sensing leaders generally do not trust their intuitive side, and intuitive leaders tend not to trust their sensing side, when they collaborate with colleagues of the other preference, they tend not to trust them either.

Nevertheless, a business has to look to the future – ideas and possibilities (iNtuition) – while at the same time being practical and realistic (sensing), and attending to the day-to-day detail of the business. Keeping an eye on relevance and reality in the here and now is essential, as is the ability to learn from experience. However, leading a business also involves looking ahead, and seeing what might be coming up around the corner. Therefore, a successful organization needs different kinds of leaders to supplement each others' personal competences, or – especially if it is a smaller business – someone who is capable of mobilizing different sides of him or herself despite his or her preference.

**Truth or tact? Thinking versus feeling**
When leading a business, there are always tough decisions to make. Logical reasoning and analytical skills (thinking) are essential steps that underpin a business. But as the business is run by and with people – and often for people, it is also essential that successful leaders practise and apply emphathetic skills. This is not assumed to come naturally to the tough, action-oriented leader. However, ensuring a leadership style that includes deep listening, that factors in interpersonal warmth and that appreciates and values others' contributions (feeling), pays dividends. If this dynamic is not in balance, there can be serious consequences in terms of the emotional well-being of individuals and the organization.

Most decisions involve both thinking and feeling processes, and difficult decisions are those in which the decision-maker is in conflict between the thinking and the feeling side. In such situations, the dominant preference will take over. Whereas thinking leaders predominantly judge a situation and others based on logic and reason, the more emotionally attuned feeling leaders' judgements are predominantly based on extenuating circumstances. The cognitively oriented thinking type is usually impersonal and seems to suppress or even ignore feelings. This type is seen as brief and business-like. In contrast, the affectively oriented feeling type has a tendency to undervalue and ignore thinking that is offensive to the feeling judgements. Such a person typically makes decisions based on his or her moral code and will take the human impact of a decision into account.

## Imbalance leading to dysfunctional leadership

Traditionally the leadership literature has assumed that at the heart of effective and successful leadership there is a specific set of human characteristics. From this understanding the four type preference dimensions are commonly used in, for example, leadership career-counselling, life-coaching and personal development, despite the fact that the instrument is lacking convincing validity data.

Personality is neither as unique as some psychologists seem to suggest, nor as universal as some behaviourists would have it. Moreover, different types of leaders perform better in different situations, which is why it cannot be claimed that any one type of leader is 'the best', nor is there any one best 'leadership type'. Expressed in layman's terms: one person's laid-back style is another person's lack of motivation. Moreover, differences in style can lead to a great deal of misunderstanding and resentment and in this process others' feelings are likely to get hurt, or swept under the carpet.

Essentially, leadership is about overcoming the challenges arising from the organization and its environment and in this process leadership boils down to reflections and choices made under the influence of both darker and brighter emotions. Anticipating that we never will be fully able to apprehend the non-conscious system that motivate or guide (leadership) behaviour, we still believe that leaders are both unique and have common qualities that can be studied. In the following case example, we are using the MBTI® lens despite its limitations both in regard to classifying people into archetypes but also – and more importantly – to show the inseparability of the darker and the more compassionate side of leadership. Despite the rather functionalistic approach inherited in the MBTI® lens, the lens has remained essentially unchanged for almost three-quarters of a century. Here the lens is used as a stepping stone for discussing leaders' – and followers' – personalities and behaviours.

We adhere to the belief that ideally all four type preference dimensions need to be in play depending on the specific situation. However, embracing the complete spectra of styles is not easy, especially since leaders – and followers – tend to favour one approach over the others and do not consciously strive to ensure that the other perspectives are also sought out and taken into consideration. As we will show in the following case example, if there is not a balanced approach to leadership, a one-sidedness of the organizational dynamics is likely to spiral out of control – often with seriously damaging results both for the individuals caught up in the leadership struggles, as well as for others who are swept along. This shadow side of an overused leadership style is shown in the following illustrative case example that demonstrates how the tendency to polarize around archetypes of leadership undermines the complexity of leadership. The case example describes two different leaders and how they both needed the ability to adapt and bring into play different leadership and personality styles in response to different situations. The case example shows that it is impossible to predetermine which style is most valuable as it depends on the specific context of the situation and of the relations. Hereby this study demonstrates how categorization of leaders is difficult and that most leadership styles vary in time and place, and in the context of different relations. Whether one or the other style is most valuable is impossible to predetermine as it depends on the specific context of the situation and of the relations.

## METHODOLOGY

Based on field research, the chapter focuses on the influence of leadership style on follower emotions. Several types of data were collected during this study and were triangulated during analyses (Denzin 1989). Data collected included: type indicator scores, observation field notes, traditional in-depth interviews and oral narratives told by employees about important work-life experiences. To evaluate leadership style, a MBTI® type preferences audit of 24 senior managers of the case organization was conducted. It is anticipated that the MBTI® is a 'still photo' of a discrete moment in time, just as it is anticipated that conceptualizing the MBTI® constructs as stable individual differences would be an error. However, although there might be good reasons to cast a critical eye on the MBTI® typology it is still a useful instrument to constructively open a reflection on leadership style. As most behaviour is habitual and unconscious, establishing a common language on leadership style can help when describing differences. Simplified codifications provide distinctions between complex examples of phenomena (Scott 1991), which in our case mean different approaches to leadership. In this chapter, the common language and simple codifications are not meant to function as universal rules or as universal characteristics of leadership differentiations. Instead they are used as points of reference in a reflexive manner. Consequently, the importance of the narratives' point of view is stressed, as the study is built on the assumption that also co-leaders and followers' point of view must be taken into account in order to understand leadership functionality.

Follower emotions are evaluated through a combination of qualitative interviews and follower narratives conducted and collected during a consultancy project by one of the authors during the period from 2005 to 2010 at an electronic manufacturing business based initially in Scotland. The informal, in-depth interviews were conducted with internal and external participants in the business at the time. The interviews were supported by narratives told by employees, who were not experienced story-tellers and therefore not inclined to be especially entertaining or amusing. Their narratives were attempts to convey simply and seriously the most important experiences of their own working lives. Although the narratives were fitted to some extent to the situation, they were essentially monologues (Labov and Waletzky 1967; Labov 1981). The narratives that form the focus of this work could be compared to a decontextualized sociolinguistic interview with the interviewer forming an ideal audience.

Based on the assumption that the reportability of an event will vary widely depending on the reporter as well as the immediate social context, observations were also part of the data collection. Although the observer has only a segment of what is happening accessible, observation still contributes to a broader understanding of a phenomenon. The following reconstructed narrative is therefore constructed based on observational field notes made during a prolonged and persistent engagement with the organization by one of the authors combined with a triangulation of data as mentioned above. The study uses a reconstructed narrative to provide a nuanced comprehension of the situations explored and analyzed (Czarniawska 2004). The intention with the following case narrative is to make readers feel as if they were there, in the field. The case description balances between factual and fictional work as it translates the reality of the case organization into a discourse. In its narrative form, the case description is both an image of reality and a representation of the real. Or as expressed by Zavarzadeh (1976, p. 193): 'The reality of the outside world is a conventional reality in that the members of the community agree to regard certain events as real'.

# THE CASE: A RECONSTRUCTED NARRATIVE

## The Golden Years

It all began when the family-owned electronic manufacturing business sold out to venture capitalists who appointed a young brash streetwise managing director (in the following called David). David was inspirational, visionary and action oriented – the personification of a JFDI leadership behaviour, which often is referred to as the (Just F***ing Do It) style of leadership within the mainstream books on personality theories that dominates the shelves of airports' book stores. Within a period of five years David developed a global manufacturing footprint and a clear strategy on how to continue to grow the business. Much of this success was down to the leadership, the vision and the drive of David.

David's leadership strategy was to recruit in his own image. He trusted and hired action-oriented, extraverted, fun-loving obsessive employees who were prepared to put the business before everything. As one of the respondents from the case study explained; 'David tells me to do it, and I do it because when David says for me to do it, you just f***ing do it. Last year I was going to go on holiday to the Caribbean with my wife and I cancelled it five times because David told me to'.

David was the paternalistic and tyrannical leader, but at the same time he was also one of the lads. The company was led by the values of 'work hard, play hard'. 'Work hard' was by the employees unofficially translated to; 'You can sleep when you're dead. And no-one here has a hangover'. 'Play hard' meant going out with the lads for heavy nights in the town, and singing the company song.

David's style of communication was a reflection of his leadership style. He would send out ill-spelled, ungrammatical, fiery emails to all and sundry at all hours of the day and night. As one respondent explained: 'The emails would burn a hole in your motherboard'. As an employee, you would have to be accessible at any hour of the day or night, 7/7, 365/365.

The company held quarterly world-wide conferences always convened at weekends, attended by 25–30 of the senior managers and directors. The general perception was that you were honoured to be invited, but you would arrive in fear and trepidation. As explained by one of the respondents: 'It was like bringing your school report home to Dad. Even if you'd got 95 per cent for mathematics, the focus would be on what you'd got wrong'. Another respondent explained: 'People were ritually humiliated. You wouldn't be listening to others, as you'd be awaiting your turn and rehearsing your defence; or trying to get your shots in before you were shot down yourself. But it was all ok – because at the end of the day you'd go out together and get gloriously drunk'.

No doubt that David would lead the conference from the front, and he would annihilate anyone publicly if he had taken against them. For example, it was the annual party at the end of a spectacular year. The women were in the spa while the men were in the bar. David and the HR director started to 'debate the issues'. The HR director told David he was wrong about something. The verbal disagreement swiftly turned into fists thumping the bar, and David's pointing fingers poking the HR director in the shoulder. They ended up on the floor of the bar, punching the hell out of each other. The next morning the HR director was fired.

The obvious question then is why did David get away with such bullying and autocratic behaviour that bears no relationship to the modern tenets of the servant leader? He got away with it because he had a vision for where the company needed to be in the future, and he got results. His energy and drive were inspirational: singing the company song you felt that you could go back and climb vertical walls if you had to for the next three months. You would do it better next time. David gave his management team the confidence, the motivation and the va va voom to go that extra mile, yet again. This company culture translated into bottom-line success and an increase in turnover from £20 million to £55 million in just a few years.

But this management style was unsustainable. It was built purely on David's personality and sense of ego. The problem with this style of leadership is that you cannot keep whipping people to get results with escalating demands of performance. Fear will only take a company so far. It also annihilated healthy debate and challenge. Every decision had the 'What will David say' indicator built into it. And this translated into: 'Just do it, and do it now. Do it my way, or hit the highway'. In the JFDI organization there is no place for considered reflection or reasoned debate. You would be considered to be dragging and a drag. Any attempt at reasoned reflection brought the inevitable response: 'We'll get f***ing nowhere with you thinking like that … pick yourself up and get going'.

**After Five Years of Success**

The consequences of leading by fear and intimidation were starting to build up under the surface, and the leadership style even had an effect on the commercial frameworks underpinning the successful growth of the company. The growth of the company had primarily been due to one phenomenally successful external client relationship that after few years accounted for 50 per cent of the business and as such represented a potentially dangerous business practice. By the end of five years, employees were running on burned-out energy resources, and there was nothing but ego and drive to underpin any sustained endeavour.

Intelligent people can sense when things need to change, but do not always know what to do about it. At a point two-thirds along in this period of growth, David knew he needed to do something about getting what was now a global management team to work more coherently together. There were two prime company behaviours that David saw that he needed to address. One was the passive attitude of the senior management team that translated into a lack of vision and short termism that was prevalent. The second was the lack of reflection. His analysis was insightful, but the moment of lucid perception was quickly translated into the knee-jerk response of what were now ingrained behaviours of the only way to do things: 'the let's do it', and 'let's do it now' solution. 'Let's have the team development weekend in China!' Secretaries ran around for weeks trying to arrange visas and travel. A training agenda was hastily drawn up.

**The Show-down**

David's strategy was not focused on supporting the development of leadership skills in others, as he wanted to be part of every decision-making process. This became clear when, for example, the board identified that a part of the business could be set up as a separate business, with a separate managing director reporting into the board. David agreed with the idea – but demanded that he should have control of the new business. When he was told that it would report to the chairman, he demanded that it would be 'my way or the highway'. Ultimately, however, David left the company, suddenly, angrily and with no warning signs. There was no time to recruit a new CEO externally, and therefore an internal candidate stepped into the role, bringing with him his reflective and introverted way of leading.

The company that had apparently been kept going by the sheer energy and visionary leadership of one person changed and became a different kind of environment. Suddenly reflection, considered opinions and listening became valued and rose up from across the entire company. George, the new CEO, overcame his qualms about stepping into the role because he did not have David's talents, and he decided to bring to his team a new leadership style based on totally different values. Almost overnight it became acceptable to spend time reflecting and discussing. Decisions did not have to be made instantly and as a result the quality of the decision-making seemed to improve. Listening was the order of the day and the voices that had been silenced in the action packed days of the 'JFDI' leadership style were heard. New perspectives were welcomed and new strategies developed as a consequence of unleashing previously unheard voices of experience and knowledge.

A new euphoria prevailed in the company as reflection and a measured pace had found its place. However, euphoria is not enough. The new momentum still required sustained externally focused energy, which comes so easily to the extraverted leader, but much less easily to a detail conscious reflective thinker. In a cost-conscious business fighting to get ahead in the tough world of venture capital funding amid a global downturn, the road to a balanced business is fraught with the dangers of reverting to the comfort of a mono-type focus.

## ANALYSIS AND DISCUSSION

### MBTI® Profiles

Despite different type preferences both David and George were the victims and perpetrators of the blind side of leading in their own image. They both demonstrated intolerance, albeit this being demonstrated very differently. Also, they were both intensely social creatures, who actively needed interaction with followers, although their styles were very different. David, being an extravert, took action, held meetings and was constantly on the rush. George also held meetings in which, however, listening and consensus were key words as opposed to David's talking and 'my way or the highway' approach. Hereby this study demonstrates how categorization of leaders is difficult and that most leadership styles vary in time and place, and in the context of different relations. Whether one or the other style is most valuable is impossible to predetermine as it depends on the specific context of the situation and of the relations. The tendency to polarize around archetypes of leadership as often done by practitioners using the MBTI® typology undermines the complexity of leadership (Ellis and Abrams 2009). A leader might have a preferable style, which is likely to be a mix of rationality and irrationality and of the conscious and the subconscious. The ability to adapt or bring into play different personal styles in response to different situations is unarguably the most powerful leadership capability that can be possessed.

Understanding archetypical styles, however, can be seen as a stepping stone that supports generating a common language on leadership and in achieving personal awareness and adaptability, which is a prerequisite for adapting behaviour. Moreover, understanding styles helps recognize behaviour and type in others. Putting aside the limitations within the MBTI® type preferences, research shows that different type choices and archetypes are not evenly distributed across populations. Yet research into type preferences and leadership across Western organizations consistently shows that there is an overrepresentation of extravert, thinking, and judging preferences in leadership structures (see Table 4.1).

*Table 4.1   Leadership type preferences*

|  | Percentage of each type | | | | | | |
|  | Extraverts vs. Introverts | | Sensors vs. iNtuitives | | Thinkers vs. Feelers | | Judgers vs. Perceivers | |
|  | E | I | S | N | T | F | J | P |
|---|---|---|---|---|---|---|---|---|
| International Leaders (*) | 63 | 37 | 50 | 50 | 86 | 14 | 65 | 35 |
| UK national representative sample (**) | 53 | 47 | 76 | 24 | 46 | 54 | 58 | 42 |

*Sources:*    (*) Carr et al. (2004); (**) adapted from the UK national representative sample, OPP, available at: http://www.opp.eu.com/German_data_supplement.aspx#type (Howard, 2008)

Anticipating that the psychologies of leaders are shaped and transformed by interaction between the individual leaders and their followers, and that different types of leaders are best suited to lead in particular situations, the literature on type preferences as well as the traditional leadership literature still seems to emphasize preferences for logical, solution-centred and goal-driven achievement (Lemmergaard and Muhr 2011). This overrepresentation of extravert, thinking and judging preferences in leadership positions naturally influences leadership style, motivation and the mere ideas of what leadership is all about. Whether a leader leads as an MBTI® extravert or an MBTI® introvert tends to be demonstrated most clearly in his or her communication style. Extraverts influence others quite naturally by engaging with them: talking, networking and taking action. Introvert leaders present the results of their thoughts (their ideas, plans, vision or values) – often in writing – after having had time to think it through. Extraverts tell others – and show in their body language and actions – what they think and how they feel. They want and need to engage with others. Introvert leaders, however, need and take time to reflect. They communicate when they are ready to.

The MBTI® thinkers-type makes up only half of the population, yet they occupy the overwhelming majority of leadership positions. Thinkers, independent of cultural background, make up about 86 per cent of middle managers, nearly 93 per cent of senior managers, and more than 95 per cent of executives (Kroeger et al. 2002). Mainly two socio-historic and psychological explanations have been given here. First, workplaces have long been male-dominated, and two-thirds of men have a thinking preference (Knowlton and McGee 1994; Myers–Briggs 1980). Second, there is a natural tendency for individuals to clone themselves in hiring and nurturing new personnel, hereby Thinkers replace and surround themselves with other Thinkers (Haslam et al. 2011). Thinkers employ cause-and-effect logic to reach a conclusion, they are analytical and problem-oriented, and they have a drive towards rightness, competence and objectivity. As leaders, Feelers tend to make subjective or circumstantial decisions focusing more on the individuals impacted by an issue than on the precedent or policy designed to deal with the issue in the first place.

The MBTI® judgers-type is decisive and emphasizes closure, structure, schedules and order for which reason they usually fit the stereotype of what many believe a leader should be. A judging leader is well-suited to systems that are strongly oriented toward decisive action, rigid schedules and the accomplishment of tasks. This is in contrast to perceivers who are flexible and like to keep decisions and plans open, preferring to continue exploring possibilities and options long after the judgers have set off on their plan of action.

In the case organization, a MBTI® type preferences audit of the 24 attendees of the senior management meeting in China was conducted, and the results demonstrated a strategy which could be labelled 'hiring in your own image' as 23 of the 24 senior management team had a preference for extraverted/taking action energy. The psychological types in Table 4.2 are represented as percentages, and compared with statistics for a general UK population, and a group of international managers.

From the MBTI® analysis of the 24 senior leaders it appears that the function of feeling – which underpins interpersonal relationships – was present in the case company more so than in many management populations. However, as is abundantly evident from the behaviours

*Table 4.2   Type distribution chart*

|              | Case study | gen pop** | mgt pop* |              | case study | gen pop** | mgt pop* |
| ------------ | ---------- | --------- | -------- | ------------ | ---------- | --------- | -------- |
| Extraversion | 96         | 53        | 63       | Introversion | 4          | 47        | 37       |
| Sensing      | 58         | 76        | 50       | iNtuition    | 42         | 24        | 50       |
| Thinking     | 37.5       | 46        | 86       | Feeling      | 62.5       | 54        | 14       |
| Judging      | 62.5       | 58        | 65       | Perceiving   | 37.5       | 42        | 35       |

*Sources:*   * Carr et al. (2004); ** adapted from UK national representative sample, OPP,
available at: http://www.opp.eu.com/German_data_supplement.aspx#type
(Howard, 2008)

within the company, it was not accessed, and did not influence the management style. This was significantly due to David's dominant 'do it my way' style, which was exacerbated by the tendency of the feeling preference not to handle disagreement with active conflict, nor to talk about emotions, values and feelings. The feeling preference is to suppress conflict by seeking consensus and wanting to assume that everything is ok; or wanting things to return to being ok as soon as possible. So feeling will not stand up, head to head, against thinking to defend values, emotions and people-centred issues.

The company's policy of recruiting in its own image created multiple problems. The tough leadership style meant that employees either fitted in or they did not, they adapted and adopted the dominant style, or they left of their own accord or they were fired. In general, employees were insecure and staff retention therefore became an issue. The company's reputation of having 'a revolving door' policy meant that potential employees were reluctant to join the company and the talent the company needed was difficult to attract. The following table (Table 4.3) summarizes from a theoretical point of view the behaviours that would be likely to be present – or missing – within such a group of leaders.

However, the implications of whether such behaviour is present or missing are not easy to detect, as leadership is a combination of Dr Jekyll and Mr Hyde. As this chapter demonstrates, leadership is an uneasy resemblance of good and evil, as leaders' – as well as followers' – personalities cannot be outlined in law-like generalizations. Especially, this case demonstrates that uncritical usage of typology measures underestimates emotional fluctuations and individual differences in leaders' actions and behaviours. The understanding of leadership as logical,

*Table 4.3    Theoretical summary of the behaviours that would be likely to be present – or missing – within a group of leaders*

| What's Present | What's Missing |
| --- | --- |
| ACTION | REFLECTION |
| Let's do it | What do we need to do? |
| Let's do it now | What's the strategy? |
| We're busy | What's the priority? |
| Just get on with it | What else could we do? |
| | What's the vision? |
| | What are we doing well? |
| | What are we missing? |
| MAKING DECISIONS | THOUGHTFUL FRAMEWORKS |
| That's what we'll do | Gives focus |
| Let's get on with it | Links the activity to the vision |
| Next! | Provides criteria for success, not just targets to achieve |
| | Establishes new processes for new products and new directions |
| | Solid foundations for sustainable approach |
| INTERPERSONAL RELATIONSHIPS | HANDLING CONFLICT |
| Warmth | Tough-minded critique against objective criteria |
| Collaboration | Openly challenging behaviours and problems |
| Cooperation | Balancing collaboration with logic |
| Acknowledgement | |
| Support | |
| Integration of new people | |
| PRACTICAL EXPERIENCE AND DETAIL | EMBRACING CHALLENGE AND CHANGE |
| Knowing what we do | New visions |
| Knowing what we've done before | New markets |
| Practical action | New opportunities |
| Knowledge and experience | New threats and challenges |
| | Insightful meaning and understanding |
| | Reflection on long-term possibilities |
| | Sustained innovation and implementation of new processes to achieve new directions |

solution-centred and goal-driven is sometimes confusing to the point where the understanding of the nature of leadership is oversimplified. Each combination of leadership style, emotion and follower context creates a unique setting of leadership opportunities and challenges. Therefore conceptualizing styles and emotions as stable individual differences would be an error. Even if it could be claimed that an individual leader emphasizes a particular style, he or she would consciously and unconsciously display different patterns of both positive and negative emotions, which would influence followers' emotions and actions. A related problem is that patterns of styles must bear some relevant relationship to the characteristics, activities and goals of followers. As expressed by Stogdill (1948, p. 64): 'Leadership must be conceived in terms of the interaction of variables which are in constant change and flux'.

**Style and Emotions Analysed**

Was David a failure as the strong achievement-oriented leader? Absolutely not! His powerful energy catapulted the company into the successful global business that delivered profit to shareholders. However, the single-minded focus on ensuring that everyone behaved and thought in the same way was in this case example a recipe for disaster. This is following a more conventional line of thinking, that the best businesses change their leaders at specific stages in their development bringing broader thinking and change in their wake. Businesses that stand still or fail to address the market changes are the ones that wither and die. The problem in the presented case was the extremes that got out of control and went too far. In such an energy-charged company, things could – and did – escalate quickly into trouble. Under the leadership of David, the values of achievement were clear and were passionately felt. The vacuum left behind on his departure started to be filled by reflective energy, with the whole team involved in the discussion about the definition of the new values of the company. However, this debate was raw and untutored. There was no natural draw to develop a people-centred business where people speak from the heart. Will the business succeed? The jury is still out.

On the basis of the presented case study one criteria for understanding leadership is to move beyond the individual level, as we must view and understand leadership in the interplay between leaders and followers. Leaders and those who translate their ideas into action are mutually dependent. A leader's capacity to influence others always depends on who those others are. The team has to be stimulated, and to learn and be encouraged to make decisions that do not always have to be right. The more reflective CEO is less certain about being right in everything so is willing to listen and to appreciate the benefits that come with difference. But the danger is that the swing from the 'in your face' 'JFDI' style of leadership to a leadership based on introversion and reflection will be too extreme. The followers still need to know that they are being heard. They want their efforts to be seen and appreciated. They need strong and confident direction. They need to be engaged with as people. So the energy has changed, and perhaps people-centred values will start to emerge authentically, but it is not by any means guaranteed.

Besides matching those they lead, leaders must also, as this study demonstrates, have an appropriate fit with their environment (Hannan and Freeman 1977; Carroll 1988). As such leadership is not a quality of leaders alone, but rather of the relationship between leaders and follow-ers. In this complex interplay between leaders, followers and context the dominant presence of leadership personality types plays an important role. Yet no clear understanding exists that distinguishes effective leaders from ineffective leaders. We do not claim that the MBTI® type indicator provides the answer to this complex question, but merely point to its usefulness in putting personality types on the agenda. Focusing on type differences using the MBTI® can help in facilitating communication that fosters an understanding of different opinions and behaviours.

As a self-descriptive inventory the MBTI® can provide leaders – and followers – with a relevant dichotomy that can support a critical reflection on behaviour and emotion. By measuring leaders' stated preferences by asking them what they like to do and how they see themselves behave in various situations, leaders are helped to understand their own types' preferences – and inherent blind-spots. Hopefully they will be able to use this knowledge constructively. Understanding that others' behaviours stem in part from their personality type can sometimes defuse an emotion-laden situation and promote tolerance and acceptance for expressions of various cognitive styles.

## CONCLUSIONS

A central contribution of this chapter is the extent to which it illustrates that leadership style is not a simple question of method, susceptible to 'quick fix' solutions. We have discussed some of the nuances of leadership style, behaviour and emotion to draw the attention of the reader to a set of complex but vital questions. These questions include: having seen some aspects of the challenges of leadership through the lens of type, what can organizations do to recognize what is happening before it is too late? What interventions need to be made to address the issues? Or is this just the way it is? Is this the way it needs to be?

The MBTI® is frequently used to develop insights into individuals' preferences which drive motivations, behaviours and emotion and which have an ongoing effect on follower interactions and organizational dynamics. According to the MBTI® index, each personality type has distinct strengths that complement other types, which is why leaders should resist the temptation to simply recruit in their own image. Successful leadership has to break through the non-diverse and excluding constraints of 'do it my way', recognizing the importance of followers and their relationship with leaders. Sensitizing leaders and followers about how and why individuals behave differently tends to make leaders and followers more tolerant of peoples' different natures, taking into account individual diversity and difference, helping individuals build on their existing strengths and approaches as well as developing less-preferred styles and behaviour. Had David been aware of and faced up to the potential consequences of his strengths and blind spots, he could have developed a deliberate and thought through strategy to ensure that the business nurtured and encouraged the voices of the people-centred qualities it required. Not only that, the influence of thoughtful reflection would have been tangible, supporting the resolutely action-focused leadership style that took the business so far. Task and achievement driven organizations have to learn to let through the emotional and people/feeling function that is crucial to building and sustaining morale – especially in challenging conditions. So-called 'good' leaders actively develop their balanced team through self-awareness and team-awareness. Balanced leadership has to be developed from within, and talent needs to be fostered at the individual, team, and organizational level – especially within top teams and executive leadership.

Especially in the macho world of business, when we must deal with problems, we instinctively resist trying the way that leads through obscurity and darkness. We wish to hear only of unequivocal results, and completely forget that these results can only be brought about when we have ventured into and emerged again from the darkness. To penetrate the darkness we must summon all the powers of enlightenment that the consciousness can offer (Jung 1930). George, the new CEO, reflected on his past experience of successful organizations and planned to recruit an HR director who he believed would bring with them the people-focused skills and empathy that he knows he lacks. Not only that, he plans to recruit a marketing director to bring more creativity to the team. Businesses that stand the test of time do not take the effectiveness of their teams for granted but plan for them, work at it and have the humility to recognize that their skills alone, no matter how powerful, are never enough to get the best results.

Despite it being a rather functionalistic tool, the MBTI® inventory might help leaders to see themselves from 'above'. Hereby they might be aware of their own behaviours and how they affect others. By paying attention to emotional signals, leaders might be able to affect their behaviours if the situation so demands. As this chapter demonstrates, one cannot fully understand leadership without trying to integrate and understand emotions, from often subjective and different, often seemingly irrational, personal perspectives.

# REFERENCES

Adams, J.A. (2005), *Transforming Leadership*, New York: Cosimo Books.

Ashkanasy, N.M. and C.L. Cooper (2008), *Research Companion to Emotion in Organizations*, Cheltenham, UK, and Northampton, MA, USA: Edward Elgar.

Bayne, R. (2003), 'Love, money and studying', *The Psychologist*, **16** (10), 529–31.

Blass, E. and J. Hackston (2008), 'Future skills and current realities: how the psychological (Jungian) type of European business leaders relates to the need of the future', *Futures*, **40** (9), 822–33.

Carr, M., J. Curd and F. Dent (2004), *International Managers from MBTI® Research into Distribution of Type*, Hertfordshire: Ashridge Management School.

Carroll, G. (1988), *Ecological Models of Organizations*, Cambridge, MA: MIT Press.

Case, P. and J. Gosling (2010), 'The spiritual organization: critical reflections on the instrumentality of workplace spirituality', *Journal of Management, Spirituality and Religion*, **7** (4), 257–82.

Case, P. and G. Phillipson (2004), 'Astrology, alchemy and retro-organisation theory: an astro-genealogical critique of the Myers-Briggs type indicator', *Organization*, **11** (4), 573–95.

Coe, C.K. (1991), 'The MBTI: a tool for understanding and improving public management', *State and Local Government Review*, **23** (1), 37–46.

Cohen, J. (1983), 'The cost of dichotomization', *Applied Psychological Measurement*, **7** (3), 249–53.

Czarniawska, B. (2004), *Narratives in Social Science Research*, London: SAGE.

Denzin, N.K. (1989), *Interpretive Interactionsim*, Newbury Park, CA: SAGE.

Ellis, A. and M. Abrams (2009), *Personality Theories – Critical Perspectives*, London: SAGE.

Famaprasad, A. and Mitroff, I. (1984), 'On formulating strategic problems', *Academy of Management Review*, **9** (4), 597–605.

Fineman, S. (2000), *Emotion in Organizations*, London: Sage.

Fleenor, J.W., C.D. McCauley and S. Brutes (1996), 'Self-other rating agreement and leader effectiveness', *The Leadership Quarterly*, **7** (4), 487–506.

Forer, B.R. (1949), 'The fallacy of personal validation: a classroom demonstration of gullibility', *Journal of Abnormal and Social Psychology (American Psychological Association)*, **44** (1), 118–23.

Gardner, W. and M. Martinko (1996), 'Using the Myers-Briggs type indicator to study managers: a literature review and research agenda', *Journal of Management*, **22** (1), 45–83.

Greenbaum, D.G. (2005), *Temperament Astrology's Forgotten Key*, Bournemouth: The Wessex Astrologer, Ltd.

Hannan, M. and J. Freeman (1977), 'The population ecology of organizations', *American Journal of Sociology*, **82** (5), 929–64.

Haslam, S.A., S.D. Reicher and M.J. Platow (2011), *The New Psychology of Leadership: Identity, Influence and Power*, New York: Psychology Press.

Howard, C. (2008), 'What "type" of training do trainers like to deliver?', *Training Journal*, 1 November.

Jastrow, J. (1915), 'Antecents of the study of character and temperament', *The Popular Science Monthly*, **86** (June), 590–614.

John, O.P. (1993), 'The search for basic dimensions of personality: a review and critique', in P. McReynolds and J.C. Rosen (eds), *Advances in Psychological Assessment*, vol. 17, New York: Plenum Press, pp. 1–37.

John, O.P. and S. Srivastava (1999), 'The big five trait taxonomy: history, measurement, and theoretical perspectives', in L.A. Pervin and O.P. John (eds), *Handbook of Personality, Theory and Research*, 2nd edn, New York: The Guilford Press, pp. 102–32.

Jung, C.G. (1921[1971]), *Psychological Types, A revision by R.F.C. Hull*, New York:Princeton/Bollingen.

Jung, C.G. (1923), *Psychological Types*, New York: Harcourt Brace.

Jung, C. (1930), *The Stages of Life, In Collected Works 8: The Structure and Dynamics of the Psyche*, New York: Princeton/Bollingen.

Kirk, G.S., J.E. Raven and M. Schofield (1983), *The Presocratic Philosophers*, 2nd edn, Cambridge: Cambridge University Press.

Knowlton, B. and M. McGee (1994), *Strategic Leadership and Personality: Making the MBTI Relevant*, Washington, DC: Industrial College of the Armed Forces National Defense University.

Kroeger, O., J.M. Thuesen and H. Rutledge (2002), *Type Talk at Work*, New York: Dell Publishing.

Labov, W. (1981), 'Speech actions and reactions in personal narrative', in D. Tannen (eds), *Analyzing Discourse: Text and Talk*, Georgetown University Round Table, Washington, DC: Georgetown University Press, pp. 217–47.

Labov, W. and J. Waletzky (1967), 'Narrative analysis', in J. Helm (eds), *Essays on the Verbal and Visual Arts*, Seattle, WA: University of Washington Press, pp. 12–44.

Lemmergaard, J. and S.L. Muhr (2011), 'Everybody hurts, sometimes: emotions and dysfunctional leadership', *European Journal of International Management*, **5** (1), 1–12.

Lewis, P., and T.O. Jacobs (1992), 'Individual differences in strategic leadership capacity: a constructive/developmental view', in R.L. Phillips and J.G. Hunt (eds), *Strategic Leadership: A Multi-Organizational Level Perspective*, Westport, CT: Quorum Books, pp. 119–38.

McCaulley, M.H. (1990), 'The Myers-Briggs type indicator and leadership', in K.E. Clark and M.B. Clark (eds), *Measures of Leadership*, West Orange, NJ: Leadership Library of America.

McCrae, R. and P. Costa Jr. (1989), 'Reinterpreting the Myers-Briggs type indicator from the perspective of the five-factor model of personality', *Journal of Personality*, **57** (1), 17–40.

Mendelsohn, G.A., D.S. Weiss and N.R. Feimer (1982). 'Conceptual and empirical analysis of the typological implications of patterns of socialization and femininity', *Journal of Personality and Social Psychology*, **42** (6), 1157–70.

Myers I.B. (1980), *Introduction to Type: A Guide to Understanding your Results on the Meyers-Briggs Type Indicator*, Paulo Alto, CA: Consulting Psychologists Press.

Myers, I.B. and M.H. McCaulley (1985), *Manual: A Guide to the Development and use of the Myers-Briggs Type Indicator*, Palo Alto, CA: Consulting Psychologists Press.

Myers, I.B., M. McCaulley, N.L. Quenk and A.L. Hammer (1998), *Manual: A Guide to the Development and Use of the Myers-Briggs Type Indicator (3rd Edition)*, Palo Alto, CA: Consulting Psychologists Press.

Paul, A.M. (2004), *The Cult of Personality – How Personality Tests are Leading Us to Miseducate Our Children, Mismanage Our Companies and Misunderstand Ourselves*, New York: The Free Press.

Petersen, V.C. (2006), *MBTI – Distorted reflections of personality?*, The Aarhus School of Business CREDO/Department of Management working paper 2006-5, , Denmark.

Podsakoff, P. and D. Organ (1986), 'Self-reports in organizational research: problems and prospects', *Journal of Management*, **12** (4), 531–44.

Quenk, N. (2002), *Was That Really Me?: How Everyday Stress Brings Out Our Hidden Personality*, Paulo Alto, CA: Davies-Black Publishing.

Ramaprasad, A. and I. Mitroff (1984), 'On formulating strategic problems', *Academy of Management Review*, **9** (4), 597–605.

Rehn, A. (2010), 'The creature comforts of management – on morality and empathic response in economic exchange', in S.L. Muhr, B.M. Sørensen and S. Vallentin (eds), *Ethics and Organizational Practice – Questioning the Moral Foundations of Management*, Cheltenham, UK, and Northampton, MA, USA: Edward Elgar, pp. 163–80.

Roush, P.E. and L. Atwater (1992), 'Using the MBTI to understand transformational leadership and self-perception accuracy', *Military Psychology*, **4** (1), 17–34.

Scott, J. (1991), Social Network Analysis, London: SAGE.

Snowden, D. and M. Boone (2007), 'A leader's framework for decision making', *Harvard Business Review*, 85 (11), 68–76.

Stogdill, R.M. (1948), 'Personality factors associated with leadership: a survey of the literature', *Journal of Psychology*, **25** (1), 35–71.

Walck, C.L. (1992), 'The relationship between indicator type and "true type": slight preferences and the verification process', *Journal of Psychological Type*, **23**, 17–21.

Wilson, N. (2006), *Encyclopaedia of Ancient Greece*, London:Taylor & Francis Group, LLC.

Zavarzadeh, M. (1976), *The Mythopoeia Reality: The Postwar American Nonfiction Novel*, Chicago, IL: University of Illinois Press.

# 5. Leadership in a family business: kinship and emotional control

**Emma L. Jeanes**

## INTRODUCTION

This chapter explores the concept of leadership in a small family-run organization using the metaphor of the family, incorporating broader notions of kinship structures. It presents a case of a reluctant leader who is perceived as a leader by virtue of being the authority figure. Typically leadership literature has focused on extreme and relatively uniform characteristics of leadership, such as those exhibited by the so-called great leader or heroic leader (Nanus 1992), or more recently, the narcissistic (Kets de Vries and Miller 1985; Maccoby 2000) or bullying leader (Kärreman 2011). The case presented in this chapter, however, demonstrates the need to take a more nuanced approach towards understanding leaders and leadership. In this case the leader is more appropriately described as average in his leadership capabilities (Meindl et al. 1985; Alvesson and Sveningsson 2003a, 2003b), and relies upon a range of relational devices (consciously or otherwise) to enact – or substitute for – his leadership role. The case presented demonstrates a leader negotiating a set of complex and uncertain roles. He moves between roles such as that of a father-figure, a naughty boy, or even a victim, to name a few. The study argues for an understanding of the father-figure as an archetype of leadership located in the context of the 'family' in order to fully appreciate the fluid and contradictory roles the 'father' plays. The case also demonstrates how the family culture gave rise to a particular set of emotions and dysfunctions as would be found in any familial or kinship relationships – highlighting the need for studies of leadership to focus on both the leader as an authority figure as well as the relationships between the members of the kinship. Only through such a focus will a more nuanced and richer understanding of emotions be gained in what might at first glance be described as a patriarchal form of leadership.

The family metaphor and the notion of the leader as the 'father' emerged from the data collected for this study. The father-figure is not directly recognizable as a paternalistic leader or a classic archetype father-figure (Steyrer 1998). Instead the leader demonstrates a more complex character who (like any father) does not always play the role of 'the man in charge' when considered in the broader network of familial relations, yet at the same time retains some level of authority simply by virtue of being the father. In effect the infantilization implied in the family-metaphor is not limited to the positions of the 'children'.

The chapter is structured as follows. First, the study is placed in the context of the broader field of leadership research; specifically in the area of research focused on emotions and emotional leadership. Second, the chapter explores the emotional context of the family, familial relationships and the role of a family culture. Third, the case study organization and the use of the family-metaphor are introduced, before reflecting on the specific aspects of interest to this argument, namely: the leader, family and kinship relations, and attempts to bridge the leadership 'gap'. The chapter concludes with a discussion and reflections on the role of the father-figure and family metaphor in exploring the emotional and complex nature of leadership.

## LEADERSHIP, EMOTIONS AND THE FAMILY

This study acknowledges, but does not dwell upon, the trait theories of leadership, behavioural styles, contingent leadership theories (and related typologies) and transformational or charismatic leadership (for a review, see Grint 2005; Parry and Bryman 2006). While these established approaches in the leadership lexicon continue to have an impact, there has been a shift towards approaches that look 'post' these accounts of leadership – with post-heroic being the most recognizable example. Broadly speaking the post-approach refers to the desire to go beyond *the* leader to consider shared or distributed forms of leadership (Gronn 2002; Pearce and Conger 2003), even alternatives to leadership (Manz 1986; Manz and Sims 1991), as well as reassessing leadership as being something a lot more humble than previously entertained (Storey 2004). The attraction to this focus on everyday leadership – distributed or otherwise – is that it captures leadership as experienced by most people. Heroic, transformational, charismatic or otherwise notable leaders have often been written about because they are the exception, not the rule.

These approaches give rise to existential questions regarding leadership, such as whether and when it exists. This highlights the inherently socially constructed nature of leadership, a phenomenon that is situated in the eye of the beholder and constitutes what is, or isn't, leadership to them (Bresnen 1995). Consequently it focuses on followers in a dyadic relationship (Graen and Uhl-Bien 1995) and positions followers and leaders in a dialectical relationship rather than treating followers as predictable respondents (Collinson 2005). Moreover, the co-constructed nature of leadership enables more attention to be given to the emotional and relational nature of leadership.

Emotions in organizations have received increasing attention in organization studies (Newton 1995; Fineman 2003), in particular in relation to emotional labour (Hochschild 1983) and emotional intelligence (Goleman 1996). More specifically emotions in leadership have been assessed in the context of heroic (Nanus 1992), toxic (Walton 2007) and bullying (Kärreman 2011) forms of leadership, to name a few recent archetypes. The literature has explored both the positive (George 2000; Goleman et al. 2004) and negative impact of these emotions (such as the bullying or toxic leader) and the effect of this emotional form of control. The tendency to polarize around an archetype of leadership (whether good or bad) neglects the fact that most leaders are more difficult to categorize, and may vary in their approach in time and place, and in the context of different relations. Casey (1999) explored this emotional form of control in the context of a family culture – demonstrating its peculiar strand of emotional discipline. The notion of family embeds the leader – in this case, and more typically, the father-figure – in the context of dynamic family relations, highlighting the importance of context in studying emotions in leadership and going beyond the leader–follower relation.

Exploring leadership in family business reveals a wealth of research on the role of the family in the business and on issues of succession. However, despite the growing body of literature in this field, there have been suggestions that the family still remains neglected as a variable in the organization and performance of (family) business, particularly when considering the extensive work in the field of family science and research on family life (Dyer and Dyer 2009). Consequently, explorations of leadership in family business research fail to give sufficient attention to the nature of relationships and their role in creating the emotional climate for leadership. The emotional-familial ties intertwined within a business context typically comprised also of non-family members indicate the complexity of relations at stake. Issues of for example succession, legacy and fairness are often more problematic due to these relationships. The combination of the familial and business context has consequently attracted the attention of scholars from outside of the traditional business disciplines, including those with a background in psychology, family therapy and other social sciences (Walsh 1994). Issues of leadership are explicitly addressed in terms of the role of the founder (entrepreneur) in following through on their vision and playing a central role in developing the organizational culture (Schein 1995). However the role of leadership in and of the emotional family climate has received limited attention.

The idea of a family culture is not restricted to family business as many small organizations are operating with similar kinship relationships (Ram and Holliday 1993). Indeed describing a business as a family business has become a marketing tool. The familial metaphor has also become a recruiting call, as a way of demonstrating a caring and inclusive community in which to work (Casey 1999). Once in the organization, such discursive devices can act as a powerful means of eliciting commitment and love for the organization (Kunda 1992; Barker 1993). The head of the familial organization is typically a father-figure, a leader who has authority by virtue of his position as well as (perhaps at times despite of) his personal style.

Steyrer (1998) draws on the work of Neuberger (1990) in developing his archetypes of leadership, one of which is the archetype of the father, which involves fatherly love, wisdom and care (1998, p. 818):

> In Neuberger's sense, the image of the father contains both the 'despotic sovereign-father' and the 'infantilizing benefactor' ... Corresponding to the despotic sovereign type, he appears 'superior, strong, knowing, great and paramount, stable, dependable and reliable'. As an infantilizing benefactor, he appears to his followers both as someone 'understanding, forgiving, benevolent, protective, caring' and 'strict, demanding, punishing, threatening, predominant and castrating' (Neuberger 1990, p. 44 f. *passim*, quoted in Steyrer 1998, p. 818)

Steyrer argues that these archetypes (father, hero, saviour and king) acquire 'symbolic functions' (p. 823). In the case of the father, this includes the admissibility of emotions and a centralized authority (Steyrer 1998) where 'what father says goes'. These symbolic functions are central to the leadership role and to follower behaviour.

The chapter explores a case study of this form of emotional leadership – drawing on the context of the family firm, family culture and father-figure archetype – providing a more contextualized account of this emotional leadership (and means of control). In doing so, it seeks to remedy some of the criticisms of leadership research (see Alvesson and Spicer 2011, pp. 18–20). First, it seeks to focus on the followers (Meindl 1990) while recognizing the problems with leader–follower binaries (Gronn 2002). Much of the literature on leadership lays emphasis on the leaders at the expense of situating the leader in the context of leader–

follower relations, as highlighted above. Here leadership is understood from the perspective of the follower rather than imposing leader-attributed claims for meaning-making (Uhl-Bien 2006). Consequently, it also seeks to give more attention to the reactions and actions of the followers, which in turn influence the leader and their leadership. By focusing on the voice of the followers, the research aims to avoid imposing an external interpretation of what the leadership meant to them (Meindl 1995). Second, the study seeks to give more weight to the context of leadership. As a professional organization, the leader–follower dynamic is influenced by the norms and expectations of the particular profession (Bryman et al. 1996), as well as the (organizational) cultural context of the firm, and the interrelationships between its members. These contextual dynamics are also potential sites for leadership substitutes, which can explain why 'gaps' in leadership may not result in organizational inertia.

## THE CASE STUDY

The case study explores the leadership of Mortimer Balmes, the managing director and principal of a medium-sized firm of solicitors (referred to as *Balmes*) located in a small town in the UK. The firm had two members of the family at the head of the organization: Mortimer, and his wife, Simone. Simone was in charge of the administration of the firm, and also had a substantial financial stake in the organization. The narrative presented is based on data collected over a six-month period, and reflects on the leadership in *Balmes* over a two-year period. Data was collected through a series of (recorded) interviews conducted off-site. Seven formal interviews were conducted, in addition to a number of informal follow-up conversations. The interviews were conducted during and after the respondents' time working in *Balmes*. What follows are the accounts of three employees of the case organization (Michael, Ruth and Kate – all pseudonyms) drawn from the legal side of the organization.

Confidentiality and anonymity are paramount, and accordingly certain details of this case are disguised, including the use of pseudonyms. There are limitations to the data. In particular, the lack of voice given to the principal means that only views of 'followers' are being explored. Given the nature of the case, it would not have been possible to approach the leader without revealing that there were other participants in the project, which could have jeopardized their positions. Consequently, the focus of this analysis is on how leadership is perceived and made sense of rather than on the intentions of the leader (Meindl 1990).

The data analysis draws on the metaphor of the 'family' to assist in making sense of the 'follower' experiences. This metaphor was explicitly raised by one of the interviewees as an analogy and family-derived labels for people's roles in the organization were employed by another interviewee as a device for making sense of their experiences. Consequently, as the interviewees' use of the family metaphor demonstrated their own construction of meaning, it was decided that the metaphor was a robust means through which to explore the dynamics. However, it is equally acknowledged that this focus may act to limit the scope of analysis, and thus the discussion of the data seeks to go beyond the frame by including quotations that allow for alternative interpretations. In developing the metaphor of the family, the notion of family in Aristotle's *Politics* is employed in which the family (*oikos*) is understood as a form of community in which members are involved in a common life, defined by a friendship and/or love that forms the basis of the kinship. The family unit is the basis for *polis*. As such kinship is founded in the familial relations, but through broader forms of association it provides the basis of wider community relations extending beyond the *oikos*. In a similar manner, the familial unit in the organization extends beyond the immediate spousal relationship to include others through kinship, and at the same time exclude those who do not accept the terms of friendship – who remain 'outside' the family (Ram and Holliday, 1993).

## Data Analysis: The Leader

The principal was clearly identified by all interviewees as the head of the organization, and the one from whom they would expect a sense of vision. This was not by dint of his personal demeanour or charisma, but through a more traditional sense of hierarchy. Indeed the interviewees' descriptions of Mortimer were far from what might be anticipated when thinking of a leader, including phrases like 'un-self-assured', 'easily persuaded' and 'incoherent'. When describing his style it was commented that 'he doesn't really want to be the boss' (Ruth). Mortimer was often described as appearing physically uncomfortable, particularly when faced with difficult decisions: 'he becomes a bit nervous … clicking his fingers … rocks on chair and sort of looks down and doesn't make eye contact' (Michael). In the company of young women: 'he found it very difficult to communicate with them. He'd sort of stand there and shuffle' (Ruth). Despite being in a position of authority, Mortimer appeared to lack confidence, as demonstrated by Ruth's job interview:

It was the most bizarre interview I've ever had ... the interview ... it was a case of ... I went, I sat down. He sort of mumbled his way through what he did and he thought I was too qualified to be an admin person and he'd like to offer me a paralegal position and would I be interested and that was in about ten minutes. There wasn't anything about: tell me about yourself, biography, anything. That was just it. (Ruth)

Despite the failure of Mortimer to live up to the implicit leadership archetypes (Lord et al. 1984) Mortimer was still seen as the leader:

It would come down to him in the end when a decision had to be made – I think he had to sort of be pushed ... I could never work it out. He was very much the boss, but because he was so quiet and withdrawn ... you wouldn't know where you stood. (Kate)

The organization was also described as lacking any clear sense of purpose or identity:

[A] bit disorganized really, not sure where it's going or how it's going to get there. (Kate)

[I]t's just ticking boxes ... it is what it is. (Michael)

[M]anaged like a home ... like an extension of the home. (Ruth)

The lack of purpose, direction and communication was clearly consequential and played an important part in employees' decisions to leave the organization. Despite his reticence in the role, Mortimer was keen not to give up the position. A proposal that gained some traction, in which Mortimer would relinquish his role as the principal and become a consultant (retaining his financial interest), and where Troy, a senior solicitor, would take over the management of the organization was discussed but came to nothing, ultimately resisted by Mortimer who was reluctant to give up his role.

**Family and Kinship**

The nature of relationships between employees and the husband and wife team were best characterized as fluid, unstable and often emotionally intense. The organization expanded considerably during the period of study, and this had consequences for the manner of engagement between the principal and his wife, Mr and Mrs Balmes, and their staff. A turning point was the appointment of a personnel manager, discussed below. During this period the organization went from being a relatively informal organization in which employees were not even required to 'book units' (chargeable hours) to being an organization that was increasingly target-driven. During this time the employees noticed a change in the degree of familiarity between themselves and the Balmes', shifting from an informal and open atmosphere, to a more complex and conflictual combination of distance and familization. While efforts were made to develop some more formal systems and means of measurement and reward, sensitivity remained towards *Balmes* being seen as a friendly and informal place to work.

Simone was viewed as 'hyper-sensitive'. Her position was exacerbated by the lack of clarity of her role within the firm. Unlike many experiences of spouses in the workplace who find their role marginalized and not compensated (Poza and Messer 2001), Simone was generously remunerated despite not having a clear role or turning up to work on a regular basis. She was noted for attending when she pleased, dressing casually and was blamed for the 'bad atmosphere' in the office. She was also prone to more extreme emotional displays:

> The Christmas party... the year before last... there was some sort of issue ... that resulted ... I don't think [Simone] could sit by [Mortimer], or something – she's very insecure ... she walked out crying and then there was a domestic, one of my colleagues said '[Ruth] I felt so sick ... it was just horrible'. (Ruth)

Despite these awkward events, the employees believed there was a desire or neediness on the part of Simone, in particular, to be liked. However Simone also had a habit of ignoring staff whom she felt were critical of the Balmes' or the firm (see Ram and Holliday 1993) resulting in the creation of in-groups and out-groups which were widely recognized (Graen and Uhl-Bien 1995). For example she would organize cakes for birthdays or occasional 'bowling days out' to boost morale, but there were 'long faces' if the efforts of the Balmes' were not appreciated, and the names of those who did not participate after Mortimer's 'cajoling and expressed disappointment' were noted down. Mortimer was also accused of acting 'the victim' when responding to Simone's emotional state.

Loyalty to Mr and Mrs Balmes and the firm was central and was most apparent when employees chose to leave the organization:

> He leaned over and he said 'don't you love us anymore?' And I went 'no' and I'm thinking you're my manager, my employer asking me, 'don't you love me?'... it was the most bizarre, bizarre, bizarre ... (...) ... and then I wasn't talked to for the whole of December. (Ruth)

> Emotions run high with [Mrs and Mr Balmes], you cannot provide a counter view against anything that [Mortimer] and [Simone] might say without it being taken personally ... You are then ostracized and that has been seen and highlighted ... when people have left the organization, or when they have handed their notice in ... When they are pleaded with not to go ... I remember [X] was offered more money and I remember [X] and [Y] were asked to stay, and they were almost begged to stay and when they didn't it turned into ... almost in the same conversation gone from being their very best friends to offering them the world to 'pack your bags, let me see what's on your computer' ... no congratulations. (Michael)

Often the departure of an employee was followed by a staff meeting, arranged at short notice, described as a 'rallying cry'. These events were efforts to keep other employees 'on board' and motivated, but were also seen as reflecting the insecurity and rejection experienced by Mr and Mrs Balmes. The emotional uncertainty served to inhibit employees, such that participation in meetings was often muted. All three interviewees commented on how colleagues would 'sit and complain' but typically stay silent in meetings: 'people don't like to rock the boat'. Given the implicit pressure for agreement and the consequences of not agreeing, and the 'killing off' of family members on their resignation (see also Casey 1999, p. 170), such silence was perhaps unsurprising. The bonds of kinship were hierarchical and, when these roles were challenged, this invoked heavy sanction. There was also evidence of the infantilization of the workforce:

> If you look at it from a family perspective, you've got mum and dad, yes, [Mortimer and Simone], and then there's all their children. We were all treated the same ... like being in a family ... like being a child in a family of this patriarch and matriarch ... very strange. (Ruth)

> I was made to feel like a ten year-old child behind the bike sheds with a box of cigarettes. (Michael)

Some of the efforts to manage the office had a nursery school feel to them which appeared to encourage what Casey (1999, p. 173) has called a 'regression':

> [T]his issue of booking units – then [Simone] brought in ... if people made their units or went over their units they would end up having stickers ... like you know like you've been to the dentist today and if you were seven you would have a dentist sticker saying 'I was brave at the dentist'. Well it was like that sort of sticker and she went along and stuck it on people ... I am 45 years old ... you don't motivate people by giving them stickers. Well, the

youngsters accepted it, because they wanted a training contract and they didn't want to rock the boat. (Ruth)

Simone played the role of an untrusting parent, finding it hard to trust her 'children' when they were out of sight. Michael experienced this when working off-site (with the Balmes' approval) and finding himself having to justify his time the following day. Ruth noted the lack of trust and inflexible working hours, and the feeling of being 'watched'. Yet at the same time the infantilization of the principal was also evident. Both Simone and the accountant, Julie, were seen to 'tell him off in front of everybody like a child'. Ruth went on to say 'I could never work out if he quite liked that sort of thing – that naughty boy sort of thing – or whether he was embarrassed ... but he allowed ... it, and I thought this was awful'. Julie, the trusted accountant who was privy to the private as well as business finances of the Balmes', was clearly part of the inner group and treated 'a bit special' and as part of the core emotional kinship group (Carsrud 1994) giving her a privileged position in influencing the organization and perhaps explaining her freedom to scold Mortimer.

The intensity of the emotions were felt by the employees during their time in the organization, and yet at the same time all of the respondents indicated that they had stayed in the organization beyond the point at which they felt they should have left it. Kate indicated she 'got comfortable ... complacent', and Ruth stayed despite the fact that latterly during her time at *Balmes* she used to cry each day before coming to work. But this intensity became most apparent afterwards:

> It was very intense when you're inside the organization... I think it almost feels like I was in ... as a part of a family and now not being inside it, not being part of it, now I can look at it as being a part of an organization ... which allows me to, I suppose, be able to think about it as more of an organization rather than a family, so some of my views have changed. (Interviewer: 'did you think of it as a family at the time?') I suppose I probably did in the sense that I carried a lot of the sensitivities; a lot of the responsibilities for the way that people, particular [Mortimer] and [Simone], felt. (Michael)

Michael, the most senior respondent, perhaps felt the intensity of the organization most keenly as he experienced the most significant change in his relationship with Mr and Mrs Balmes. When he arrived he was quickly invited to join the management team, and made to feel an important member of the organization. He worked long hours and sought to make a positive impact on the organization. When he perceived his efforts to develop the organization were thwarted, and not recognized, he felt the sense of rejection keenly. Over time the relationship broke down and a mutual distrust developed. It seems likely that they felt his lack of trust, illustrated by when he asked an administrative assistant for his total billable hours. In this case the administrative assistant was told off for revealing the details, and Michael assumed that it was deemed a breach of trust for him to question their assessment of his performance.

But there was also a sense of expectation and disappointment felt by others:

> When I left I found it really difficult and I sort of felt like they were trying to promise me things that they couldn't really offer – that was probably the most upsetting for me. (Kate)

There was also a resigned acceptance of the idea that things would not get better:

> 'Nothing would ever change' I think was the buzz phrase that we used to hear going down the corridor from the fee earners on our way out from the meeting. (Michael)

## Bridging the (Leadership) Gap?

The literature on leadership substitutes suggests we may find alternatives to the need for leadership, particularly in a professional organization. However the situation in *Balmes* was more complex. While there were clearly some examples of mechanisms that helped the firm operate, none were a complete substitute for Mortimer. First, over the duration of the two-year period in question, two individuals played what could be termed a substitute leader role. These individuals were called upon to act in a leadership capacity particularly when there was a need to communicate with staff. The first of these was a short-lived position held by a personnel manager brought in, in part, to make the organization more professional in its approach and to cope with its expansion in personnel. This working relationship was not successful, and the manager left a few months later after being given 'the bullets to fire'. After the failure of this relationship the Balmes' were seen to 'make amends':

> I know they tried afterwards ... well, they would ... on a Friday ... we'd have cakes ... that type of thing, again, like a child ... if a child is upset you try to comfort them, and then you try to distract them on to something else. (Ruth)

However the arrival of the personnel manager was seen as a turning point for Ruth: '[Mortimer] and [Simone] detached themselves from us'. Upon the departure of the manager, one of the longer-serving solicitors was called in to become the 'right-hand man' of Mortimer. This can be looked upon as a means of ensuring that *Balmes* had a management structure that extended beyond the principal. However, a management team – set up under the personnel manager some months earlier – was at the same time effectively (though not officially) disbanded. Instead, the senior solicitor – Troy – became the 'voice piece' for Mortimer. Troy was recognized as both having some leadership capacity, but also limitations within his role:

> [L]atterly [Troy], the man with no remit if I may put it that way, is used as a confident and a crutch ... that [Mortimer] relies and leans on with any areas of contention concerning staff or meetings ... or anything that needs to be vocalized. (Michael)

Troy was seen to 'legitimize' Mortimer's decisions, and act as a 'buffer', but was not seen to be influential in the decision-making, despite being called into the office on a regular basis, and taking on the role of conducting meetings. Mortimer was felt to be 'getting [Troy] to do his dirty work for him'. To an extent Troy acted as a substitute leader, but at the same time failed to achieve a status of leader by virtue of his role as the 'middle man'. In effect Troy was 'called off the subs bench' when required but failed to be appointed to a more permanent position. Indeed he was never given an official position or job description, nor was anything announced to the employees; his changing role was observed by his colleagues:

> [Troy] does have a propensity to report back to [Mortimer] and [Simone] when they have their little cozy meetings ... certainly at least three times a day ... I suppose he feels his remit has changed, his ... job description's not changed ... on the couple of occasions that we've talked about it ... he kind of shrugs his shoulders and says it's not really up to me it's up to [Mortimer]. (Michael)

Yet Michael also observed how Mortimer would often speak to Troy several times a day about things that Simone did not seem to be privy to, in part suggested by the fact that Mortimer came to Troy's office, rather than inviting Troy to the (more private) office he shared with his wife. The quote also reflects a degree of the 'paranoia' articulated by Ruth who felt that, following the arrival of the personnel manager, there was a greater sense of 'being observed' and fearing that colleagues were 'reporting back' on your behaviour (see Casey 1999, p. 172).

In addition to the role of the personnel manager and Troy, other potential substitutes for leadership can be found throughout the organization, not least in the nature of the work. The professionalism of the organization was located in the working practices of individual solicitors and their paralegals more clearly than the organization as a whole, as will be seen in the following. The organization relied heavily on an external referral agent for the case load. The agency was paid a fee per case (for referring the business) – a fee that they returned if the file had to be closed without further action, and consequently there was pressure not to close files. The use of this referral agency was problematic for the interviewees:

> The way in which the clients were referred to us was another thing I didn't like … You'd basically get people who had been promised all kinds of things and then you'd speak to them and have to say to them 'no, sorry, that's not the case' so people were lied to, basically … I found it frustrating that we continued to deal with the same company, despite all the problems, but due to the workload they were referring, they weren't willing to look elsewhere. (Kate)

The bonus structure for closing files also provided an incentive – and personal interest – in settling files. This and other examples were given as evidence of a lack of professionalism in the organization, even though, as we'll see below, there was a self-guided professionalism that substituted for this lack in the organization's procedures. In addition to these questionable practices, there was criticism of the lack of systems that might guide behaviour. It was clear that there was no sense of direction for the organization from the perspective of the employees: no team briefings, and performance reviews that were either not conducted, or undertaken many months late. There was a failure to follow through on pay rises or bonuses for many months after they were due to start; in the early days salaries were not paid on time. On a day-to-day basis they felt the lack of a case management system, a lack of supporting legal references and databases and a lack of career structure – particularly for junior members of the legal team. Perhaps most starkly of all was the perpetual promise of training contracts for the paralegals that never materialized. The lack of consideration for what might be considered the hygiene factors of the organization were also indicative – including detached toilet seats, unclean towels, limited heating and lighting in the paralegal room (referred to by the Balmes' – much to Ruth's frustration – as the 'playroom' despite all the work that was being done), a stench from waste pipes in the back office, and having to move a brown piece of paper between windows during the day in the typists' office, in lieu of blinds. The lack of attention to these issues, and the lack of investment in the firm generally, was a cause of disquiet. The risk of questioning these factors could result in being ignored, by Mrs Balmes in particular, so many such annoyances were not vocalized.

However, the volume of work, and the specific nature of the work, ensured that on a daily basis employees knew what was expected of them, even though this was not always clearly articulated from the start:

> I was given 150 files. They said 'these are your files ...' (Interviewer: 'no training?') No, nothing ... I've never worked in a paralegal position before ... so it was just a case of picking up the file, putting it down, reading the next ones until I got an understanding of what was required. (Ruth)

Michael described the employees as the firm's 'support structures' and it was evident that for all the interviewees their colleagues were the best thing about the organization: 'the staff are loyal' and 'great colleagues'. The work was described as limited (in the areas of law covered) and 'repetitive' which also helped the organization function without additional direction, and the pressure to meet targets (the allocated number of billable hours per day) kept employees focused: 'so busy... no time', 'all hands to the pump'. In this way the familial camaraderie between employees played an important role in the functioning of the firm, and the individual professionalism also steered employee's actions. On a day-to-day basis the professional work ethic served to keep the organization functioning:

> The company is led almost by forfeit...it works because of the foot-soldiers ... because they know their jobs ... (...) ... so effectively (Mortimer) deals with the decisions which keep the strings of the puppet alive, barely, but the puppet is really operated by the foot-soldiers. (Michael)

Despite the tensions, there was also an appetite for employees to step in and assist Mortimer, demonstrating loyalty:

> He has before him, and it's almost like he can't see the nose on his face, some very, very secure and some loyal members of senior staff ... that would take up that gauntlet for him and work with him. (Michael)

Nonetheless while the individual professionalism of the practitioners ensured their case load was managed, it did not substitute entirely for the leadership of the organization, nor overcome the consequences of the principal's approach to leadership. Consequently the organization felt the effects of a reluctant leader.

# DISCUSSION

In this case the family-kinship metaphor locates the nature of leadership in the relations rather than in the individual. Comparable to the patriarch of the family who plays many roles – from the man-in-charge, to the cuckolded husband, the doted upon and teased father, and man at risk of the Oedipal drive to take the place of the father – the principal of this organization was in turn the father-figure and patriarch, the naughty boy, the victim, and the vulnerable and resented weak leader. Just as the dynamics in a family are complex, co-produced, fluid and able to take many forms (see Kertzer 1991) so are the dynamics in the leader–follower relations. The archetype father-figure leader needs to be understood in the context of the family, replacing the static ideal of this role with a fluid, relational one – while at the same time retaining the importance of the perceived authority underpinning these relations. The principal was in one moment the leader and father-figure; but in the next the nervous and dependent child in search of someone to take charge. These shifts were context, mood and event-related. This suggests that leadership is not merely distributed but a process that one dips in and out of: a leader is not actively a leader (engaged in leadership) all of the time.

Furthermore the family analogy also reminds us that families comprise a set of co-determined and co-produced emotional relations that are at times functional and at other times dysfunctional. This case demonstrates not only the infantilization of the workforce, but also the infantilization of the father-figure – at times cuckolded by some of the senior administrative staff and pitied by others – at other times seen as the man in charge and the one employees wanted to impress. This stands in contrast to the archetype of the father-figure presented by Steyrer (1998). Steyrer's archetype is not a uni-dimensional figure, being both 'despotic-sovereign' and 'infantilizing benefactor', but he remains the patriarchal head. By exploring the emotional control exerted by the family in the context of the broader familial relations, this study shows how the archetype is challenged. It has been argued that this organization demonstrates heightened levels of emotions, exhibited by the leader and through the kinship relations.

It is also interesting to reflect on whether this could be seen as an example not just of emotional leadership but also as an example of emotionally dysfunctional leadership. In the literature on the family, functionality (or otherwise) refers to whether the family unit remains workable (able to stay together and resolve any issues while maintaining a degree of well-being among the family members). This is contingent on the family and its own beliefs as to what is functional, as well as being contingent for each family member (Walsh 1994, pp. 179–80). In the context of a family business, these workable systems are even more complex, combining the functioning of the family (kinship relations) with the functioning of the firm.

From the perspective of many in the organization, the arrangement – particularly the spousal partnership – was dysfunctional and unworkable. However on a day-to-day basis there was some functionality, much as a normal family has abnormal dynamics. Clearly for some, the dysfunctionality was too much, and resulted in emotional strain or changes in behaviour. In these cases the interviewees ultimately left the organization. Nonetheless there were many other examples of employees who 'kept their head down' and carried on. In some cases this reflected a degree of ambivalence towards the kinship in which the lack of resistance demonstrated a desire 'not to rock the boat' rather than a sense of commitment (see Casey 1999, p. 169). There was little evidence of active resistance to the culture (with perhaps the exception of Michael), or a counter-culture apart from employees' 'bitching'. Ultimately resistance to the 'infantilization struggle' (Casey 1999, p. 171) was achieved by leaving the organization. This was despite some palpably deep emotional reactions being reflected in the interviews demonstrating their endurance of discomfort over a period of time, and also their personal commitment to the 'family'.

Understanding the kinship structures enables us to see how the firm functioned (became self-leading to an extent) but at the same time demonstrates the limitations to this emotional climate. With no clear vision, or values and a lack of strong leadership – the classic father-figure archetype – the leadership substitutes merely served to keep the organization operating on a day-to-day basis but were not able to lead the organization in new directions or articulate a clear sense of direction for the firm in its current position.

The familial-kinship metaphor is not the only possible way of exploring this case, and the reliance on it as a device for understanding their experiences as adopted by some of the interviewees may have framed their accounts such that other interpretations and events may have been excluded. Further, the case is reliant on respondents who were clearly unhappy in the organization, all of whom eventually left during the process of data collection. This inevitably biased account that draws only on the perspectives of (disaffected) 'followers' is a limitation to this study's capacity to give a full account of leadership (Alvesson 2011). Nonetheless the metaphor utilized also provides interesting insight into this emotional, familial context and positions the leader in the nexus of kinship relations and organizational context to understand better the nature and effect of this emotional leadership.

## CONCLUSION

In conclusion, the chapter has sought to demonstrate the importance of situating the understanding of leadership in the broader network of relations – beyond that of leader–follower relations. Going beyond the metaphor of the father-figure, and considering the family as a set of intertwined relationships extends our understanding of leadership, and its substitutes. In this case, the relations between employees, and between employees and the leader were the source of tension, but also of the organization's survival. These relationships were influenced in part by their identification with (as well as resistance to) the familial dynamic. The contradictory positions also parallel those found in the family, where there are bonds of love and in extremis, feelings of hate. As a result the chapter also concludes with some reflections on the use of metaphors which focus on the leader at the expense of the situational aspects of leadership, and in particular the broader relations in which this leadership is enacted. Lastly, this chapter explores the use of the 'familial' as a device for emotional control, and in particular for demanding trust from its followers.

The chapter attempts to demonstrate the importance of considering context in the study of leadership, and in particular the network of relations that constitute, shape and constrain the process of leadership. It also points to how the use of metaphors needs to go beyond the leader metaphor to reflect upon leadership in the context of broader relations. In essence it argues that by bringing the network of relations to the fore researchers can better understand the nature of leaders and leadership. Such an approach also helps expose the contradictory positions held by leaders, revealing the ambiguities in their identities and activities and helps to avoid oversimplified accounts.

## NOTES

1.  Whether this constitutes a family business depends on the definitional criteria, however it is the family culture and dynamic which is of interest. For a review of what constitutes a family business, see Winter, M., M.A. Fitzgerald, et al. (1998), 'Revisiting the study of family businesses: methodological challenges, dilemmas, and alternative approaches', *Family Business Review*, **11** (3), 239–52.
2.  Care must also be taken not to 'normalize' dysfunctional relationships – see Walsh (1994)

# REFERENCES

Alvesson, M. (2011), 'Studying leadership – taking meaning, relationality and ideology seriously' *Department of Business Administration Working Paper*, Lund, Sweden: Lund University.

Alvesson, M. and A. Spicer (eds) (2011), *Metaphors We Lead By*, Abingdon: Routledge.

Alvesson, M. and S. Sveningsson (2003a), 'The good visions, the bad micro management and the ugly ambiguity: contradictions of (non-)leadership in a knowledge intensive company', *Organization Studies*, **24** (6), 961–88.

Alvesson, M. and S. Sveningsson (2003b), 'Managers doing leadership: the extra-ordinization of the mundane', *Human Relations*, **56** (12), 1435–59.

Barker, J.R. (1993), 'Tightening the iron cage: concertive control in self-managing teams', *Administrative Science Quarterly*, **38** (3), 408–37.

Bresnen, M.J. (1995), 'All things to all people? Perceptions, attributions, and constructions of leadership', *Leadership Quarterly*, **6** (4), 495–513.

Bryman, A., M. Stephens, and C. Campo (1996), 'The importance of context: qualitative research and the study of leadership', *Leadership Quarterly*, **7** (3), 353–70.

Carsrud, A.L. (1994), 'Meanderings of a resurrected psychologist, or lessons learned in creating a family business program', *Entrepreneurship, Theory and Practice*, **19** (1), 39–48.

Casey, C. (1999), '"Come join our family": discipline and integration in corporate organizational culture', *Human Relations*, **52** (2), 155–78.

Collinson, D. (2005), 'Dialectics of leadership', *Human Relations*, **58** (11), 1419–42.

Dyer, W.G. and W.J. Dyer (2009), 'Putting the family into family business research', *Family Business Review*, **22** (3), 216–19.

Fineman, S. (2003), *Understanding Emotion at Work*, London: SAGE.

George, J.M. (2000), 'Emotions and leadership: The role of emotional intelligence', *Human Relations*, **53** (8), 1027–55.

Goleman, D. (1996), *Emotional Intelligence: Why it can Matter more than IQ*, London: Bantam.

Goleman, D., R. Boyatzis and A. McKee (2004), *Primal Leadership*, Boston, MA: Harvard Business School Press.

Graen, G. and M. Uhl-Bien (1995), 'Relationship based approach to leadership: Development of leader–member exchange theory of leadership over 25 years', *Leadership Quarterly*, **6** (2), 219–47.

Grint, K. (2005), 'Problems, problems, problems: the social construction of "leadership"', *Human Relations*, **58** (11), 1467–94.

Gronn, P. (2002), 'Distributed leadership as a unit of analysis', *Leadership Quarterly*, **13** (4), 423-451.

Hochschild, A.R. (1983), *The Managed Heart: Commercialization of Human Feeling*, Berkeley, CA: University of California Press.

Kärreman, D. (2011), 'Leaders as bullies: leadership through intimidation', in M. Alvesson and A. Spicer (eds), *Metaphors We Lead By*, Abingdon, UK: Routledge, pp. 162–79.

Kertzer, D.I. (1991), 'Household history and sociological theory', *Annual Review of Sociology*, **17**, 155-179.

Kets de Vries, M. and Miller, D. (1985), 'Narcissism and leadership: an object relations perspective', *Human Relations*, **38** (6), 583–601.

Kunda, G. (1992), *Engineering Culture: Control and Commitment in a High-Tech Corporation*, Philadelphia, PA: Temple University Press.

Lord, R.G., R.J. Foti and C.L. Devader (1984), 'A test of leadership categorization theory: internal structure, information processing, and leadership perceptions', *Organizational Behavior and Human Performance*, **34** (3), 343–78.

Maccoby, M. (2000), 'Narcissistic leaders: the incredible pros, the inevitable cons', *Harvard Business Review*, **78** (1), 91–102.

Manz, C.C. (1986), 'Self-leadership: towards an expanded theory of self-influence processes in organizations', *Academy of Management Review*, **11** (3), 585–600.

Manz, C.C. and H.P. Sims (1991), 'Superleadership: beyond the myth of heroic leadership', *Organizational Dynamics*, **19** (4), 18–35.

Meindl, J.R. (1990),' On leadership: an alternative to the conventional wisdom', in B.M. Staw and L.L. Cummings (eds), *Research on Organizational Behavior*, London: JAI Press, pp. 159–203.

Meindl, J.R. (1995), 'The romance of leadership as a follower-centric theory: a social constructionist approach', *Leadership Quarterly*, **6** (3), 329–41.

Meindl, J.R., S.B. Ehrlich and J.M. Dukerich (1985), 'The romance of leadership', *Administrative Science Quarterly*, **30** (1), 78–102.

Nanus, B. (1992), *Visionary Leadership. Creating a Compelling Sense of Direction for Your Organization*, San Francisco, CA: Jossey-Bass.

Neuberger, O. (1990), *Führen und Geführt Werden*, Stuttgart, Germany: Enke.

Newton, T. (1995), *'Managing' Stress: Emotion and Power at Work*, London: SAGE.

Parry, K. and A. Bryman (2006), 'Leadership in organizations', in S.R. Clegg, C. Hardy, T.B. Lawrence and W.R. Nord (eds), *The Sage Handbook of Organization Studies*, London: SAGE, 447–68.

Pearce, C. and J. Conger (2003), *Shared Leadership: Reforming the Hows and Whys of Leadership*, Thousand Oaks, CA: SAGE.

Poza, E.J. and T. Messer (2001), 'Spousal leadership and continuity in the family firm', *Family Business Review*, **14** (1), 25–36.

Ram, M. and R. Holliday (1993), 'Relative merits: family culture and kinship in small firms', *Sociology*, **27** (4), 629–48.

Schein, E.H. (1995), 'The role of the founder in creating organizational culture', *Family Business Review*, **8** (3), 221–38.

Steyrer, J. (1998), 'Charisma and the archetypes of leadership', *Organization Studies*, **19** (5), 807–28.

Storey, J. (2004), 'Changing theories of leadership and leadership development', in J. Storey (eds), *Leadership in Organizations: Current Issues and Key Trends*, London: Routledge, pp. 11–38.

Uhl-Bien, M. (2006), 'Relational leadership theory: exploring the social process of leadership and organizing', *Leadership Quarterly*, **17** (6), 654–76.

Walsh, F. (1994), 'Healthy family functioning: conceptual and research developments', *Family Business Review*, **7** (2), 175–98.

Walton, M. (2007), 'Leadership toxicity: an inevitable affliction of organisations', *Organizations & People*, **14** (1), 19–27.

Winter, M., M.A. Fitzgerald, R.K.Z. Heck, G.W. Haynes and S.M. Danes (1998), 'Revisiting the study of family businesses: methodological challenges, dilemmas, and alternative approaches', *Family Business Review*, **11** (3), 239–52.

# 6. The emotional rollercoaster: leadership of innovation and the dialectical relationship between negative and positive emotions

## Stephan Schaefer and Alexander Paulsson

### INTRODUCTION

Although leadership literature has included its link to emotions (see Lemmergaard and Muhr 2011 for a discussion), there has not been much discussion – and research for that matter – on the interrelationship between leadership, emotions and innovation (Lockyer and McCabe 2011). Opposed to formalized processes and routine tasks, innovation is an uncertain and highly ambiguous endeavour (Kline and Rosenberg 1986; Poole and Van de Ven 2000). Intuitively, then, participation in innovative processes should involve a variety of emotions, such as fear, anxiety, hope, frustration, anger and exhilaration. The interrelationship between leadership, emotion and innovation is therefore worth further investigation, and will be the topic of this chapter.

As will be demonstrated in the following, because of its assumed ability to achieve change, transformational leadership is often argued to be the ideal leadership approach to facilitate innovation (Sosik et al. 1998; Van de Ven 1986). Transformational leadership, however, has received a lot of criticism for its lack of moral foundation. As a response to this criticism the concept of authentic leadership was developed (Bass and Steidlmeier 1999). Authentic leadership, which is based on ideas from positive organization scholarship (POS), assumes that positive emotions are preferred since negative emotions are generally considered to be dysfunctional (Cameron and Caza 2004). This unilateral theoretical development raises interest in the interrelationship between leadership, emotions and innovation and we will therefore discuss the preference for positive emotions from a critical perspective. We will question whether only positive emotions such as excitement, relatedness and optimism lead to successful leadership of innovation and suggest that negative emotions such as anger, fear and anxiety play a constructive role as well. Although, our focus lies on innovation processes, we will not argue that it could not be relevant for other leadership contexts as well. However, for matters of simplicity, and viable empirical illustration of the emotional mechanisms we discuss, we have chosen to limit the scope of this chapter to the leadership of innovation.

To investigate the interrelationship between leadership, emotions and innovation the chapter is structured as follows: In the first section we form the foundation of our main argument by discussing the links between emotions and leadership in innovation processes. We then dive deeper into the issue by providing an overview of the prevailing leadership literature and connecting it to emotions. To illustrate how positive and negative emotions are interrelated in leadership of innovation, we discuss a case study of a company known for its innovative capability. Before our concluding remarks, we discuss our findings, which suggest that positive and negative emotions in the leadership of innovation can be conceptualized as a dialectical relationship.

## BETWEEN CREATION AND DESTRUCTION: EMOTIONS, LEADERSHIP AND INNOVATION

Innovation is a pivotal concept in management research and has become increasingly popular over the last decades (see, for example, Crossan and Apaydin 2010 for an overview of the field). The origin of the concept is usually traced back to Schumpeter (1934), who argued that innovation is instigated by 'creative destruction'. Creative destruction is often embodied by a 'creative destructor', who as an entrepreneur destroys the equilibrium of an economy or an industry through his or her innovative activity. This constant struggle with an inert environment – attempting to break routines and business-as-usual – enables, according to most innovation theorists, economic growth and technological progress (Fagerberg 2003; Kline and Rosenberg 1986; Nelson and Winter 1977). The act of 'creative destruction', however, often involves a noticeable impact on an organization, as big changes most likely are accompanied by emotional turmoil and resistance. After all, 'destruction' is usually linked to something familiar ceasing to exist in its original and trusted form (Shah 2000). The term 'creative', in contrast, implies a possible resurrection, leading to a positive outcome in the interest of organizational leadership. This double-edged characteristic of innovation, implied by Schumpeter, suggests a noticeable emotional impact on its leadership processes. We suggest the metaphor of an emotional rollercoaster as an appropriate way to understand and unpack the emotional dynamics of the leadership of innovation. A rollercoaster ride induces a simultaneous and relatively short-time experience of exhilaration, fear, joy and satisfaction (Rutherford 2000). This, we purport, aptly captures the emotional dynamics related to leading innovative processes.

Broadly speaking, leadership research can be characterized by dichotomous claims of it being either something positive and beneficial (Avolio and Gardner 2005; Bass and Steidlmeier 1999) or toxic and dysfunctional (Ashforth 1994; Conger 1997; Einarsen et al. 2007; Padilla et al. 2007). The former characteristic is connected to a set of particular positive emotional responses such as, for example, excitement or relatedness (Bass 1985) or optimism and hope (Avolio and Gardner 2005). The latter inter alia instils, for example, fear (Lockyer and McCabe 2011). Accordingly, there is a fixation in the literature on either positive heroic leaders or dysfunctional narcissistic psychopaths (see the discussion in Lemmergaard and Muhr 2011). In relation to innovation and creativity, leadership research pinpoints positive feelings such as optimism as relevant for engendering innovation (Humphrey 2002), which draws inspiration from positive organizational scholarship (POS) and forms the conceptual base for authentic leadership research (Avolio and Gardner 2005).

The existing literature emphasizes positive emotions and leaves little, if any, room for a discussion of the possible functionality of negative emotions. However, we will stress in the following that emotions such as fear, anxiety and anger can, to put it metaphorically, 'push the buttons' for innovation. In this way, negative emotions like fear or frustration can be constructive because they function as catalysts for finding novel solutions to problems. As Fineman (2006, p. 272) argues, 'negative emotions can constructively modulate individual expectations and performance to positively enhance outcomes'. Just as positive emotions might be functional drivers of leadership, so might feelings of anxiety and fear – especially when leading innovative processes.

The dichotomy between positive and negative leadership traditionally emphasizes a bipolarity of emotions. We, however, oppose this bipolarity and argue that a dynamic of emotions develops which is not necessarily bipolar. We view leadership as a dynamic social interaction as opposed to a dualistic leader–follower construct (Collinson 2005; Fairhurst 2001). An interactive or dialectic perspective on leadership emphasizes the co-creation and mutually constitutive outcomes of leadership processes. It acknowledges that leadership cannot be reduced to a dualism between the leader and follower but that 'it is more relation and group based, dependent on fluid, multi-directional interactions and networks of influence' (Collinson 2005, p. 1422). In alignment with such a perspective we argue that in the interaction between leaders and subordinates an interdependent dialectic relationship between negative and positive emotions develops which impacts innovative outcomes. Such interplay between negative and positive emotions complicates a neat separation of positive and negative leadership styles, and accordingly also the distinction between dysfunctional and functional leadership for innovation. The concept of a dialectical relationship between positive and negative emotions thus challenges concepts of leadership, which assume a bi-polarity of emotions such as the authentic leadership concept (Avolio and Gardner 2005). We argue that leadership research has neglected these implicit emotional dynamics, encapsulated in Schumpeter's oxymoronic notion of 'creative destruction', and we aim to resurrect them. In the following section, we will delve deeper into the different parts of this dynamic and refine and develop our argument further.

**Creation: The Leadership of Innovation**

As explained above, transformational leadership is often suggested as an applicable way to 'lead' innovation processes (Buckler and Zien 1996; Van de Ven 1986) because leading innovation is concerned with facilitating the creation of something novel which requires unleashing the latent creative potential of followers (Amabile 1988) – a hallmark of the transformational leadership concept (Bass 1985). Critiques of transformational leadership, however, have questioned its moral foundation, leading to the development of authentic leadership, which eschews the negative and immoral side of leadership impregnating it with an all-encompassing positivity. It is this one-sided emphasis on the positive emotions in leadership, which will be the focus of the following discussion of transformational and authentic leadership.

Transformational leadership aims to establish a strong emotional bond between leaders and subordinates. Based on this relationship the leader aspires to transform and heighten the subordinates' attitudes and needs so that they transcend self-interests for the common collective good (Avolio et al. 1999; Bass 1985; Bass and Avolio 1993). The effects of transformational leadership are believed to be higher intrinsic motivation and performance, which allegedly conduces creative efforts (Jung 2000; Mumford et al. 2002; Sosik et al. 1999). Numerous scholars have argued that autonomy and empowerment is required for solving problems in an innovative and creative way, thereby eschewing the creation of formal rules and bureaucracy (Burns and Stalker 1961; Dodgson et al. 2008;

Kimberly and Evanisko 1981; Storey and Salaman 2005). Therefore, leaders are not only supposed to promote and communicate inspirational visions, but also to 'empower others to take greater responsibility for achieving the vision'. (Bass and Avolio 1993, p. 113). Related to this, Brown and Eisenhardt (1995) propose the concept of 'heavyweight leaders' in new product development. Consider also in this respect the following description of leadership in innovation by Roberts (1984):

> This type of leadership offers a vision of what could be and gives a sense of purpose and meaning to those who would share that vision. It builds commitment, enthusiasm, and excitement. It creates a hope in the future and a belief that the world is knowable, understandable, and manageable. The collective energy that transforming leadership generates, empowers those who participate in the process. There is hope, there is optimism, there is energy. (cited in Van de Ven 1986, p. 3)

Providing meaning, symbols and visionary myths for engendering and sustaining innovation is thus key (Buckler and Zien 1996; Van de Ven 1986). Leadership creates a vision by stressing positive emotions, which empowers and motivates employees to innovate and take the liberty of divergent thinking. An innovative organizational culture instigated by leadership should be warm and welcoming with a focus on establishing trust and care (Elkins and Keller 2003).

Transformational leadership, however, has been criticized for its disregard of ethics and moral grounding, begging the question whether transformational leaders need to act on a legitimate moral basis (Ciulla 1995). The question of whether transformational leadership encompasses all leaders, even morally dubious ones such as Stalin or Hitler, prompted Bass and Steidlmeier (1999) to develop the concept of authentic transformational leadership challenging so-called pseudo or inauthentic transformational leadership. An authentic transformational leader is supposed to transform his or her subordinates based on sound and moral principles. 'It is the presence or absence of such a moral foundation of the leader as a moral agent that grounds the distinction between *authentic* versus *pseudo*-transformational leadership' (Bass and Steidlmeier 1999, p. 186, emphasis in original). Bass and Steidlmeier's (1999) call for a positive moral grounding of transformational leadership in this way laid the foundation for the authentic leadership literature (Avolio et al. 2009).

The concept of authentic leadership is closely related to positive psychology (Seligman and Csikszentmihalyi 2000) and its derivative: positive organizational scholarship (POS) (Avolio et al. 2009; Roberts 2006). In general, POS scholars believe that by foregrounding positive feelings and optimism, individuals will draw upon their authentic inner-most virtues of honesty and trust, which eventually leads to better performance and heightened creativity (Seligman and Csikszentmihaly 2000). Positive personal constructs, such as authenticity and honesty, are assumed to engender positive organizational outcomes (Roberts 2006). Authentic leadership scholars emphasize how positive emotions can enable far-reaching transformations of subordinates (Avolio et al. 2009). These positive emotions are related to 'confidence, optimism, hope and resiliency' (Avolio and Gardner 2005, p. 322). However, Cameron and Caza (2004, p. 731) claim that: 'POS is not fashionable advocacy for the power of positive thinking. Although it does espouse an unequivocal bias concerning positive phenomena, POS does not ignore the presence of negative, challenging, or contrary aspects of organizations'. While they do acknowledge negative organizational aspects they still claim that positivity and concomitant affective states will help to overcome nega-tively evaluated situations.

In general, authenticity is a popular concept and has gained consider-able influence in the last decades (Giddens 1991). Most ideas on authenticity are based on essentialist assumptions, ascribing a fundamen-tal and stable authentic core to individuals. Turning inwards and connect-ing with your inner self allegedly discloses your true character, traits and fundamental personal values. This idea of authenticity assumes a stable self-identity characterized by some fundamental core traits. This assump-tion has been contested, however, as identity constructions might as well be fragmented, ephemeral and inconsistent (Sveningsson and Alvesson 2003) and as such will discount the claim that we possess an inner core that we need to get in touch with. Most of the literature on authentic leadership, however, assumes an essential stable system of values and morals, which the leader purportedly can tap into to make informed and ethically sound decisions (Avolio and Gardner 2005; May et al. 2003). The literature on authentic leadership contends that 'authentic leaders exhibit a higher moral capacity to judge dilemmas from different angles and are able to take into consideration different stakeholder needs' (May et al. 2003, p. 248). The authentic leader seems to possess a constitu-tional quality of differentiating between right and wrong using universal innate positive values to make the right decisions for the common good. A capacity of authenticity apparently seems to be one of the key concepts and specifies the predominant essentialist view. Describing characteristics of authentic leaders, Avolio and Gardner (2005) mention positive psycho-logical capacities as a key element. According to them positive psycho-logical capacities can lead to positive outcomes and the generation of concomitant positive emotions. The psychological capacity in combination with a positive organizational context and certain triggers 'can play a crucial role in developing individuals, teams, organizations, and communities to flourish and prosper' (Avolio and Gardner 2005, p. 324).

The predominant view on emotions in authentic leadership is hence inspired by an essentialist conception. This line of thought is based on findings that some basic emotions are universal and the same across cultures (Ekman and Friesen 1971). This stands in contrast to interpretative approaches, which purport that emotions are culture specific and embedded in social relations. Take the concept of optimism as an example, which is repeatedly mentioned in the authentic leadership literature as a desirable outcome: optimism should generally engender positive emotions – in particular anticipation or excitement. The authentic leadership literature tells us that true optimism is based on the leader's inner core values and beliefs. May et al. (2003) for instance argue that optimism communicated by a leader can be received unambiguously by subordinates. 'If all leaders act in accord with their core beliefs and values, then what they say is exactly what they mean' (May et al. 2003, p. 249). We, however, question this explanation. How can we know that the display of optimism is directly connected to anticipation and excitement? What if subordinates perceive the display of optimism with anxiety and trepidation? Anticipation then might stem from existential anxiety or angst reflecting on one's ability to realize personal freedom? (Heidegger 1927). Or less positive: what if the subordinates' anticipation is staged and acted out; conforming to institutional pressures?

The bottom line is that the authentic leadership concept rests entirely on positive emotions as the medium, which engenders positive organizational outcomes. In terms of innovation, authentic leadership would encourage the creation aspect of the innovation process emphasizing positive emotions. However, a critical view on such an assumption raises the question of whether a focus on positive emotions is always the best option and whether negative emotions instead could be a viable alternative. After all, an exclusive emphasis on positivity seems to be rather superficial, as negative emotions have and should have a place in organizations, and as we will show even hold the possibility of being productive and functional.

## Destruction: Going Downhill on the Emotional Rollercoaster

'Necessity is the mother of invention' is a common saying, which alludes to a connection between emotions and innovation. It implies that when being hard-pressed and anxious, the seed of an innovation, an invention or an idea, might be around the corner to 'save' you. To provide another and a related example, let's turn to a proverb, which conveys a message of great emotional impact: 'The fear of the Lord is the beginning of wisdom'. This frame of mind has been the hallmark of Calvinist work ethics, which imbued work-life until the late 20th century, and to a certain degree still does today (Ehrenreich 2009). Leadership in this tradition becomes necessary in order to draw attention to necessities (Van de Ven 1986) or even create the fear or awe of the leader who is deified (Gabriel 1997). Negative emotions become functional for the organization, as in fearing the deified leader you will devote your entire self to labour and toil possibly creating something novel.

The widespread preoccupation with positivity discussed above has led to a negligence of the relationships between negative emotions and leadership in processes of innovation. Granted this, how could one discuss the possible functionality of negative emotions without being labelled a sadist or chronically pessimist? To claim that a leader, in one way or another, ought to spread a culture of negative emotions seems intuitively wrong. However, those who do study this nexus claim that negative emotions induced by leaders – for example fear – can lead to innovation (for example, George 2000; Lockyer and McCabe 2011; Maccoby et al. 2004). Additionally there are arguments, which might not pertain directly to the constructive role of negative emotions for the leadership of innovation, but which are implied by studies on positive thinking and death awareness (Ehrenreich 2009; Reedy and Learmonth 2011).

In her analysis of the positive thinking movement in the US, Ehrenreich (2009) argues that a narrow focus on positivity suppresses potentially constructive negative emotions. Excessive optimism, she claims, facilitated the occurrence of fateful events, such as 9/11 or the financial crisis, because leaders such as George W. Bush and or others denied negative thoughts and eschewed information which could have indicated a possible attack or the collapse of the financial markets. An obsession with positivity eventually builds up a 'reflexive capacity for dismissing disturbing news' (Ehrenreich 2009, p. 11). Suppressing negative thoughts outright, however, leads to the neglect of other possibilities and ideas with a latent creative potential. We are not claiming that pessimism or negative emotions by themselves lead to innovation but the limitation on only positive thinking restricts the proposition of novel ideas, which might be based on negative notions. Pessimism might lead to innovative outcomes insofar as one is able to assess different alternatives and possible novel solutions to threats. In simple terms, they can be facilitators and eye openers for novel solutions. In the case of 9/11 for example the possibility of an attack might have triggered ideas on how government agencies share information to ensure the surveillance of possible threats.

Closely connected to excessive optimism is the constructive role of negative emotions, which have caught the attention of scholars who have focused on the awareness of death as perhaps the strongest negative thought one could have. Research on death awareness in organizations, and a concomitant arousal of fear, thus adds some further substance to our argument. Grant and Wade-Benzoni (2009), for example, discuss antecedents and consequences of death awareness in organizations and its practical implications. They claim that death awareness, if it results in prolonged reflection, can have powerful positive effects on motivation in organizations. Their conclusion is that death awareness does not automatically engender destructive behaviour. Instead, they suggest that managers should be sensitive to mortality cues and react appropriately by encouraging reflection rather than suppress them.

Based on Heidegger's ideas about death, Reedy and Learmonth (2011) argue that fear might lead individuals to realize their own potential, while breaking out of the institutional frame of an organization. Emotions like anxiety and fear can thus have positive and emancipatory effects as they stimulate reflections on mortality. Additionally, frame-breaking experiences may potentially lead to the search for new solutions or actions, which will ensure long-term survival. Evoking fear of death – although only in the form of a symbolic death, as in the death of an organization or the death of one's career – is of course a rather dramatic approach. It showcases, however, how people react to the arousal of fear and related negative emotions, which in the end might be constructive for innovation. Anxiety and death awareness are thus feelings, which could be affected or engendered by leaders – intentionally or unintentionally – and which would possibly lead to constructive and novel outcomes. As already hinted above leaders walk a thin line by raising anxiety levels and possibly fear. The main message is that leaders should not suppress negative emotions at all costs but allow for reflections on negative issues and thus open spaces for a pessimistic outlook as well.

In order to empirically illustrate how leaders and subordinates balance positive and negative emotions on the one hand, and creation and destruction in innovation on the other hand, the following section will show the emotional dynamics of leadership processes at a high technology company: Technovator.

# CASE STUDY: TECHNOVATOR

Technovator is a recently established 50/50 joint venture comprising two successful players in the high technology sector. It is an engineering-driven company with approximately 8000 employees working globally. The core business is supplying high technology products integrating software and hardware components.

## Methodology

This study is based on 63 in-depth interviews with engineers and managers as part of a project on the leadership of innovation. The purpose of the research project was the investigation of roles and forms of leadership processes in innovation. The project comprised multiple case studies in various companies, one of which was Technovator. The research site was the R&D department, which is divided into multiple sub-departments linked by common large development projects. All interviews were conducted by one of the authors during a two-year period. The main bulk of interviews were conducted with managers at the headquarters where the main R&D offices are located while some interviews were conducted at other local sites. Each interview lasted on average 60–90 minutes. The interviews were recorded and subsequently transcribed. The analysis of the empirical material was based on phenom-enologically inspired methods (Smith et al. 2009) and focused mainly on the experiences of leaders in processes of creativity and innovation. During the analysis of the interviews and iterations to the literature other themes emerged from the empirical material, one of which indicated a conjoint existence of positive and negative emotions in innovation. This theme was followed up by reviewing the extant literature. The analysis does not follow a strictly grounded theory approach but is rather based on iterations between theory and empirical material which is commonly referred to as abduction (Alvesson and Sköldberg 2009).

## Leadership in Technovator

Technovator ranks as a highly innovative organization using common indicators such as R&D expenses and the number of patents. Close to 90 per cent of Technovator's staff is working within R&D and it has a large portfolio of patents. Innovativeness is one of the core brand values associated with Technovator because the company has created products that can be classified as radical or discontinuous as they had a disruptive impact on the market (Garcia and Calantone 2002). Most of Techno-vator's innovations, however, can be described as incremental which means they are significant improvements in processes or technologies which do not necessarily have a disruptive impact on the market as such. Technovator's facilities are spread out over various sites but common projects link the development work of these sites together. Teams and projects are distributed physically but usually led by a manager from the main site. The organizational culture is informed by a first-mover rather than a 'me-too' attitude which is also based on the fact that all employees are trained engineers and there are only a few people with different backgrounds working in marketing or HR. Technovator has no formal innovation policy and leadership of innovation is not governed by any formal rules or specific norms. Accordingly, most of the managers in the R&D department develop their own 'style' of leading innovation due to the lack of clear guidelines. Leadership 'styles' in Technovator's R&D department thus vary across the sample of interviewees from the description of a leader emphasizing positive emotions to others who spread fear and panic.

One interviewee's description of the leadership style of her superior for instance comes close to the ideal of a transformational leader. Her description depicts the leader as someone who would transform sub-ordinates' full potential for a better cause.

> His only task was actually to promote these different guys and girls. Coach them, push them to perform the things they were best at doing. He didn't have any competence in a particular area but he was very good at making them feel good about themselves. [...] He is very good at leading because he thought that every individual possesses something really good. I mean, he had some employees who were not high-performers but he found something that he could have full confidence in them doing. I think that he had full confidence because he looked at the special skills everybody had and he assigned them so they could do that. I think he had full confidence in his employees. (Employee A)

The subordinate describes an example of a leader who instils confidence in his employees and who uses positive emotions to reinforce innovative behaviour. It is a description depicting empathy and emotional intelli-gence. She confirms the prevalent view in the literature that positivity and a display of confidence would lead to innovative outcomes. A leader, according to this particular interviewee, is supposed to deliver positive feedback and encourage the generation of ideas. Similarly, a manager within the product management division of the R&D department recounts:

I mean my people they have ideas all the time, and for some of them you actually take a deep breath and you go for them. [...] You face a choice. [...] We have a reasonably competitive solution, and we will be done in 12 months. And then we have this other new completely unproven concept, and if that works we could make a much better radio. But it may take two years to get it completed. And you only have people to do one solution. So I mean, do you take this leap of faith and go for the new architecture and the unknown (Manager A)?

This manager points to the choices leaders face in innovation processes and to the trust leaders need to exhibit when they support an idea proposed by a subordinate. Leaders must 'take a deep breath' and display confidence and trust in their subordinates. Trust is based on engendering positive emotions as leaders strive to pull out the best from their subordinates and show it to them. Such consistency in behaviour and a positive attitude are important according to the head of an R&D division.

You need to have very consistent behaviour. [...] If people know which type of reaction to expect and they see that actually in my way of acting then they will start trusting it and then they will dare. You get that by consistent behaviour. [...] Again, as I said before, a more positive attitude is vital. (Manager B)

These attitudes expressed by employees and managers are well received by engineers working under his leadership. They appreciate positivity and the trust they are receiving for developing new solutions. One engineer talks about the possibilities to take time off for working on new ideas.

I also think that the managers have been more and more open to let the developers spend some time if they have an idea, of course, you have to tell them first what your idea is and then if they think it sounds good then they say: 'Okay, you can spend a week on it.' (Engineer B)

This engineer's attitude is discernible in other departments as well. Engineers appreciate trust and optimism. At the same time and within the same R&D department, however, a somewhat different leadership style is apparent. A leadership style which emphasizes fear and panic, alluding to the possibility of an 'organizational death' resulting from increased competition. A department manager describes the leadership style of his division manager in the following way:

His leadership is completely different from what I am used to. I like him. If you take everything he says seriously you could be a bit insulted, but I have learned what to listen to and what not to. He has a very high drive. He has a very strong ambition. He can make things happen in a very short period of time. That is what I like about his leadership style. (Manager C)

This manager is being very careful talking about his superior and phrases his perception in rather positive terms – probably in order not to 'say too much'. But the subtext of his statement and the way he uses the words 'you could be insulted' insinuates that this particular leader most likely arouses anxiety and fear in people, a view that many of the other interviewees also expressed in informal conversations, such as during lunch breaks, which were observed by the researcher. One story that was repeatedly retold was that this particular manager would publicly 'crucify' subordinates during meetings demanding immediate results. Delivery of novel solutions and new ideas was one of such immediate results and he would relentlessly pursue it. This leader was arousing anxieties concerning a possible crisis; concerns which spread to other sites of Technovator as well. A design manager similarly describes feelings of fear and panic in innovation processes and how negative emotions impact on them:

> I have observed that when we have developed innovative technology, or methods, in the past, we had to struggle, to overcome obstacles. You know, a major issue – that would threaten it all. There was a fear of a terrible waste of efforts. [...] [Innovation is] squeezed, squeezed out by fear or panic. (Manager D)

This interview excerpt depicts a leadership style, which stands in stark contrast to the arousal of confidence and optimism in subordinates displayed by the leaders described above who were aiming to arouse positive emotions. Fear and anxiety are prevalent and fostered by leaders in other departments at Technovator to overcome obstacles in the innovation process. Consider the depiction of another design manager with regard to the atmosphere in Technovator.

> You pick anyone in this company; and he [sic] will have an extreme sense of what competition is. Competition is a struggle. We are struggling for life, so there is fear, a fear to dissatisfy the customer, a fear to be beaten by competition. I am sure that all people are very aware that innovation is the only escape on a long term basis. I am sure. You can pick anybody, from the highest manager to the lowest level operator. (Manager E)

The observation that competition and tight deadlines lead to panic and potential new solutions is reiterated by the observation of an R&D manager in one of the projects concerning his development team which was affected by tight project deadlines. Like the previous manager quoted he remarks that his engineers feel the pressure and by the prospect of missing project deadlines they 'squeeze out' innovation.

> There are people who have really gotten [very annoyed] by sitting and waiting: 'I have to wait for two hours for this tool to complete and that's ridiculous. I am very stressed by the project; I want this software tool to work faster'. And because of that they initiate a new process or new tool. (Manager F)

The idea that fear and anxiety would lead to innovation is expressed by the above quoted manager, who is talking about the source of innovation.

> It can be [a solution] to a technical problem, for the fear that the whole company is going down. It can be menace from the customer to go to next door. Then I'm sure, people start to do their best and turn to innovation, not turn on – you know – protecting the old habits. (Manager E)

The short case illustration shows a juxtaposition of fear and panic, on the one hand, as well as confidence and trust in the leadership styles of innovation on the other. Still, Technovator's managers engender innovation and generate ideas. A manager captures the essence of innovation leadership at Technovator quite well in the following way: 'It [Leadership of innovation] is a little bit of dictating and a little bit of supporting and coaching. Making us move into the right direction'. In this quotation the manager hints at the two interrelated processes of arousing opposing emotions simultaneously. Leadership of innovation is not only about providing support and inspiring confidence, it is also about telling people what to do and possibly arousing negative emotions. With this empirical illustration as a basis it is exactly this dialectic of positive and negative emotions we aim to discuss in the following.

## DISCUSSION: THE EMOTIONAL ROLLERCOASTER OF LEADERSHIP

> It was unbelievably loud, rattling, terrifying: an emotional episode the likes of which I had never before experienced. But as the speeding train neared the end of the course, my fear rapidly melted into something else altogether – a sense that it was OK to howl with delight like everyone else, to let go, to have fun. Once you got the hang of it, the Shooting Star didn't seem too bad after all. (Rutherford 2000, p. 9)

In this quote Rutherford relates his emotional experiences of a roller-coaster ride and the simultaneous presence of emotions during and after the ride. Much like the rollercoaster the innovation process is a 'ride' in which fear and frustration emerge alongside joy and optimism and in which developments look bright and possibly gloomy at the same time. For most of us, rollercoasters are both scary *and* fun. The rollercoaster ride is determined by a fixed track, much like a leader who provides a vision of the company. While the way uphill fills us with great expectations, the steep downhill gives us a sense of both fear *and* joy. Simultaneously two opposite emotional reactions are triggered, both negative *and* positive. Eschewing these vital emotional dynamics of innovation delivers a somewhat one-sided picture for leaders in organizations. In the following we therefore suggest the emotional rollercoaster metaphor as a way of understanding the *dialectical relationship* of positive and negative emotions in leadership processes of innovation.

The case study of Technovator illustrated the coexistence of negative and positive emotions and their conjoint effect on innovation outcomes. Both negative and positive emotions are interconnected in the quest for innovation. Positive and negative emotions stand in a dialectic relationship in which they overlap, reinforce integrate and possibly synthesize to generate something novel and innovative. This conclusion confirms Fineman's (2006: 274) argument that a focus on positivity is one-sided, eschewing crucial simultaneous emotional dynamics, which are constructive in organizational contexts. Our study supports Fineman's claim that there is a 'continual dialectical relationship' of positive and negative emotions. In Technovator this dynamic is present in the display of confidence and in the need to show consistent behaviour towards subordinates. Yet simultaneously another emotional dynamic is discernible in the leadership processes. Leaders also spread fear and panic, which drives engineers to come up with innovative solutions indicating a relationship between negative emotions and innovation. This dynamic implies in general a coexistence of positive and negative emotions in innovation processes, which are facilitated by the leadership of innovation.

Our conclusions regarding a dialectic relationship of positive and negative emotions lend empirical support to the critique of authentic leadership and its conceptual foundation POS. If we accept the argument that positive and negative emotions are dialectically related three problematic issues in relation to the authentic leadership concept arise: the question of possibility, desirability and ambiguity. We will discuss each in turn.

As we have seen, scholars claim that authentic leaders would promote positive feelings and optimism drawing upon their authentic innermost virtues of honesty and trust (Roberts, 2006). Without denying the multifaceted and intricate aspects of organizational life, scholar's espousing authentic leadership claim that honesty and trust eventually leads to creativity and innovation, and eventually to positive organizational outcomes (Roberts 2006). This argument implies a bipolar view on emotions (Green et al. 1993). A bipolar view argues that negative and positive emotions are located at opposite ends of a continuum. Bipolarity is mainly an issue for statistical measurement of emotions and indicates a reciprocal relationship. For instance, if we feel less positive feelings of love, we gain more negative feelings of hate. We trade in love for hate moving along the bipolar scale. Bipolarity as such is not undesirable. There are in fact many meaningful bipolar constructs such as for example hot and cold. Nevertheless, there might be reason to believe that a bipolar structure in emotions is artificially created (Cacioppo et al. 1997). An alternative perspective on the relationship between emotions is to view them as independent and unrelated constructs. Independency implies that emotions can be experienced simultaneously. Love and hate can then be felt at the same time, which Pratt and Doucet (2000) refer to as 'emotional ambivalence'. Our findings are thus in line with the previously cited research, which proposes that there is an occurrence of joint emotional experiences refuting the bipolarity claim.

The claim that positive emotions should be foregrounded to enable human flourishing and unleash all positive human potential (Fredrickson and Losada 2005; Roberts 2006; Seligman and Csikszentmihalyi 2000) implicitly assumes that negative emotions can be crowded out and replaced by positive emotions. In the positive thinking movement, negative emotions, people and situations are threats which should be avoided (Ehrenreich 2009). This one-sidedness, however, cannot be upheld in the face of our empirical case study. Emotions do seem to occur simultaneously and thus appear to be independent constructs (Larsen et al. 2001). Other scholars have challenged the one-sided focus of POS. Lazarus (2003, p. 173) for instance argues that POS has distorted and emphasized the dichotomy between positive and negative emotions too much:

> I think positive psychologists are constantly congratulating themselves for having discovered positive character traits all by themselves. This typology of positive and negative, which the positive psychology movement seems to be stuck with, is unproductive because the realities of life usually fall in between and, to be even more precise, most people seek to integrate the extremes of positive and negative, thereby making the best of the negative and often creating positive out of negative.

The refutation of bipolarity thus questions the mere possibility of authentic leadership. If there is emotional ambivalence how would we be able to crowd out negative emotions and replace them with positive ones? Apart from questioning the possibility of authentic leadership, questions of its desirability arise as well.

Our empirical illustration challenges the predominant view that innovation is solely facilitated by the removal of negative emotions. Moreover, removing negative emotions could be undesirable in innovation. The authentic leadership concept would thus eschew important features of the innovation process. It is a truism that achieving particular outcomes such as innovation requires hardship and struggle – the infamous 'blood, sweat and tears'. This process is certainly informed by hope and optimism, but at the same time also by fear and anxiety. Only stressing authenticity and positive emotions is a cul-de-sac, creating a detached view on the hardship of innovation and its empirical reality. The fear of failure, termination and loss of self-esteem indisputably spurs innovation and creativity. A strict focus on positivity in leadership suppresses a vital component of the innovation process and might thus not be desirable. As Ehrenreich (2009) has argued and we have seen in the case study, the suppression of negative feelings might have consequences, which restrict creative solutions. Technovator is a highly innovative company, which has produced innovative products, which were 'squeezed out by panic and fear'. Feigned optimism might have led to the acceptance of a situation with perhaps detrimental consequences.

Lastly a dialectical relationship between positive and negative emotions also questions the proclaimed unambiguous relationship between authentic leadership acts and reactions by subordinates and thus the validity of the concept's constructs stemming from POS. Related to the basic concept authenticity we can ask ourselves why the leader in the Technovator case study who spread fear and panic cannot be regarded as an 'authentic' leader? Authenticity is always related to positive emotions rather than leaders actually being themselves. Hackman (2009) demands conceptual clarification of various constructs in positive psychology but we would argue that the validity question of concepts in positive psychology and authentic leadership needs to be extended to incorporate the acceptance of ambiguity and complexity. The assumptions that authentic positive emotions can be transmitted to subordinates needs to be questioned. This relationship is certainly more complex and ambiguous than conceptualized. The essentialist core to the conceptualization of emotions in leadership might simplify complex relationships.

In general, a dialectic of positive and negative emotions also challenges the distinction between functional and dysfunctional leadership.

Authentic leadership which builds on trust, care and harmony is usually deemed to be functional while fear and anxiety are considered dysfunctional (Lockyer and McCabe 2011). While there certainly are leaders who exhibit pathological tendencies and destructive traits, the clear-cut distinction between functional and dysfunctional, at least as they are related to a dichotomy between positive and negative emotions, needs to be at least questioned in its distinctiveness. The relationship is far more complicated than claimed, as it can be built on multiple emotions all believed to be dysfunctional or functional. Our discussion of the importance of negative emotions does therefore not imply that we believe leaders should strive to arouse negative feelings. Rather, we claim that negative feelings, whether we want them or not, will always play a vital part in innovation processes and should therefore be taken seriously by leadership. In this respect it is of course essential to act ethically, which would be a discussion beyond the scope of this chapter.

## CONCLUSION

The purpose of this chapter was to discuss and analyse the nexus of emotions, leadership and innovation. To meet this purpose, we first discussed the literature on leadership of innovation. We showed that the leadership of innovation literature mainly builds on the concept of authentic leadership. Authentic leadership is strongly influenced by the concept of POS, which claims that in organizations positive emotions should be in the foreground. This claim has been critiqued from various angles as demonstrated in this chapter. Scholars have inter alia challenged the essentialist notion of emotions in POS and the unambiguous transmittal and reception of positive emotions. Based on this critique we presented arguments, which point to the functionality of negative emotions, and their relation to innovation. We illustrated this through a case study of a high technology firm.

From the case study we drew the conclusion that emotions in the leadership of innovation stand in a dialectical relationship. In innovation processes, both positive and negative emotions are present. This finding challenges the authentic leadership literature on the dimensions of possibility, desirability and ambiguity. The possibility of authentic leadership is questioned on the basis of its bipolarity assumptions and the ability to crowd out negative emotions. With a view to the constructive effect of negative emotions in innovation we also questioned the desirability of suppressing negative emotions and lastly acknowledging the ambiguity of the innovation process authentic leadership might draw on too simplified and less developed constructs. A dialectical relationship also challenges the distinction between functional and dysfunctional leadership. The assumption that positive emotions are linked to functional leadership, and negative emotions to dysfunctional leadership, has to be rethought – at the very least in the leadership of innovation. These emotional dynamics have to some extent been implied by Schumpeter (1934), when he was talking about the simultaneous act of destroying and creating something new. Positive and negative emotions certainly have a joint effect on this process.

To capture these dynamics, we suggested the metaphor of an emotional rollercoaster. Even though a rollercoaster follows a laid out track, the 'ride' usually simultaneously arouses emotions such as joy and fear. This is, we argued, reminiscent of the relationship between leaders and followers in the innovation process.

# REFERENCES

Alvesson, M. and K. Sköldberg (2009), *Reflexive Methodology – New Vistas for Qualitative Research*, London: SAGE.

Amabile, T.M. (1988), 'A model of creativity and innovation in organizations', in B.M. Staw and L.L. Cummings (eds), *Research in Organizational Behavior*, Greenwich, CT: JAI Press, pp. 123–67.

Ashforth, B. (1994), 'Petty tyranny in organizations', *Human Relations*, **47** (7), 755–78.

Avolio, B.J. and W.L. Gardner (2005), 'Authentic leadership development: getting to the root of positive forms of leadership', *The Leadership Quarterly*, **16** (3), 315–38.

Avolio, B.J., J.M. Howell and J.J. Sosik (1999), 'A funny thing happened on the way to the bottom line: humor as a moderator of leadership style effects', *Academy of Management Journal*, **42** (2), 219–27.

Avolio, B.J., F.O. Walumbwa and T.J. Weber (2009), 'Leadership: current theories, research, and future directions', *Annual Review of Psychology*, **60** (1), 421–49.

Bass, B.M. (1985), *Leader and Performance: Beyond Expectations*, New York: Free Press.

Bass, B.M. and B.J. Avolio (1993), 'Transformational leadership and organizational culture', *Public Administration Quarterly*, **17** (1), 112–21.

Bass, B.M. and P. Steidlmeier (1999), 'Ethics, character, and authentic transformational leadership behavior', *The Leadership Quarterly*, **10** (2), 181–217.

Brown, S.L. and K.M. Eisenhardt (1995), 'Product development: past research, present findings, and future directions', *The Academy of Management Review*, **20** (2), 343–79.

Buckler, S.A. and K.A. Zien (1996), 'The spirituality of innovation: learning from stories', *Journal of Product Innovation Management*, **13** (5), 391–405.

Burns, T. and G.M. Stalker (1961), *The Management of Innovation*, Oxford: Oxford University Press.

Cacioppo, J.T., W.L. Gardner and G.G. Berntson (1997), 'Beyond bipolar conceptualizations and measures: the case of attitudes and evaluative space', *Personality and Social Psychology Review*, **1** (1), 3–25.

Cameron, K.S. and A. Caza (2004), 'Contributions to the discipline of positive organizational scholarship', *American Behavioral Scientist*, **47** (6), 731–9.

Ciulla, J.B. (1995), 'Leadership ethics: mapping the territory', *Business Ethics Quarterly*, **5** (1), 5–28.

Collinson, D. (2005), 'Dialectics of leadership', *Human Relations*, **58** (11), 1419–42.

Conger, J.A. (1997), 'The dark side of leadership', in R.P. Vecchio (eds), *Leadership: Understanding the Dynamics of Power and Influence in Organisations*, Notre Dame, IN: University of Notre Dame Press, pp. 215–32.

Crossan, M.M. and M. Apaydin (2010), 'A multi-dimensional framework of organizational innovation: a systematic review of the literature', *Journal of Management Studies*, **47** (6), 1154–91.

Dodgson, M., D. Gann and A. Salter (2008), *The Management of Technological Innovation*, Oxford: Oxford University Press.

Ehrenreich, B. (2009), *Smile or Die: How Positive Thinking Fooled America and the World*, London: Granta Publications.

Einarsen, S., M.S. Aasland and A. Skogstad (2007), 'Destructive leadership behaviour: a definition and conceptual model', *The Leadership Quarterly*, **18** (3), 207–16.

Ekman, P. and W.V. Friesen (1971), 'Constants across cultures in the face and emotion', *Journal of Personality and Social Psychology*, **17** (2), 124–9.

Elkins, T. and R.T. Keller (2003), 'Leadership in research and development organizations: a literature review and conceptual framework', *The Leadership Quarterly*, **14** (4–5), 587–606.

Fagerberg, J. (2003), 'Schumpeter and the revival of evolutionary economics: an appraisal of the literature', *Journal of Evolutionary Economics*, **13** (2), 125–59.

Fairhurst, G.T (2001), 'Dualisms in leadership research', in F.M. Jablin and L.L. Putnam (eds), *The New Handbook of Organizational Communication*, Thousand Oaks, CA: SAGE, pp. 379–439.

Fineman, S. (2006), 'On being positive: concerns and counterpoints', *The Academy of Management Review*, **31** (2), 270–91.

Fredrickson, B.L. and M.F. Losada (2005), 'Positive affect and the complex dynamics of human flourishing', *The American Psychologist*, **60** (7), 678–86.

Gabriel, Y. (1997), 'Meeting God: when organizational members come face to face with the supreme leader', *Human Relations*, **50** (4), 315–42.

Garcia, R. and R. Calantone (2002), 'A critical look at technological innovation typology and innovativeness terminology: a literature review', *Journal of Product Innovation Management*, **19** (2), 110–32.

George, J.M. (2000), 'Emotions and leadership: the role of emotional intelligence', *Human Relations*, **53** (8), 1027–55.

Giddens, A. (1991), *Modernity and Self-Identity*, Cambridge: Polity Press.

Grant, A.M. and K.A. Wade-Benzoni (2009), 'The hot and cool of death awareness at work: mortality cues, aging, and self-protective and prosocial motivations', *Academy of Management Review*, **34** (4), 600–22.

Green, D.P., S.L. Goldman and P. Salovey (1993), 'Measurement error masks bipolarity in affect ratings', *Journal of Personality and Social Psychology*, **64** (6), 1029.

Hackman, J.R. (2009), 'The perils of positivity', *Journal of Organizational Behavior*, **30** (2) 309–19.

Heidegger, M. (1927), *Sein und Zeit*, Tübingen, Germany: Niemeyer.

Humphrey, R.H. (2002), 'The many faces of emotional leadership', *Leadership Quarterly*, **13** (5), 493–504.

Jung, D.I. (2000), 'Transformational and transactional leadership and their effects on creativity in groups', *Creativity Research Journal*, **13** (2), 185–95.

Kimberly, J.R. and M.J. Evanisko (1981), 'Organizational innovation: the influence of individual, organizational, and contextual factors on hospital adoption of technological and administrative innovations', *Academy of Management Journal*, **24** (4), 689–713.

Kline, S.J. and N. Rosenberg (1986), 'An overview of innovation', in R. Landau and N. Rosenberg (eds), *The Positive Sum Strategy: Harnessing Technology for Economic Growth*, Washington, DC: National Academy Press, pp. 275–304.

Larsen, J.T., A.P. McGraw and J.T. Cacioppo (2001), 'Can people feel happy and sad at the same time?', *Journal of Personality and Social Psychology*, **81** (4), 684–96.

Lazarus, R.S. (2003), 'The Lazarus manifesto for positive psychology and psychology in general', *Psychological Inquiry*, **14** (2), 173–89.

Lemmergaard, J. and S.L. Muhr (2011), '"Everybody hurts, sometimes: emotions and dysfunctional leadership', *European Journal of International Management* **5** (1), 1–12.

Lockyer, J. and D.A. McCabe (2011), 'Leading through fear: emotion, rationality and innovation in a UK manufacturing company', *European Journal of International Management*, **5** (1), 48–61.

Maccoby, M., J.H. Gittell and M.A. Ledeen (2004), 'Leadership and the fear factor', *MIT Sloan Management Review*, **45** (2), 14–18.

May, D.R., A.Y.L. Chan, T.D. Hodges and Bruce J. Avolio (2003), 'Developing the moral component of authentic leadership', *Organizational Dynamics*, **32** (3), 247–60.

Mumford, M.D., G.M. Scott, B. Gaddis and J.M. Strange (2002), 'Leading creative people: orchestrating expertise and relationships', *The Leadership Quarterly*, **13** (6), 705–50.

Nelson, R.R. and S.G. Winter (1977), 'In search of useful theory of innovation', *Research Policy*, **6** (1), 36–76.

Padilla, A., R. Hogan and R.B. Kaiser (2007), 'The toxic triangle: destructive leaders, susceptible followers, and conducive environments', *The Leadership Quarterly*, **18** (3), 176–94.

Poole, M.S. and A.H. Van de Ven (2000), 'Towards a general theory of innovation processes', in A.H. Van de Ven, H.L. Angle and M.S. Poole (eds), *Research on the Management of Innovation: The Minnesota Studies*, Oxford: Oxford University Press, pp. 637–62.

Pratt, M.G. and L. Doucet (2000), 'Ambivalent feelings in organizational relationships', in S. Fineman (ed.), *Emotion in Organization*, London: SAGE, pp. 204–27.

Reedy, P. and M. Learmonth (2011), 'Death and organization: Heidegger's thought on death and life in organizations', *Organization Studies*, **32** (1), 117–31.

Roberts, L.M. (2006), 'Shifting the lens on organizational life: the added value of positive scholarship', *Academy of Management Review*, **31** (2), 292–305.

Rutherford, S. (2000), *The American Rollercoaster*, Mendota, IL: Andover Junctions Publications.

Schumpeter, J.A. (1934), *The Theory of Economic Development*, Cambridge, MA: Harvard University Press.

Seligman, M.E. and M. Csikszentmihalyi (2000), 'Positive psychology: an introduction', *The American Psychologist*, **55** (1), 5–14.

Shah, P.P. (2000), 'Network destruction: the structural implications of downsizing', *The Academy of Management Journal*, **43** (1), 101–12.

Smith, J.A., P. Flowers and M. Larkin (2009), *Interpretative Phenomenological Analysis – Theory, Method and Research*, London: Sage.

Sosik, J.J., S.S. Kahai and B.J. Avolio (1998), 'Transformational leadership and dimensions of creativity: motivating idea generation in computer-mediated groups', *Creativity Research Journal*, **11** (2), 111–21.

Sosik, J.J., S.S. Kahai and B.J. Avolio (1999), 'Leadership style, anonymity, and creativity in group decision support systems: the mediating role of optimal flow', *The Journal of Creative Behavior*, **33** (4), 227–56.

Storey, J. and G. Salaman (2005), *Managers of Innovation: Insights into Making Innovation Happen*, Malden, MA: Blackwell.

Sveningsson, S. and M. Alvesson (2003), 'Managing managerial identities: organizational fragmentation, discourse and identity struggle', *Human Relations*, **56** (10), 1163–93.

Van de Ven, A.H. (1986), 'Central problems in the management of innovation', *Management Science*, **32** (5), 590–608.

# 7. Happily working until they drop: when there is no longer a balance between stress and fun – a task for leadership

**Yvonne Due Billing**

## INTRODUCTION

In contemporary society, it is not uncommon that people seem to live to work rather than work to live. Many people are highly committed to their jobs and their personal and social identities are closely connected to what they do for a living. They often enjoy the fruits of this engagement; perhaps working in places with positive work cultures, which create well-being for employees. They are highly committed to the teams they work in and they work hard. However, for some employees this commitment may lead to self-entrapment; an area which seems to be overlooked in the leadership literature. Although there is a focus on how to improve workplaces there has not been much attention paid to the problem of entrapment. It is strange – Burke et al. (2011, p. 338) suggest, along with other researchers – 'that we know surprisingly little about [...] how leaders create and handle effective teams'. In their review of team leadership Burke et al. consider the importance of facilitating performance management, but they do not discuss the problem that workers' willingness to work hard may result in over-commitment and may lead to self-entrapment.

On the basis of a study of knowledge workers in an IT/design organization situated in Copenhagen (referred to as Design IT), this chapter argues that leadership faces a problem if it is not attuned to the strains experienced by team workers in the organization. The employees at Design IT were highly committed to their work and generally displayed high work satisfaction, but there were also employees who were close to – or already had experienced – a breakdown. The tensions between work satisfaction and breakdown were related to high work

127

pressure and, for some employees, also to conflicting demands for time from the organization and their families. These tensions are important to try to resolve, not only because the employees' health is at risk but also because it is essential if the organization wishes to retain its employees.

It is crucial for an organization to understand what causes over-commitment and the tensions that follow. Ignoring these tensions may, in the long-run, be fatal to an organization and its workers as tensions may result in stress and burnout. Consequently, tensions that are reported as stressful call for attention and special leadership. Leaders should be sensitive enough to be able to 'read' and understand the emotional state of employees. They should try to manage the apparent paradox; that instead of leading to more freedom, autonomy may lead to over-commitment and entrapment (King 2004), which in turn may lead to stress and burnout.

This chapter discusses organizational (over-)commitment and how a missing balance – i.e. a feeling of incapacity to control the context – between stress and fun can be dysfunctional as it leads to burnout. First, the chapter will briefly look at the existence of tensions in relation to work and work–family. Second, the studied organization – Design IT – will be presented. The focus of this presentation will be on how Design IT's employees reacted to the tensions they experienced at work and how leadership seemed to be impotent when it came to dealing with these tensions. The chapter closes with a discussion about the increasing difficulties of dealing with the missing balance between fun and stress. Although the employees have autonomy at work and are in control of their working hours they do not necessarily feel 'in control'. Feeling 'in control' is a precondition for feeling that there is a balance. This problem is not unique to the studied organization but is more or less a precondition in what Rosa (2005) calls a high-speed society. As such, the problem is a much more general issue, which should not be individualized.

## TENSIONS AT WORK

Since industrialism there has been an evolution in ways of working. The content of work has changed and for many people work is identity-creating and gives life meaning (Florida 2001). Some would even claim that work provides us with the ultimate meaning to our lives or, as expressed by Beck (2002, p. 63), that work provides us with everything which is sacred: 'prosperity, social position, personality, meaning in life, democracy, politically cohesion. Just name any value of modernity, and I will show that it assumes the very thing about which it is silent: participation in paid work'.

At the same time that work is becoming increasingly important as a symbol of social status and a core part of most people's identities, employees are also becoming much more responsible for their own work, that is many workers are expected to be able to self-manage (Quigley and Tymon 2006). Significant parts of contemporary work are organized in project groups and many employees work in teams. It is then no longer a manager who controls and gives orders but the team members and their colleagues. This change does not eliminate control and surveillance. They still exist, just in different forms, for example through performance measurements and assessments for promotions and allocation of attractive work tasks (Alvesson 2000). To work in teams, then, is not necessarily just freedom from control. Team workers control themselves and do the 'surveillance' themselves (Barker 1993). Surveillance has become self-surveillance, or self-technology (Rose 1999) meaning that power relations have become blurred and power structures have become much more complex than in traditional hierarchical organizations. Personal development and responsibility are given to the individual as a way of enhancing his or her freedom. However, freedom and power go hand-in-hand (Foucault 1982), and as argued by Marx, workers may have their freedom but they are also chained to the work, and there may be no opposition. Power may therefore not even be observable, and may be at its most effective when least observable (Lukes 1982). Leadership practices have been internalized. However, this delegation of leadership practices is not without problems, and there is a price to pay for being free and autonomous. For example, the employees are responsible for how much time should be spent on a given work task – and often also for how many tasks to take on – which means that they themselves hold the responsibility and get the blame if a project is not finished on time (see also Muhr et al. 2012).

According to Sennett, working in teams seems to provoke a special morality, as employees have to work hard to prove their worth. In Sennett's own words: 'the good team player does not whine' (Sennett 1998, p. 115). It is not unusual for knowledge workers to be committed and work hard (Alvesson 2000). These workers like what they do, 'it is simply a matter of intrinsic work motivation associated with the qualities of the work content', that is the work implies 'a high degree of work morality and job commitment' (Alvesson 2000, p. 1104). Besides this, Alvesson also points to other relevant aspects, for example that these jobs are often highly paid, and in return the employees accept long work hours. More importantly, however, is that these employees identify with the organization to a higher degree than other types of workers. Their self-image or identity as a corporate member is therefore strong.

Organizations will, of course, strive to recruit 'ideal workers' (Acker 1992). That is employees who are fully committed to the job and the organization (see, for example, Meriläinen et al. 2004). This means, for example, that employees with care commitments outside the organization may face dilemmas or tensions between the time demands of the job and family life. These employees, who are often women, may find it difficult to live up to the norms of working in the organization. A powerful discourse in society is the gender-stereotypical expectation from families and mass media that women should be the primary caregivers. Women are socialized into structures, where certain gender norms are reproduced (Kugelberg 2006), and their habitus (Bourdieu 1979) will then dispose them to 'appropriate' gender behaviour. This is difficult not only for individuals but also for organizations to counter-act. Women often adapt to the circumstances around them and, in periods when they prioritize family, they are therefore more likely than men to choose part-time job solutions and signal that they are tied up with family duties. Their engagement in the organization may then suffer for a period and they might be looked upon as less committed than those (mostly men) who can engage themselves totally.

The problem with this total engagement is that it can be without limits (Muhr et al. 2012). The job provides individuals with material rewards and they may also feel that they need to live up to the demands of for example customers. However, for many, work also fulfils some important personal needs. It is identity-creating and provides a sense of meaning as long as the work is under control. However, if self-managing employees cannot control their work situations and deliver on time, they face a paradoxical dilemma. The workers work according to limits that they have decided for themselves, under their own surveillance. However, being responsible for, and perhaps not meeting, the deadlines may cause the balance to tip (for some). Breakdown is the result. The 'paradise' of the freedom provided by teamwork may, for some, turn into an 'iron-cage' (Weber 1968). Kunda (1992) questions whether this form of organization represents a new form of tyranny or whether it is an enhancement of freedom. In his empirical study of a high-tech company, people seemed to be working hard and to be emotionally attached to work. Although some employees experienced the excitement of creativity, they also lived with ambiguity. Kunda states 'there are hints of a darker, less explored side: there seems to be potential for considerable suffering (...) and there are diverse populations affected very differently by "the culture'" (p. 22–23). Breakdown or burnout can easily be thought to be the result of failure to self-manage.

Burnout is a state of emotional exhaustion that can lead to loss of self-confidence, focus and enthusiasm. Burned-out employees risk becoming disconnected from their workplace and negative emotions often become their predominant reaction to difficult work situations. As decisions and attitudes are infused with emotions, understanding the role of emotion and how to manage emotions is critical in the quest for a deeper and more productive understanding of leadership. As such, it is important to understand emotions if we wish to understand the organization (Fineman and Sturdy 1999) as emotions are central to any organization whether they are healthy or toxic (Härtel 2008). According to Barbalet (1998) emotions are provoked by our circumstances and are implicated in the actor's attempt to transform these circumstances, thus emotions can be understood as the link between the structure and agency. Emotions may be a response to structural conditions in the organization. Awareness of emotions in the social context is then essential. Negative emotions arise, for example, as stress or more seriously as breakdowns, if stress is not handled appropriately. Emotion is a contested notion and there is no firm consensus regarding the social scientific approaches to emotion (see Poder 2004), so this chapter will provide no further attempts to define the concept. For further discussions of emotions at a physical, psychological and social level, see Chapter 1 in this volume or, for example, Barbalet (1998) or Fineman (2001).

Härtel and Ashkanasky (2011, p. 87) argue – quite simplistically – that a positive emotional climate is, 'where positive emotional experiences outweigh negative emotional experiences'. They define positive work environments as consisting of three dimensions: a positive organizational climate, social inclusion and an emotional climate that promotes human flourishing. A positive organizational climate relates to 'values such as openness, friendship, collaboration, encouragement, personal freedom and trust', whereas social inclusion is about 'valuing and embracing diversity of perspectives, knowledge, and mental and physical abilities'. In their discussion of a positive emotional climate, Härtel and Ashkanasky (2011) do not pay much attention to the problem of what Kunda (1992) calls the 'darker side' and which, in this chapter, is referred to as self-entrapment, meaning that people's self-commitment may lead them to over-commitment and burnout. This chapter looks into this gap in the literature on emotions and leadership. What happens in situations where the so-called darker sides of emotional engagement in the organization take over and what does this require of leadership?

## THE CASE OF DESIGN IT

The study was conducted in a well-known, successful and highly prestigious Scandinavian organization (here referred to as Design IT), which is situated in Copenhagen. The study, which was part of a larger study about identity and leadership, draws on interviews with 19 so-called knowledge workers as well as participant observation at the site of Design IT. The interviews lasted between 30 and 90 minutes. Participant observation included taking part in for example meetings, lunches and celebrations. The impression was that employees at Design IT generally enjoy working with the organization and are highly committed. However, there are also tensions and dilemmas, due to over-commitment, which has hardly been acknowledged by the leaders and which seems to be difficult for leadership to deal with. All the managers (3) and an equal number of female and male employees (8 men, 8 women) were interviewed. For anonymity reason, all names have been changed.

Design IT was started almost 25 years ago by Paul. The organization currently enjoys a positive reputation and, from its inception, it received prestigious job orders and won several design prizes. In its early days the organization mainly dealt with design but, at present, there are two more functions: web and communication. The company offers integrated solutions for other organizations. Job orders vary in size, some of the largest jobs consist of design and implementation of a corporate identity from scratch. Nowadays the organization is known as a communication company with design and web resources. The communication consultants are currently the biggest group, followed by the designers and the web developers. About 50 employees are employed in the organization in total. From the start, two-thirds of the employees were women but, following an expansion, the gender composition changed, and today two-thirds are men (whose average age is about 35). More than half of the employees do not have children.

The founder (Paul) has recently sold his remaining share of the company and is leaving the organization for another prominent job. Paul has appointed his successor (Bruce) who, shortly after his appointment, appointed a co-manager, Clara. Bruce and Clara share the leadership/management of the organization with three project leaders (two men and a woman) who represent the project groups, which are the main professional working groups in Design IT.

In the design and communication groups there is an almost equal number of men and women but, in the web group, there are no women.

The three work groups are physically separated but all situated in one large open-space office. This makes communication – especially the informal – easier and also makes the employees more visible to one another. Consequently, the level of informal communication is high between the groups and the groups also often celebrate various social events together.

The web group consists of the 'computer games boys' (also called the 'coke boys' because of their large consumption of Coca-Cola). An employee from the communication group described them as being 'in their own little world'. The design group consists of 'artists', seen (by Paul) as 'sensitive' people who are fuzzy about critique, which is often taken personally. The communication group is generally seen as some-what (semi-)academic and intellectual and is regarded as a bit superior.

The organization, like most others, is affected by competitive pressures and is said to employ only people who wish to work hard and who have creative talents, intuition, fantasy, good communication skills, ability to cooperate, etc. The employees generally like the workplace, and some of them even described Design IT as the best place they had ever worked. At the same time, however, there was also talk about stress and people seemed to find it difficult to set limits for their engagement. Tension between fun and stress seemed to be a particular issue. The next part of this chapter will focus on this particular issue.

**Fun and Stress**

As mentioned above, Design IT is a popular workplace. The employees described the organizational culture as friendly, informal and with a high degree of solidarity. They might work a lot, but the general opinion is that people worked there because the work is meaningful and interesting. As explained by Karen:

> The people but also the work is interesting. I have nice colleagues and I do interesting things (...) It is not an easy job, but you get something out of doing it. (Karen)

In a similar vein, Jane said that she had been keeping an eye on the organization for years and applied; when there finally was a vacant position. She really wanted to work at Design IT.

The organization also presented an image of a playful workplace, and many of the employees, like Henry below, said that when they were looking for work, they deliberately chose work they found fun.

> My aspiration in life is to go with the flow, do things I think are fun and
> things I enjoy. (Henry)

At the same time, most of them found their job very stressful. During the
period that data was collected, five employees were on sick leave and
several others unexpectedly resigned. One of the former project managers
(Eric) suddenly could not cope any more. He went on sick leave and
never returned. One of his colleagues described the incident in the
following way:

> He just had too much to do. He is, of course, the kind of person that likes to
> be very busy – juggling ten balls in the air – but it just became too much, all
> the customers and the projects at the same time as being the manager. I think
> that was too much. (…) I think it opened people's eyes that we are working
> closer to the edge than we thought and it should be something that we can
> talk about (…). There is an acceptance that it could happen to anyone. That
> you collapse with stress is understandable, even expected with the way we
> work. We should try to change things (…) maybe change the way that we
> have arranged the working environment. But I think now it has become a little
> more distant, I think there is a danger that we forget it. (Jens)

Eric's incident in a sense forced his colleagues to think about their own
situation and the general stress levels at the work place.

> I think, when Eric went down, it opened our eyes. We actually managed to sit
> down and think about our own lives and situations, because it has been more
> quiet now, I think we manage to plan ourselves out of the real tight issues
> (…). Not every stressful situation is bad, it is just how you deal with it that
> can be bad for you. The bad way is if you are not capable of making your
> own plan for how much work you want to do. If you are open to workloads
> then they will just pour it on you so you have to learn to say no to some jobs,
> if you haven't got the time. I think a lot of it is planning. (Mark)

However, even though they try, in theory, to use Eric's incident as a
reminder of what needs to be prevented in the future, in practice this is
difficult to uphold when work tasks are building up on their desks:

> We talk about how busy we are and we would like to be less busy but also
> from time to time people talk about, have you noticed how Michael is looking
> kind of stressed, he looks like someone who could use some help, maybe we
> should offer our help on some of the projects? (…) But everyone is working
> 120 per cent, so you do not have that extra energy to say, ok let me take one
> of your projects, because you are already just focused on solving your own
> (…). Everyone is working on ten projects at the same time (…). But I think
> we could do better than we do at the moment. (Lars)

In all the interviews one gets the impression that Design IT is a very busy workplace with high demands and where responsibility is given to the work teams. But they seem to find it hard to control their own time. They need to meet the deadlines and they work 120 per cent. One of the problems, according to Paul, is that 'the time schedules are getting shorter, the economic framework we work in is getting smaller, and the people are getting more and more expensive to hire and there are more and more clients'.

The workplace is very goal-oriented and the bottom-line discussions are about earning money and being able to compete. Making a profit and winning competitions is the dominant idea. But it is also very interesting work, and it seems to be hard to refuse to take on new orders.

> My plan is to say, 'No thank you' to more customers, but it is very hard to say, 'No', if it is interesting, if it is worth my own time. If they say, 'There is this new very exciting thing you can do for us', I can't say, 'No'. (Peter)

A lot of the work is very exciting and it is not always possible to foresee what a job means in terms of hours at the point when it is taken on. As Jens explains, work easily becomes everything:

> When you have a really high level of activity and you are working towards deadlines on three big projects, then work becomes everything and you cannot stop thinking about it and you think about it at night and you dream about it. (…) Sometimes I get really stressed and that is not a good feeling. I know that it is a general problem here and I think it is a bigger problem than maybe management knows, or at least it is bigger than we talk about. I think there are more people who are closer to the edge than we actually think, or than we would like to think. (Jens)

When the interviewer asks what makes him think that so many of his colleagues are close to breakdowns, he answers:

> I can see it on my colleagues, when people work night after night and look really tired and they just have a stressed attitude and are running around more or less confused and trying to make ends meet. I know how they feel because I have had the same feeling in some periods. (…) [At a dinner] I talked to one of my colleagues who said that he had just started taking antidepressants because he had become very stressed, at a dangerous level. I didn't know that and I think if he has been able to walk around with that for maybe three, four, five months, and feel that way, without people noticing that he was either that close to the edge or had actually fallen over, then I suspect there might be more of our colleagues who could be going around feeling the same way. I think it is dangerous. I think the problem is that in the last two and a half years things have been going really well here and we are making more money

and clients are coming in every day and giving us projects. We don't go out asking for a project, we just get them, and that is the way it has been for two and a half years and I think the normal situation is now that everybody works at 120 per cent – that has become the normal situation. (Jens)

In a sense, constantly working overtime has become the new normal, and maybe this is why no one objects. Overtime work is not an exception anymore. Nevertheless, the employees are beginning to notice the problem, which results in a growing dissatisfaction:

> I think we have reached a situation where we are used to people working late nights. That has become the normal situation and it shouldn't be because it is only a matter of time before more people collapse with stress. But of course you can say, 'Oh, but you are making great money'. We get a bonus, so of course it is positive for me that we make that much money but I would definitely, willingly give up that bonus if it meant that we could hire five more colleagues and then get down to working just 100 per cent or 95 per cent and have room for when things are peaking in periods (...) that we could just work 110 per cent in that peak period. I would, yes, I really would wish that. (Mark)

Mark is in agreement with many of his colleagues, who would rather drop their bonuses and have reasonable working hours. The problem, however, is that many of the employees find it hard to refuse work tasks – the work tasks are 'exciting' and 'great fun' and their job is experienced as very rewarding. Some of them even seem to be dependent on work, getting a 'kick' out of working. Toftegård (2011) argues that workaholics may develop 'happiness' hormones. However, for others the imbalance between the demands and their resources results in breakdown. Their bodies physically react when there is a feeling of incapacity to control the context. A competitive culture, such as the one at Design IT, may therefore enhance performances, but it may also have many unfortunate personal emotional consequences, which, in the long run, reduce performance and efficiency.

Workplaces provide positive as well as negative experiences, but in this organization there does not seem to be an awareness of the trap into which many employees have fallen. However, some employees have taken on the role of mediators for their colleagues. It is not unusual that 'informal leaders' emerge and exercise social influence in this way (Kilduff and Balkundi 2011). At Design IT, critique was not made public but could be observed in more subtle forms in internal communication technologies, such as sports articles from the company intranet. Three colleagues initiated these (often satirical) writings, after they played football matches against other company teams. In a friendly and subtle way they tried to communicate what happened in the organization. 'We turn the culture and humour around and make it kind of ok to ridicule the bosses and ourselves (...) In the stories we cast ourselves as managers and thus ridicule ourselves'. By writing these humorous sports articles, the employees performed an inversion of the social roles and, in that way, were able to mock the organization. The writers talked about their writings as being a sort of shadow version of what had happened. The writings may therefore be seen as an attempt by some to support an ideal worker identity and constitute a collective for 'good employees' in opposition to those, who could not manage to work hard, who broke down. But the commentaries also seemed to compensate when difficult things happened, for example they sent out a message that three of the 'players' had decided to make their own soccer club (a rewriting of the fact that three key persons had left Design IT and started their own business). Frank states in the interview, 'somehow, this let off some of the steam (...) and made it easier to accept' [that employees had left]. The newsletters became very popular in the organization and many employees commented on the 'jokes' and suggested themes for the following weeks.

Joking, commenting, criticizing and getting feedback on the jokes was therefore not just a creation of a sort of masculine community commenting on sports. According to the respondents, the articles were read, followed and commented upon by many employees and most of the interviewees said that they found them funny. The articles became a way of channelling critique, which would otherwise not have been voiced. They therefore worked as a sort of coping mechanism in the sense that difficult issues were confronted humorously, helping to reduce strains and tensions. In this sense, humour as argued by Gabriel et al. (2009) dealt with contradictions and paradoxes and could be seen as a sort of 'symbolic protest'. Sport talk and soccer games are then not just 'men behaving as men'; instead the reports functioned as a way to vent frustrations and emotions. Frank exemplified this in the following way:

> They get all my frustrations out as you can tell people what you really think but in a way that no one can really be annoyed about it. (...) we are using sports words. Using their terrible ways of writing is a lot of fun but also being able to do satire on the company is part of it. (Frank)

The writings can be seen as a sort of resistance or perhaps even an (unconscious) attempt to 'glue' the organization together (for example, after key people have resigned). This way of using humour may bring

contradictions to the surface and can then be seen as emotion management in the sense that it might change emotions and create bonds
between the workers (Gabriel et al. 2009). The nature, style and content
of the articles may also reflect the fact that employees may not find it
easy to find a target for their critique. They, themselves, are responsible
for both planning and executing their work, therefore, an open critique of
management might ring hollow.

Design IT has always been a leader in its field – and wants to remain
in that position. However, the great success of the organization is also,
according to Paul, what makes people work so hard without complaining.
When asked why people stayed with the organization, Paul responded:

> Simply the success that we have had. Success is something that makes people
> stay. It is a self-supporting way of developing the business. If you have
> success then it is hard to say, 'I hate this place'. I would rather be part of the
> success than leave. (Paul)

This 'self-understanding' seems to produce cultural values, which honour
a strong orientation towards working hard and never saying 'no' to new
assignments. Even if the negative experiences might outweigh the
positive experiences for some, they tend to stay. John concludes that, for
him personally, the fun part of the job outweighs the stressful part:

> I consider it a relatively stressful job because there are a lot of deadlines and
> there is a lot of work to do. Of course it is a good thing for the company that
> there is a lot of work to do (...). There have been times where I have thought,
> 'this is too much', but they are rather short periods of time and right now,
> maybe because of my age [24], I don't have responsibilities at home. I think
> that the fun part of the job makes it worth it, but it is a stressful job. I think if
> I had kids I might think otherwise because there are a lot of deadlines and it
> can sometimes be difficult to organize the job, at least for me, in working
> hours; between nine and five. (John)

Of course it is possible to work long hours every day as long as there are
no other responsibilities. But the employees are not all young and single,
and some of them might have to change their priorities when they, for
example, have children. This added to the tension between fun and stress:

> It is very stressful. You can compare it to being a stand-up comedian
> sometimes. I have two kids at home and a house to take care of (...) and one
> month ago, I did four Annual Reports in four weeks so that is a pretty
> stressful situation (...). It is hard sometimes to cut off work and be a good
> father. That is stressful. (Carsten)

To make it particularly troublesome for some, while it was recognized that men may be(come) fathers, it was only women with young children that actually reduced their work hours (to around 32 hours a week). Just a few of the men, and the key managers (Bruce and Clara) occasionally left work early in order to pick up children from day-care. They compensated for this by working in the evenings; communicating via e-mails when the children were in bed. Although, Bruce did signal his responsibility towards his family, Design IT (like Danish society in general) was characterized by a high degree of traditional gender division. Most of the male employees' wives, according to interviewees, prioritized family over career and took the main responsibility for the children. This generally made the tension between work and family a greater issue for the female employees than the male, but the women reacted by reducing their work hours, which seemed to be more difficult for the men to do. For the women, this reduction in hours was not without consequences; they were first in line for redundancies. The following section examines the possible ways that leaders can handle or manage the complex trade-off between stress and fun.

### Self-made Demanding Structures – and No Leadership From Above?

Leadership is a contested term and a complex enterprise, especially in team organizations, where decentralized problem-solving is not uncommon and workers often adapt to circumstances rather than being 'led' from above (Alvesson 2000). According to Alvesson (2011, p. 152) 'leadership is not just a leader acting and a group of followers responding in a mechanical way, but a complex social process in which the meanings and interpretations of what is said and done are crucial'. It is often claimed that team-based organizations are characterized by high-speed, high levels of anxiety, constant challenges, constant conflicts and a high risk of breakdowns for those who cannot live up to the demands of, for example, self-management (Barnes and Van Dyne 2009; Casey 1999; King 2004). This mirrors well the situation at Design IT, where employees are supposed to be self-managed. Many of Design IT's employees have been able to cope with self-management and, thus, enjoy many of the freedoms that this entails. However, many employees emphasized that more structures and routines would make their work-life easier.

Leadership, then, is closely related to organizational culture. At Design IT there seemed to be a belief that leadership was essential for the employees' well-being. This stemmed from the idea that employees were not able to handle their time and that, for many, there was no longer a balance between work and fun.

> Well, people should be able to do things by themselves. I think a lot of people have been able to do so but I think that maybe some other things are lacking (...) such as routines and processes and stuff that would maybe make daily life easier for many people. (Lars)

It is as if the requirement of self-management at Design It has become too much. The employees expressed an appeal for somebody else to help solve their problems. These expectations were not directed to Paul, who was seen more as an entrepreneur and was said to have too little focus on leadership.

> Paul is a great inspiration but is also being very personal about the company. Sometimes [he gets] very upset if people want to leave. Like it's out of order. But it is a personal thing for him. It's his business (...) He has a very strong personality, he is very dominant. (Lars)

Instead of taking care of the practicalities and day-to-day leadership, Paul regarded himself as a visionary leader and described himself in rather fuzzy terms as someone 'who shows the way'. When he was asked to be more precise, he described his leadership as, 'walking around and inspiring people'. He was also said to make decisions on 'gut feelings'. 'He just knew' what was the right decision. He had attained an almost mythical status and was said to be immune to critique. While many of Paul's employees seemed to see leadership as an interaction with followers (for example, Peele 2005), or as a collective process (Ladkin 2010), Paul seemed to leave leadership responsibility to the employees – or the teams – themselves. Instead of acknowledging the needs of his employees and taking the desired leadership responsibility, Paul mostly focused on efficiency, and how important this was for the organization to survive.

> Working in an organization like this is a lot of things, of course, but basically it is a question of going from A to Z in the shortest amount of time (...) achieving the best solution for the client that doesn't destroy your company. How difficult can that be? It is just a question of asking the people with whom you work, 'Can you do this in another way that would be more efficient?' (...) So leading is a necessity, not leading in the original respect, but making things more efficient is a necessity if you want to survive. (Paul)

Paul expected the teams to be able to find the best way to get from A to Z themselves and to be more efficient, but the handing over of responsibility and leadership to the teams seemed to have resulted in ambiguous role distributions, and this may have been reinforced by what Paul called the 'spaghetti structures', which are 'extremely demanding'. According to Paul, this is a special way of using the work force and their capacities. As he said 'each of the account managers has a number of clients. When a job comes in they put together a group of people by handpicking whoever they want from across professional borders'. However, Paul was not engaged in this job. People management seemed to be missing at the same time as the organization was said to have what Hanne called 'a caring culture, a culture where people care'.

Exactly what care means is not that clear. Taking care indicates that employees look after each other but whether this also involves an obligation to actually intervene is another matter. The feelings of sympathy are present, but there seems to be no time to help colleagues 'who could use some help' as stated in the interview with Lars.

Many interviewees repeated that time and work pressures are too demanding and that the way they are organized in projects and the way they allocate time may not be the most efficient. One designer said that the way the organization/employees think about time and cost is one of the great barriers to creativity and to developing new ideas.

> I think our projects are actually similar to making a movie. You solve a problem for a customer, but how much is that problem solving worth for the customer? It is not dependent on how many hours you spent on the project but we sell it like that. I think actually that is a big flaw because we ought to sell it by the value (...) I don't think we would spend more time, but we would spend our time in another fashion, not wondering about time. I wonder about time all the time and that is not good for the creative phase of my work. But it is quite hard and I think we could get better solutions than we have today. (...) I think time is one of the hardest problems when making these teams. (Harry)

As mentioned, Paul is eventually leaving and some employees hope that his successors (Bruce and Clara) will be better able to provide the necessary structures in order to improve the work environment, as well as be more involved in the well-being of the employees for example through listening to their problems. Employees believe that Clara is more 'structured', 'goal-oriented' and 'good at providing feed-back'. 'She is a good manager. She is actually trained in leadership and she has a lot of experience in this' (Hans). Hans also comments that Clara has given him some feedback and sent him e-mails, and he concludes, 'this was a new thing for this company, I think'.

Hans's comment about Clara's training could be understood as an implicit critique of Paul, whose leadership style was more 'ad hoc' and based on gut feelings, if it existed at all. The new leaders both agree that their colleagues push themselves too much because they are ambitious, too loyal and that they need more attention:

> People are very ambitious and press themselves to work too hard. They seem to need more attention but also somebody that tells them that they are stressing themselves too much. (Clara)

Bruce seems to agree with Clara, as he remarks, that – in connection with the Friday beer tradition, seen by the employees as a sort of compensation for a hard work week – 'they only take half a beer, then they go back to the computer and finish their work, so they are very loyal to the work, too loyal'.

The essence of it all is that, because of their loyalty and their commitment to their teams, many of the employees at Design IT seemed not to be able to control their own time. There were many good excuses for not setting limits to their work hours; not least the fact that they are part of a great success and that they are offered very interesting job assignments, which they just cannot refuse to take on. Although there is an awareness that some individuals are 'looking stressed' and 'could need some help' there is little chance that this will be provided by any of their colleagues. It is left to the individual employee to deal with his or her problem. This, however, contradicts the statements about 'caring' and a 'caring culture'. The caring culture seemed to be more of a 'collective idea' than something practised. It did not prevent many from working themselves into a breakdown. There seemed to be a discrepancy between rhetorically describing/constructing one's organization as caring and ignoring colleagues who needed help. Caring 'ad hoc' is not sufficient.

There was, however, a growing awareness that there was a need for a better planning. At least the new leaders were aware that their colleagues were perhaps too loyal and they seemed to be interested in helping them finding a balance. As one interviewee said, 'a lot of it is about planning' and 'learning to say no to some jobs'. The founder mainly talked about efficiency and was aware of the demanding structures – he is now leaving the organization and the employees hope that the future will bring better planning, so that they do not continuously have to work overtime. Design IT needs to attend to the problem of more people 'falling over the edge' so that they can prevent breakdowns. Although it may sound paradoxical in an organization with self-organized teams, managers need to take responsibility and help with the planning.

## DISCUSSION

In many ways Design IT is a good workplace, and on the surface it lives up to most of the characteristics that Härtel and Ashkanasky (2011) use to describe a positive work environment. On this level of analysis, there can be said to be a positive organizational climate and social inclusion as well as an emotional climate that promotes human flourishing. Most employees, when first asked, described the organizational culture as caring, friendly, informal and with a high degree of solidarity. They also found the work fun and seemed to have found it seductive to work so much as the work provided them with pleasure. Besides this, many of the employees have also developed friendships with colleagues – this also could be a result of the fact that they hardly had time to establish friendships outside of work because of the time spent at work. For many their work seemed to make up the foundation for their social existence, which then became defined by the organization and, according to Kunda (1992, p. 67), implied that they incorporated this role, becoming one with the organization by 'making it part of one's self'.

Although the level of flexibility and room for creativity is high, the employees still have to develop ideas that pay off. They must make profit and to do this they need to work hard and to be creative and original. All this is identity-producing and gives them status (and high wages). However, there are no limits, formalized structures, predictability and rules, which could have provided some protection from stress (Billing 2005, 2006). It is the individual employee's own responsibility to set the limits. This is difficult as they are part of a great success and they are offered very interesting job assignments, which they just cannot refuse to take on. Failure to control their own time has led to incidents of employees suddenly breaking down and, after sick leave, some of these employees never returned.

In this organization there has not been an awareness of the entrapment that many of the workers seemed to have been locked into. This is a sign that the organization is not healthy and unfortunately the idea about caring seems to be more a mantra than reality. Design IT, like most other organizations, is influenced by competitive pressures, and therefore they are inclined to employ people who wish to work long hours. The capitalist economic system is based on competition and on efforts to eliminate competitors. The need to constantly increase growth and be ahead produces cultural values that honour a strong orientation towards maximum performance. It is important to meet deadlines if the organization wants to survive and, therefore, working long hours is hard to avoid. The problem is that people's devotion to working hard might lead to self-entrapment and they might also easily be exploited. This work orientation is reinforced at Design IT by the pressure of wanting to be ahead and, as a result, it is a stressful workplace, especially for employees with commitments outside the organization. The existing imbalance is damaging and better balance is necessary to stop the present production of unhealthy employees. It would, however, be naïve to think that all the organization's and the employees' problems are due to dysfunctional leadership. The problem is that in contemporary society there is a tendency to support the discourse of the ideal employee, who sacrifices his or her personal needs in the interest of the organization. Capitalist organizations are instrumental and oriented towards profit, and the separation between work and private life, experienced in the beginning of industrialism when production and reproduction were split, also means that everything concerning private life is left to people to take care of themselves.

An awareness of the kind of tensions that are experienced in organizations can add to our understanding of leadership problems and help us to see what we should pay attention to. At Design IT there are dilemmas and contradictions that cause tensions that need to be taken seriously. The main paradox is that the employees are willing to work hard and accept a long-hours culture, despite the fact that this affects their health, because the work is fun. Using the term 'fun' indicates that this is a workplace where people, in fact, enjoy working. Sometimes, however, play at work contradicts people's ideas about what happens at work. To use another paradoxical term, play becomes 'serious play' (see also Sørensen and Spoelsta 2012) and, for some, autonomy and flexibility led to self-entrapment. For many of the employees the stakes are too high, they act against their own interests when they work until they drop. The negative consequences of the pleasure work provides must be dealt with. Of course it is possible at times to work hard, but not all the time, at other times there is a need for more flexibility, especially for those with care commitments.

The organization's leaders should deal with the unfortunate consequences of the workaholic attitude and discuss and initiate changes to hold a balance. They should also be aware that sometimes there is a need for time-out, if the organization wants to retain its employees. Leaders need to pay attention to each individual and the entrapment that some of them have fallen into. Leaders at least need to be emotionally capable of understanding what constitutes balance for each individual employee. At the same time, this problem should not be individualized as it is a more general problem. The danger, however, is that it can easily be turned into a personal problem.

There are no easy general solutions and it is not certain that leaders know best what to do. We live in a time where work may provide pleasure and be our main source of identity but many of us also live under high time pressure, which explains the huge market for self-help books on how to escape the race (see also Pedersen 2008). Some organizations have already incorporated time-outs for the employees (like retreats, or one day off per week) so that they can regain their energy.

If work becomes everything and there is no time left for anything else but work, then employees might feel caught in a trap, whether this is self-entrapment or not. A possibility is to acknowledge that employees need time out and that there must be time to spend on something else (for example, leisure, family) so they experience that there is something other than work. This time away from work may even make employees more creative. In the examples in the study, it was clear that the employees did not want more money or higher wages; they wanted more time. The existing imbalance is damaging, and a balance is needed between stress and fun to stop the present creation of unhealthy employees. The question, which is not resolved, is how it is possible to live up to the demands of competition and at the same time to slow down. However, something needs to be done if the employees are not to become victims of their own success.

## ACKNOWLEDGEMENTS

Thanks to Mats Alvesson, Jeanette Lemmergaard and Sara L. Muhr for helpful and insightful comments on earlier drafts of this chapter.

## REFERENCES

Acker, J. (1992), 'Gendering organizational theory', in A. Mills and P. Tancred (eds), *Gendering Organizational Analysis*, London: SAGE, pp. 248–60.
Alvesson, M. (2000), 'Social identity and the problem of loyalty in knowledge-intensive companies', *Journal of Management Studies*, **37** (8), 1101–24.
Alvesson, M. (2011), 'Leadership and organizational culture', in A. Bryman, D. Collinson, K. Grint, B. Jackson and M. Uhl-Bien (eds), *The SAGE Handbook of Leadership*, London: SAGE, pp. 151–64.
Barbalet, J.M. (1998), *Emotion, Social Theory, and Social Structure*, Cambridge: Cambridge University Press.
Barker, J.R. (1993), 'Tightening the iron cage: concertive control in self-managing teams', *Administrative Science Quarterly*, **38** (3), 408–37.

Barnes, C.M. and L. Van Dyne (2009), '"I'm tired": differential effects of physical and emotional fatigue on workload management strategies', *Human Relations*, **62** (1), 59–92.

Beck, U. (2002), *The Brave New World of Work*, Oxford: Polity Press.

Billing, Y.D. (2005), 'Gender equity: a bureaucratic enterprise?' in P. Du Gay (ed), *The Values of Bureaucracy*, Oxford: Oxford University Press, pp. 257–81.

Billing, Y.D. (2006), *Viljan till Makt?* [The Will to Power?], Lund, Sweden: Studentlitteratur.

Bourdieu, P. (1979), *Outline of a Theory of Practice*, Cambridge: Cambridge University Press.

Burke, C.S., D. DiazGranados and E. Salas (2011), 'Team leadership: a review and look ahead', in A. Bryman, D. Collinson, K. Grint, B. Jackson and M. Uhl-Bien (eds), *Handbook of Leadership*. London: SAGE, pp. 338–51.

Casey, C. (1999), 'Come join our family: discipline and integration in corporate organizational culture', *Human Relations*, **22** (2), 155–78.

Fineman, S. (2001), 'Emotions and organizational control', in R.L. Payne and C.L. Cooper (eds), *Emotion at Work: Theory, Research, and Applications for Management*, Chichester: Wiley, pp. 219–40.

Fineman, S. and A. Sturdy (1999), 'The emotions of control: a qualitative exploration of environmental regulation', *Human Relations*, **52** (5), 631–66.

Florida, R. (2001), *The Rise of the Creative Class. And How it's Transforming Work, Leisure, Community and Everyday Life*, New York: Basic Books.

Foucault, M. (1982), The subject and power, *Critical Inquiry*, **8** (4), 777–95.

Gabriel, Y., S. Fineman and D. Sims (2009), *Organizing and Organizations*, 4th edn, London: SAGE.

Härtel, C.E.J. (2008), 'How to build a healthy emotional culture and avoid a toxic culture', in C.L Cooper and N.M. Ashkanasy (eds), *Research Companion to Emotion in Organizations*, Cheltenham, UK and Northampton, MA, USA: Edward Elgar, pp. 575–88.

Härtel, C.E.J. and N.M. Ashkanasy (2011), 'Healthy human cultures as positive work environments', in N. Ashkanasy, C.P.M. Wilderom and M.F. Peterson (eds), *Handbook of Organizational Culture and Climate*, London: SAGE, pp. 85–100.

Kilduff, M. and P. Balkundi (2011), 'A network approach to leader cognition and effectiveness', in A. Bryman, D. Collinson, K. Grint, B. Jackson and M. Uhl-Bien (eds), *Handbook of Leadership*, London: SAGE, pp. 118–35.

King, Z. (2004), 'Career self-management: its nature, causes and consequences', *Journal of Vocational Behavior*, **65** (1), 112–33.

Kugelberg, C. (2006), 'Constructing the deviant other: mothering and fathering at the workplace', *Gender, Work and Organization*, **13** (2), 152–73.

Kunda, G. (1992), *Engineering Culture. Control and Commitment in a High-Tech Corporation*, Philadelphia, PA: Temple University Press.

Ladkin, D. (2010), *Rethinking Leadership. A New Look at Old Leadership Questions*, Cheltenham, UK, and Northampton, MA, USA: Edward Elgar.

Lukes, N. (1982), *Power: A Radical View*, London: Macmillan.

Meriläinen, S., J. Tienari, T. Robyn, and A. Davies (2004), 'Management consultant talk: a cross-cultural comparison of normalizing discourse and resistance', *Organization*, **11** (4), 539–64.

Muhr, S.L., M. Pedersen and M. Alvesson (2013), 'Work-load, aspiration and fun: problems of balancing self-exploitation and self-exploration in work-life', *Research in the Sociology of Organization*, **37**, 193–220.

Pedersen, M. (2008), 'Tune in, break down, and reboot – new machines for coping with the stress of commitment', *Culture and Organization*, **14** (2), 171–85.
Peele, G. (2005), 'Leadership and politics: a case for a closer relationship?', *Leadership*, **1** (2), 187–204.
Poder, P. (2004), 'Feelings of power and the power of feelings: handling emotion in organizational change', PhD thesis, University of Copenhagen, Department of Sociology, Copenhagen.
Pye, A. (2005), 'Leadership and organizing: sensemaking in action', *Leadership*, **1** (1), 31–49.
Rosa, H. (2005), 'The speed of global flows and the pace of democratic politics', *New Political Science*, **27** (4), 445–59.
Rose, N. (1999), *Governing the Soul*, London: Free Association Books.
Sennett, R. (1998), *The Corrosion of Character: The Personal Consequences of Work in the New Capitalism*, London: Norton and Company.
Sørensen, B.M. and S. Spoelstra (2012), 'Play at work: continuation, intervention and usurpation', *Organization*, **1** (19), 81–97.
Toftegård, B. (2011), 'Forebyg stress', www.forebygstress.dk/blog/artikel-forsta-arbejdsnarkomani, accessed 14 March 2011.
Weber, M. (1968), *Economy and Society*, vol. 3, New York: Bedminster.
Quigley, N.R. and W.G.J. Tymon (2006), 'Toward an integrated model of intrinsic motivation and career self-management', *Career Development International*, **11** (6), 522–43.

# PART III

# Theoretical reflections

If one must philosophize, one must philosophize, and if one does not philosophize, one must equally philosophize; in any case therefore one must philosophize; if, then, philosophy exists, we must maintain in all ways to philosophize, given that it does exist; if instead it does not exist, even in this case we must inquire how philosophy does not exist; but, by inquiring, we philosophize, since to inquire is the cause of philosophy.

Aristotle, *Protrepticus*, Frag. 2

# 8. Introduction to Part III

## Jeanette Lemmergaard and Sara Louise Muhr

The third part of this volume explores different phenomena – ignorance, authenticity, functional stupidity and vanity – in the context of leadership and emotions. The authors of these chapters operate simultaneously at a philosophical, a theoretical and a practical level. They are not entering the debate to solve puzzles, but to raise awareness and critical thinking. From reading the chapters, which have been written with the intension of aiding reflection on our attitudes, it becomes clear that what we know about the reality of leadership and emotions is limited by our perceptual capabilities. Each chapter highlights, from a different angle, inconsistencies that many of us are likely to encounter in our attitudes towards – and opinion about – leaders.

Combining the empirically founded cases in Part II with the critical reflections in Part III, readers are invited to reflect on the distinction between leadership as an intrinsically valuable activity and an extrinsically valuable action; a distinction comparable to Aristotle's distinction between *praxis* (activity) and *poesis* (productive action). Whereas an extrinsically valuable activity is a means to an end, an intrinsically valuable activity does not involve a cost-benefit calculation. In the same manner, leadership toxicity and dysfunctionality are not simply negatively coercive or repressive connotations, but also potentially productive and enabling connotations which should be understood both extrinsically and intrinsically.

Leadership emotions can, as the chapters here demonstrate, both be seen as interference and as the nurturing of organizational life. The value of leadership as an extrinsically valuable action lies in achieving efficiency. In viewing leadership as an intrinsically valuable activity our interest is directed towards the activity itself. Here the mere intellectual thinking about leadership and emotions is motivated by curiosity in just the same manner as moral activity is motivated by a sense of duty without regard for cost-benefit calculations.

Characterizing leadership as having an intrinsic value does not mean that leadership has no practical results, and as most human activities also leadership activities have both intrinsic and extrinsic value. Rationality–emotionality are not dichotomies akin to good–bad for organizations just as well as toxicity and dysfunctionality are not exceptional 'bad apples', but rather institutionalized rules or manifestations of systemic functions. The reflexive and critical exploration of this part goes beyond what the empirical material presented in Part II of this volume was able to say, and the readers are encouraged to think, and think again about leadership and emotions. This final part of this volume invites the readers on a journey simulating intellectual curiosity.

In Chapter 9 Nathan Harter discusses leaders' ignorance and their suppression of criticism. Inspired by Socrates, Harter demonstrates how leaders by ignoring evidence of doubt and uncertainty risk relying on inadequate beliefs, which are likely to result in insufficiently supported and erroneous decisions as well as unethical behaviour. Harter demonstrates how Socrates' response to the originating experience of doubt and uncertainty in ancient Athens continues to inform the contemporary scene, where ignorance in the face of volatility, uncertainty, complexity and ambiguity is widespread, indisputable and unnerving.

In Chapter 10, Sverre Spoelstra suggests that the underlying premise of leadership studies is the use of uselessness, which he philosophizes on both epistemologically and historically. In this chapter the uselessness of leadership is viewed upon as something that is seen as a good or end in itself and as something that becomes part of a larger function that promises superior business performance. Spoelstra argues for a move away from business in leadership studies as business is no longer considered to offer redemptive powers in its own right. The faith in the capitalist entrepreneur is shattered; business now needs the help of, for example, virtue ethics, religion or new age spirituality to legitimate itself. This argument is made drawing upon the concept of the gift as the outside of business, and by looking at some examples of popular leadership concepts that offer versions of this gift. Then, Spoelstra continues by suggesting that this move away from business, towards givenness, marks a transition from the scientific towards the religious.

In Chapter 11, Mats Alvesson and André Spicer philosophize on how leadership often works through prompting stupidity in both followers and leaders. They demonstrate the stupidity of believing that leadership has a large impact on organizational life and how perhaps leadership talk actually stupifies the members of the large and expanding leadership industry. The more emphasis there is on leadership, the more there are elements of followership and subordination. This marginalizes the use of critical reflection about the activities one is being led to accomplish. In this sense, functional stupidity is a key element of the idea of leadership, and leadership can therefore be viewed as stupidity management. Furthermore, Alvesson and Spicer also demonstrate how acts of leadership and broader discourses of leadership sometimes may not be as powerful as many assume. Instead of being taken on by individuals in organizations, ideas about leadership are often simply grandiose talk, which the audience treats with a mixture of mild amusement, distain and boredom.

Finally, in Chapter 12, Alf Rehn indicates that vanity needs to be reassessed in an age of mediatized business, and that many phenomena that are today highlighted as part of the modern leaders' toolkit need to be analysed from the perspective of vanity as well. Rehn claims that the contemporary leader needs to balance the productive and the pathological aspects of vanity. He argues that vanity may be a sin, but it may also lead to a strange kind of beatification. Whereas under-exhibited vanity seems to be equivalent to unprofessionalism, over-exhibited vanity does not seem to be a disqualification to a leadership position. Instead, the vain leader may have become a fellow traveller for leadership, a constant companion in an age of personal brands and mediatized business.

# 9. Socrates' mission against reproachable ignorance: leaders who refuse to acknowledge their ignorance and instead suppress criticism

**Nathan Harter**

## INTRODUCTION

Leaders who refuse to acknowledge their ignorance and instead suppress criticism create conditions for dysfunctional leadership. By ignoring evidence of their own doubt and uncertainty, they persist in inadequate beliefs. By suppressing criticism from others, they avoid acknowledging their own doubt and uncertainty. They also prevent the critical thinking that can transform doubt into more adequate beliefs. It is the absence of doubt that contributes especially to unethical behaviour, as leaders go heedlessly toward outcomes they will regret and others will condemn. Finally, by suppressing criticism, they prevent followers from developing their own powers to think critically and improve morally as a result of open, frank dialogue. This leaves followers no better-off and probably inhibits their contributions. For these reasons, we might label leaders who refuse to acknowledge their ignorance and instead suppress criticism as pseudo-leaders (Heidegger 2002).

Fields of inquiry lying alongside leadership studies such as political science, organizational behaviour, economics and law have investigated the tension underlying this phenomenon. Oksenberg (1998), for instance, describes as a 'classical dilemma' in politics the choice between suppressing dissent, on the one hand, and bolstering political participation as a way to establish legitimacy, on the other. Neither choice always works. Larson and King (1996) characterize dissent in organizations as part of its 'negative feedback loops' necessary to avoid information distortion, yet they note that at some point the organization has to make and implement decisions. Dissent can delay execution and distract from going forward. Argyres and Mui (2000) approach the topic from a cost-benefit analysis, finding that dissent in a learning organization helps a firm manage knowledge as a competitive advantage, yet managers must enforce the firm's rules of engagement somehow. They recount the behaviour of Apple Computer's chief of engineering back in the 1980s who responded to disfavoured proposals by 'yelling and screaming' without any apparent obligation to resort to evidence or logic (Carlton 1997, in Argyres and Mui 2000, p. 14). Rhode (2006) exhorted lawyers to engage in what is referred to as 'moral counselling (sic)' as a way to help clients avoid the temptations of the sort that result in liability and scandal. It is her contention that lawyers should adopt a more confrontational posture toward their clients' unethical choices. These investigations in related fields of inquiry can prove to be useful in leadership studies, and, in fact, Edward Elgar Publishing (2008) devoted an edited book as part of its *New Horizons in Leadership Studies* series to examining this very relationship of leadership to the experience of dissent (Banks 2008). Evidently, the question poses a problem for contemporary leadership in different domains, exposing the prevalence of a type of leadership that ultimately proves dysfunctional.

Leaders failing to encounter their own ignorance and repress criticism are in this context referred to as pseudo-leaders. They are leaders by definition, but in practice they are not fulfilling what in this chapter, based on Socratic philosophy, is defined as ideal leadership. Already, Socrates confronted this kind of pseudo-leadership in ancient Greece over two thousand years ago. He took it upon himself to confront this incomplete behaviour and teach the young people of Athens how to avoid it. His unique approach has influenced European culture ever since and still proves relevant. This paper introduces what Socrates taught about leadership – not least the risk inherent in adopting his approach to combat pseudo-leaders. Then, the chapter describes three attempts in the literature on leadership studies that seek to bring the lessons of Socrates forward to the present day. These attempts can be referred to as the legitimation of doubt, critical thinking and ethics. By understanding the subtleties inherent in these attempts, contemporary leaders are helped to understand how they might be victimized by other pseudo-leaders. Also by understanding the nuances of pseudo-leadership, leaders are hopefully able to reflect on their own ignorance and suppression of criticism, and hereby be able to understand the act of leadership in a different – and more nuanced – way.

## THE 'APOLOGY OF SOCRATES'

Socrates took it upon himself as an ordinary citizen to examine Athenian leaders in order to discover what they knew about their responsibilities. After a number of contentious interviews in full view of other citizens, these leaders had failed to demonstrate a satisfactory understanding of their leadership – an outcome that amused many, but angered the leaders. One of the best known leaders of Athenian democracy at the time finally joined in prosecuting Socrates on the charges of impiety and corrupting the youth, for which Socrates stood trial and delivered the defence known today as Plato's *Apology of Socrates*.

Socrates' complete philosophy of leadership is impossible to reconstruct. He never wrote anything on the subject, so we must rely on secondary sources – especially the accounts of contemporaries Plato and Xenophon, whose texts in Greek are now thousands of years old. Even though Plato is probably the more reliable guide to what Socrates believed (Benson 1992), there is much evidence that as he continued to write his philosophical dialogues using Socrates as the main character, Plato gradually inserted his own beliefs and got away from anything we might refer to as an authentic philosophy of Socrates (Benson 1992). Nevertheless, the *Apology* was not only one of the first works of Plato – presumably written before he started insinuating his own beliefs into the dialogues – it was also written while many of those who had attended the trial were still alive and could dispute Plato's version of events. In addition, the *Apology* is not a typical dialogue in which Socrates asks a series of questions hoping to elicit answers from an interlocutor; rather, it is a set of three speeches laying out in strict prose what Socrates thought he had been doing for all those years. In other words, it is in the *Apology* that Socrates explains both why he had been confronting the political leaders of Athens and what he had concluded as a result of his inquiries.

Using the translation of Thomas and Grace West (1984), we can examine Plato's account of Socrates' own words, spoken in a public forum as he sought to refute the charges that threatened him with the death penalty. Strengthening the plausibility of Socrates' claims as recounted in the *Apology* is the fact that many of the jurors that day would have witnessed the behaviour for which he had been charged, so Socrates had little incentive to lie about his activities (Thomas and Grace West 1984, 19d). Apparently, as a younger man Socrates had enjoyed a reputation as (a) a clever man who studied many things and (b) a loyal soldier of Athens. However, this was before an oracle disclosed that no one was wiser than he (Thomas and Grace West 1984, 21a). Such a prophecy puzzled Socrates, who doubted it could possibly be true, given that he regarded himself as possessing no wisdom at all (Thomas and Grace West 1984, 21b).

In order to interpret the meaning of the oracle, Socrates sought out the wisest men in Athens, beginning with its politicians (Thomas and Grace West 1984, 21c–e). It was his purpose to elicit their wisdom in response to his questions. What he discovered was that the leaders could not give an account of their knowledge about leading Athens. He asked them, for example, about courage, justice and virtue. The politicians were demonstrably not wise at all, despite their reputations, and the more he investigated, the more he came to understand what the oracle had meant: no one was wiser than Socrates because no one at all was wise; the only difference was that Socrates *knew* he was not wise. This was disturbing then, just as it can be disturbing today, for as Ackoff (1986) observed, 'Those who do not know but think they do are more dangerous ... than those who do not know – but know it' (p. 130). The leaders in ancient Athens did not realize their limitations or hid them from the public, content to give the impression of wisdom. It is even the case that Socrates started to believe the leaders were the most deficient of all (Thomas and Grace West 1984, 22a). It would not be too far-fetched to construe the prosecution of Socrates as an attempt by the leaders to silence him and cover up their inadequacies.

If Socrates despaired of finding anyone possessing wisdom, then who should lead? Plato was to answer that question elsewhere by suggesting the character of the philosopher-king, nurtured carefully in a strict regime as depicted in *The Republic* (Plato 1968). If anyone is wise, it would be the philosopher, and if leadership should be entrusted to the wise, then philosophers should govern. But so far as we know from the *Apology*, Socrates never took that position. It is helpful to wonder, therefore, what conclusions Socrates himself did make.

Socrates interpreted his life's mission as a result of the oracle to help ordinary people *become* wise first by recognizing their ignorance (Thomas and Grace West 1984, 23b). He undertook philosophy therefore as a means for improving his fellow citizens. The practical problem is that no one has reason to seek wisdom if he or she believes they are already wise. Thus, they must confront their 'reproachable ignorance' (Thomas and Grace West 1984, 29b). Socrates took it upon himself by means of questioning to help others see that. He even told the jurors at his trial that what he had been doing in posing these questions served the interests of Athens. 'I suppose that until now', he said, 'no greater good has arisen for you in the city than my service to the god' (Thomas and Grace West 1984, 30a–b). Accordingly, he was construing his activity as a benefit to the city – literally a 'gift' (Thomas and Grace West 1984, 30e and 31b) – and therefore the highest political good.

Socrates then answered the following question: if he thought he was so gifted, why had he refrained from putting himself forward into politics as a leader? That would seem to be the obvious choice for someone who understood himself to be pursuing the highest political good. Why not stand for public office? Socrates offered two distinct reasons why he had refrained. First, he sensed that the god Apollo advised against it, and since he had been commissioned by the god in the first place, he must obey (Thomas and Grace West 1984, 31c–d). It would be impious not to obey. Second, Socrates believed that if he had put himself forward into the political process, the powers-that-be would have destroyed him (Thomas and Grace West 1984, 31d–e) – much as the same powers were now bent on destroying him in court. Socrates gave a couple of examples when he had participated in political activity and, due to his deep commitment to virtue, defied the regime at great peril (Thomas and Grace West 1984, 32a–e). He did not think it prudent to subject himself to that risk needlessly. An ethical man cannot survive long in public office.

To paraphrase Takala's (1998) interpretation of Socratic leadership, the purpose of the polis is to educate people to become good. If it had become necessary to 'educate people to become good' from outside of the electoral and governmental processes, it is no less political. That is why Socrates could allege in another dialogue by Plato that despite his absence from electoral politics he had been the only true statesman in Athens (Plato 1960; see Jaeger 1943). He had been a leader in his own right.

After the jury convicted Socrates of a capital offence, he was given a chance to suggest an alternative penalty. He responded by saying that he deserved an honour equivalent to winning the Olympics for Athens (Thomas and Grace West 1984, 36d). In other words, he remained true to his beliefs about his worth to the city, although saying this did not change the outcome. He was subsequently condemned to die.

## IMPLICATIONS FOR LEADERSHIP

### A Life of Moral Excellence

Socrates confronted leaders who proved to be ignorant. He believed that he was doing them a favour, giving them a chance to seek wisdom and pursue a life of moral excellence. As it turned out, he inspired at least some of them to retaliate instead. Not only did they persist in their 'reproachable ignorance', but they also used their influence to indict him and at the same time hope to intimidate others, so that they could continue in power without being questioned by followers. This, Plato clearly condemned. Socrates (by way of contrast) seemed more resigned to his fate. He was not even indignant (Thomas and Grace West 1984, 36e). He came to accept it as inevitable. The persecution would have happened earlier, if he had put himself forward into politics. Still, he told the jurors that what they were doing was wrong. He said that 'if you suppose that by killing human beings you will prevent someone from reproaching you for not living correctly, you do not think nobly'. He then continued: 'For that kind of release [from criticism] is not at all possible or noble; rather, the kind that is both noblest and easiest is not to strain others, but to equip oneself to be the best possible' (Thomas and Grace West 1984, 39d). In other words, the best method for avoiding reproach was to lead an irreproachable life in the first place, and this takes wisdom.

A leader will avoid criticism only by improving oneself. Not only is that practically the case; it is also the most ethical way to avoid criticism. Another way of saying this is that the best strategy for leaders is to become worthy of leadership. At a superficial level, this might be enough for prospective leaders to learn from Socrates. The problem is that he had just taken the position of a morally excellent politician who will be destroyed for his efforts. Was he advising leaders to do precisely that, which would lead to their ruin as leaders? The short answer is; yes, he was. Anderson has claimed that 'the very nature of [Socrates'] way of life was such that it must lead ultimately to the destruction of him who leads it' (1967, p. 10). If that is so, then why was Socrates saying this?

Let us state the problem simply. Socrates appears to have believed that leaders must become morally excellent in order to be released from criticism, yet he also appears to have believed that being morally excellent will result in the leader being destroyed by others. At the risk of sounding sardonic, let me remark that being destroyed is presumably the most severe form of criticism any leader could imagine. So, has Socrates contradicted himself? When Socrates argued, in the *Apology*, that being morally excellent in public office would bring destruction, he was not sugar-coating the reality. He meant literally that the leader would be inviting his death. He would certainly incur hatred. The paradox is that Socrates did not believe these to be such terrible things compared to being unjust. It was better to suffer an injustice than to commit injustice (Plato 1960). So, while these unpleasant outcomes were likely, they were not the worst that could happen. Being unethical is worse. A courageous leader who risks destruction for the sake of the Good would have transcended care for most earthly goods, such as life and reputation, since wisdom consists in caring for one's soul. And that care supersedes all others. Socrates declared that a leader's adversaries could 'kill, banish, or dishonor' the leader, yet they would not be harming him. They harm only themselves (Thomas and Grace West 1984, 30d).

It appears from what Socrates said in court that there is a direct and inevitable conflict between caring for the soul and caring for one's safety; leaders simply have to choose. This point of view runs counter to most street-level understandings of leadership as a process of bringing about change in the world. How can it be leadership to sacrifice one's career and one's societal impact for the sake of virtue? That approach would suggest that moral excellence *guarantees* the failure of leadership, the exact opposite of what most students of leadership would seek. But is that true? It may be true that the individual leader will not long survive. However, is it not possible that by making these excellent choices, the leader will have advanced the cause? We often read about martyrs, and we proclaim them to have been leaders – partly *in spite of* their sacrifice and partly *because* of their sacrifice. If leaders truly believe in something, then they must be willing to be destroyed in achieving it. Think back to historical figures such as Jesus of Nazareth (and his disciples), Abraham Lincoln, Martin Luther King Jr. and Mohandas Gandhi. They literally died for their beliefs, and the propagation of their beliefs has been nourished by their blood. That sounds awfully dramatic, however, as though Socratic leadership entails martyrdom, when in fact leaders every day have limited purposes, such as running a factory or managing an office, and they can undertake leadership without fearing danger. Often, they accomplish great things, acquire honours and die peacefully of natural causes. Socratic leadership sounds extravagant to the modern ear.

Socrates is so difficult for understanding the performance of leadership precisely because he is uncompromising. Moral excellence arising from the care of the soul will draw negative consequences from other people. You just have to expect such things as an empirical matter. But let us grant the possibility that maybe the conflict will not be inevitable. Maybe a good leader can flourish in this world. Even so, it is still true that moral excellence might bring a person into conflict with others, such that insisting on virtue threatens your success as a leader. That does happen. Even if we remove the empirical question of whether the conflict will be inevitable, it is still the case that moral excellence often appears to collide with utility. For such moments – inevitable or not – Socrates stakes out a clear position on behalf of moral excellence. His own example reinforces the point: he pursued wisdom and devoted his life to serving both his god and his neighbours, which in turn resulted in his conviction and execution. And this means that if leadership as a role itself must be sacrificed, then so be it (Machiavelli famously disagreed, of course, and took the contrary position).

Nevertheless, Socrates appears to contend that choosing moral excellence is the highest form of leadership, the purest example of leadership. It is possibly a false dilemma to say that you must choose between moral excellence and leadership. Instead, moral excellence is leadership. How can that be?

In another dialogue, Socrates is reported to have condemned nearly all of the famous leaders from Athens' past – not because they had not defended the homeland and built the economy, but because they had failed in their signal duty to improve the people morally. This, he claimed, is the proper ideal for leadership (Plato 1960). For Socrates, it mattered what the leadership was intended to accomplish. Overseeing a business or passing legislation is not leadership unless it accomplishes this purpose. Or more accurately, it is *pseudo*-leadership unless it accomplishes this purpose. If leaders do accomplish this purpose of moral improvement, then their own fates become secondary. However, if leaders do many wonderful things, yet fail in this purpose, they have failed. Whatever it is that they do, it is not leadership. Only moral improvement is true leadership.

## The Dysfunctions of Pseudo-leadership

Socrates was in a position to show that leadership contrary to what he was advising would be ill-advised. First, reproachable ignorance would leave leader and led ignorant about the good life. He had established over the course of his career that nobody was wise. Everybody was ignorant, yet most people believe they possess adequate beliefs about the good life – or they trust their leaders to know – even though nobody apparently possesses the means to know whether those beliefs are true or false. As a result, the leadership that does take place in such ignorance would likely result in undesirable outcomes, both in the social order for which the leader is responsible as well as within the souls of the leaders themselves.

A leader can influence other people. That is not to be doubted. Yet if everyone in the *polis* is ignorant of what it takes to live the good life – and few will acknowledge that ignorance – then this influence will be based on untrustworthy choices. Leaders will make mistakes. Moreover, until the consequences of their leadership become obvious, nobody will be in a position to judge. By that point, of course, it could be too late to make corrections.

Since the ultimate purpose of leadership – according to Socrates – is to improve the moral character of the *demos*, failed leadership will increase the likelihood of a populace with bad character. This alone is a regrettable outcome from Socrates' perspective, but it also lays the groundwork for harm to the leader. By contributing to the corruption of the people, the leader increases the likelihood that they will respond to his leadership injuriously. As such, they could easily turn against the leader at some point, for example, robbing him, killing him, mounting insurrection and committing treason. However, they could also defer to the leader out of ignorance and influence him to believe that he is doing a great job, when the truth is that he is not. In other words, their interpretation of the situation and of the leader's worth could very easily mislead the leader into believing what is not true, namely, that they are succeeding in their search for the good life. Living in untruth does not conduce to the good (Versényi 1963; see also Taylor 1953). Socrates apparently argued this claim strenuously throughout his life.

Of particular interest to leaders, then, their ability to gratify their own desires and gain pre-eminence in the community will simply foster a tyrannical spirit, jeopardizing the virtue of self-control, so that the leader increasingly yields to the demands of appetite, becoming enslaved to the dictates of desire, which results in a depraved condition of wanton gratification. The irony is that what might appear at first blush to be the height of freedom, i.e. doing as you please, turns out to be an enslavement of a different sort (Jaeger 1943). A leader of this sort can never be at peace (Plato 1960). Inwardly, the soul will become inharmonious, fractious, vexing. The tyrant gradually thinks he can do as he likes and make an exception for himself of the moral rules (Price 2008). In a manner of speaking, Socrates anticipated the famous admonition that power corrupts.

From where do the opinions of a leader come, if not as expressions of mere appetite? Suppose a leader who is ignorant really wants to do a good job. Socrates emphasizes that whatever else the leader chooses to pursue other than raw gratification will be inauthentic, derived from somebody else who was equally ignorant. The choices will not be grounded in knowledge. So the leader hoping to escape the tyrannical spirit and do some good in the world will consume opinions he *believes* to be true – though, without the powers of critical thinking, who knows for sure? They might sound good. People believe all sorts of things that sound good. Without the power to discern, then, what happens is that the leader becomes the unwitting mouthpiece for somebody else's agenda, somebody else's purpose. They finish reading some book on leadership and decide, 'That is what I'll do!'. The leader becomes something less than a leader and more of a surrogate for somebody else, such as a boss higher on the organizational chart or some guru. The leader becomes little more than an instrument for influencing others. The worst of it is they might have no suspicion of this. '[The ignorant leader] had only to speak beautifully, persuasively, and convincingly about something, and this he could do without the least knowledge of the truth' (Versényi 1963, p. 115).

The unwise leader therefore eventually lives in perpetual dissatisfaction, frustration and anxiety, in a *polis* that fails in its essential purpose and not only leaves everyone not only further from the good, but also less able to know what to do about their predicament. Such a person might be engaging in a process we can technically call leadership, but they are a pseudo-leader, leading everyone away from the very ends they would seek if only they knew the truth. Socrates is reported to have made this indictment directly to a wayward pupil named Alcibiades, who comes to admit that his beliefs prove that he would be incompetent to lead others, let alone his own life, so that everything he would presume to lead finally becomes wretched (Pangle 1987). That in summary is the judgement Socrates makes of such leaders; and that is why they can be considered dysfunctional.

## THE SOCRATIC APPROACH TODAY

The situation faced in ancient Athens resembles the situation many leaders face today. Johnson (1996), for example, made this point in his essay titled 'Antipodes: Plato, Nietzsche, and the Moral Dimension of Leadership'. Conditions are still ripe for pseudo-leadership. Because the indictment of pseudo-leadership and their practices persists to this day – and rightly so – some of what Socrates taught can be seen in recent efforts to inform leadership studies. This paper will mention three.

First, Socrates repeatedly claimed that he was not wise and knew nothing noble or good (Plato 1984, p. 21b and d). Nevertheless, in his case this awareness motivated him to seek knowledge, which is why he accosted the leaders of his day who presumably knew something. Once he had revealed their ignorance, however, many of them turned away in anger rather than joining him in his search. This is why Socrates was to refer to their ignorance as 'reproachable' (Plato 1984, 29b): they occupied positions of responsibility for which knowledge was crucial and, finding themselves to be ignorant, were in a position to remedy their ignorance, yet they declined (Reeve 1989). Making matters worse, they continued to hold themselves forth to their followers afterwards as

knowledgeable. If their core purpose as leaders was the moral development of their followers – which is something Socrates firmly believed –
then their pretence of knowledge shut off the opportunity to bring
everyone through the experience of doubt that made genuine inquiry
possible.

In other words, Socrates induced doubt and used that experience as a
beginning point for a shared inquiry toward knowledge. Leaders today
have been invited to do this in a short book chapter by Weick in 2001.
Titled 'Leadership as the Legitimation of Doubt', the chapter opens by
saying that admitting 'I don't know' can be a strong act of leadership
precisely because it launches a process of sense-making. Sense-making
as a process then gives direction in uncertain times (Weick 2001). Saying
'I don't know' is an act of humility, but more importantly it is an act of
honesty. For a leader to say this honestly, therefore, he must be 'deeply
aware of personal ignorance' (Weick 2001, p. 94).

Simon (1983) drew similar conclusions from his study of organizational decision-making. He concluded that we are all constrained by
what he called bounded rationality. Nobody has all the answers. We
cannot always find the optimal solution. We simply know less than we
might like under perfect conditions. The sooner leaders acknowledge this,
the better organizational decisions will become. Belasco and Stayer
(1993) made a similar claim, as they advised the organizational manager
to tell people where you are going, then admit you do not know how to
get there, so you need their help. The next step would be to start an
inquiry, posing questions in order to learn what others might be thinking
or to expose flaws in their thinking, but in either case to draw them out of
their private 'logic bubbles' and draw them in to deliberation. Martin
(2007) referred to this process as assertive inquiry, by which you seek to
understand the 'underpinnings' of somebody else's mental models by
means of questions. It originates in the sense that you may not have all
the answers; you may in fact be ignorant.

Being ignorant, however, might be difficult for someone in a leadership position to admit. By making this admission regardless, the leader
helps others face their own uncertainty. It also implies the need to go find
out together what you do not know (Weick 2001). This means that
followers are drawn into the process and not left to stand aside waiting
for the leader to figure things out alone. Weick explicitly states that the
entire group must 'stay in motion, have a direction, look closely, update
often, and converse candidly' (2001, p. 96). In other words, followers are
encouraged to undertake the search as well, which is precisely what
Socrates believed should be the case if everyone is to make progress. The
leader becomes more of a listener than a pronouncer (2001). In fact,

Weick uses language very similar to the language adopted by commentators on Socrates, namely that the goal is for each participant to become able to give an account of what they know to be true. Weick calls this outcome a 'stable rendition' (2001, p. 97).

Furthermore, Weick (2001) is trying to say that you cannot manage knowledge you do not yet trust. Maybe leaders ought to entertain the possibility they do not know what they would like to know. Then, they can share that doubt with their followers and invite them to join in a dialogue to find out, so that as a result everyone can arrive at some kind of stable rendition of the truth before even trying to make decisions. Somewhere, Socrates would be smiling.

The second effort that should be mentioned attempts to inject leadership studies with Socratic wisdom pertaining to the literature on critical thinking. Critical thinking itself is often attributed to Socrates (Paul 1995, p. 39). Ricketts (2005) recently made the case to leadership educators why they should teach prospective leaders critical thinking. He argued that leaders must learn how to engage in this process. Thus, once a leader experiences doubt, there must be some method for working through toward a satisfactory outcome, and critical thinking is one name for that method. Otherwise, a person would be left in puzzlement and might not know where to turn next. In fact, critical thinking will help *induce* doubt as a part of the method, so you do not take anything for granted.

The literature on leadership does refer to several methods for reaching a conclusion. There is material on sense-making, as we had reason to see in the work of Weick. There is also material on problem-solving, decision-making, knowledge management, strategic visioning and other interrelated processes for a leader to use as techniques in moments of uncertainty. Critical thinking can be understood as a broad category encompassing them all, for it concentrates less on thinking *about something* and more on thinking about thinking (Moore and Parker 2009). In that sense, critical thinking is (to borrow a term) *propaedeutic*. The phrase 'critical thinking' also retains some of the harsh flavour of 'challenging', 'provoking' and 'holding to account' – elements of the irritating Socratic style, which the other methods are less likely to feature. Pointing out the 'defects and deficiencies' in an assertion might seem hostile, yet just as Socrates claimed long ago this can be the greatest service you can provide others who are about to make a mistake (Moore and Parker 2009). Bennis (1989) took this one step further in his research when he found that leaders say they must reflect on their experience, which he took to mean 'having a Socratic dialogue with yourself...' (p. 61). They internalize the process of critique.

Lest we forget the role of followers in this process, there has been evidence in the literature on leadership that critical thinking is not intended for the leader alone (Graham 1991; Dvir and Shamir 2003; Moss et al. 2009). Instead, leaders are encouraged to involve followers (see for example Sashkin and Rosenbach 1993; Drath 2001; Wheatley 2002). Critical thinking is an iterative process, a collaborative process, just as Socrates exemplified in his many dialogues. It requires the involvement of other people, other minds. The benefit, he believed, would be mutual. It was not a 'clash system' (as Edward de Bono (1994) was to put it) in which one person squares off against another person in order to establish who's right and who's wrong. Rather, it was a joint exploration built on everyone's willingness to subject their various thoughts and ideas to strict standards of logic and proof. That is the heart of critical thinking. To reach that point, the leader must tolerate, if not invite, dissent. Axelrod (2008) cites 'many studies of dissent in every-day decision-making [that] have focused on decisions that were poorly conceived because of the failure of those involved to fully evaluate all relevant information, including contrarian views' (p. 4).

According to Grove (1996), former CEO and Chair of Intel, 'Fear that might keep you from voicing your real thoughts is poison. Almost nothing could be more detrimental to the well-being of the company ... I can't stress this issue strongly enough' (p. 119).

Despite institutional and psychological pressure to stand mute, dissent is inevitable anyway. Davis (1996) concluded that 'it is ... clear that even the most successful contemporary leaders are controversial and the subject of fierce opposition' (p. 168). In response to this predictable climate, leaders are being encouraged these days to open themselves to experience doubt, as Weick said, and then they are being encouraged to take that experience and think critically with their followers towards an account of what they know. By doing this, a leader would be hearkening back to the teachings and example of Socrates.

The third effort to bring forward the teachings of Socrates almost goes without saying. Socrates held that the purpose of leadership is the moral improvement of the people. In his own life, he had turned away from studying science in order to concentrate on the well-being of his fellow citizens. He believed that their well-being derives from their pursuit of moral excellence. The expanding literature today on leadership ethics retains this feature of Socratic teaching. Ciulla (1998) probably put it best when she in her book title claimed ethics to be '*The Heart of Leadership*'.

We should recognize nonetheless that leadership ethics is not just about the defensibility of leader behaviour. There is that, of course (for example Price 2008), but the literature also concerns the imperative to improve the followers – an objective which was Socrates' abiding passion. An attempt to account for this is made in Burns' (1978) depiction of transforming leadership as 'a way that leaders and followers raise one another to higher levels of ... morality' (p. 20). According to Burns this is to be done to a large extent by helping followers detect contradictions and inconsistencies in their current beliefs. That is, Burns (like Socrates) regards critical thinking as a means toward moral improvement, such that the test of transforming leadership will be the elevation of everyone's moral excellence. This means that forms of conflict, exemplified by critical thinking in dialogue, serves as the 'motor' for improvement (see however also the critique of transforming/transformational leadership in particular Chapter 1 and Chapter 10 in this volume).

Esteban and Collier (2003) have made a supplementary argument about the transition firms undergo from hierarchical structures to more participative structures of the sort envisioned by Burns, when by their nature social systems resist change and participants do not yet trust each other to engage in these open processes of dissent and dialogue. Followers must learn to participate. The burden to teach them, if only by example, falls on leaders.

Ultimately, therefore, leadership ethics is not just about holding leaders accountable. It is also about holding followers accountable as well (Kellerman 2004). This is what Socrates attempted in ancient democratic Athens. Perhaps with the growing literature in leadership studies taking up his cause, the leaders who adopt a Socratic approach will suffer a better fate than Socrates did. Even so, let there be no illusions. Human nature being what it appears to be, there is always a risk that leadership of this kind will incur hostile reactions, not least the attempt by pseudo-leaders among us to suppress such inquiries (Kellerman 2004).

Czech philosopher Jan Patočka (2002) once argued that the legacy for leaders in the modern world is to contribute toward building a social order in which a person like Socrates need not die. That is, leaders must value truth above all, and value it in all people. At the very least, they must be prepared for the day when followers will hold them to account. Woodruff, writing in *The Quest for Moral Leaders* (Ciulla et al. 2005), put it this way: leaders compatible with democratic freedoms are 'content with close public scrutiny of their actions' and 'respect the opinions of others' (p. 17). By way of contrast, a tyrant (or pseudo-leader) 'does not accept criticism', 'cannot be called to account', and 'does not listen to advice' (p. 21). Similar findings are presented in the cases presented in the first part of this volume. Also here leaders squelch instead of facilitate what Ackoff (1986) referred to as 'communicating up'. They close off avenues for discerning the truth for the sake of preserving the forms of power that put them into leadership in the first place.

## CONCLUSION

As stated in the introduction of this chapter, dealing with the complexity of leadership involves considerations of ignorance and considerations of how to deal with criticism. The chapter is inspired by Socrates and his understanding of how leaders who will not acknowledge their ignorance and instead suppress criticism are creating the conditions for dysfunctional leadership. By ignoring evidence of doubt and uncertainty in their own minds, leaders might persist in inadequate beliefs, and that can increase the likelihood of decisions that result in error and dismay. By suppressing criticism from others, these pseudo-leaders prevent acknowledging their own doubt and uncertainty. They also prevent the critical thinking that can transform doubt into more adequate beliefs. It is the absence of doubt that contributes especially to unethical behaviour, as leaders go heedlessly toward outcomes they will regret and others will condemn. Finally, by suppressing criticism, these pseudo-leaders might even prevent followers from developing their own powers to think critically and improve morally as a result of open and frank dialogue.

Happily, however, by integrating lessons on the legitimation of doubt, critical thinking and ethics, leadership thinking can continue to carry forward the teachings of Socrates to the present age. The mere idea of a perfect organization in which everyone works well with each other and is happy is unreachable. This means that Socrates' response to the originating experience of doubt and uncertainty in ancient Athens continues to inform the contemporary scene, where ignorance in the face of volatility, uncertainty, complexity and ambiguity is widespread, indisputable and unnerving. Pretending otherwise, pseudo-leaders ignore intimations of reality, disguise their limitations, inhibit participation by others, and impose an organizational climate completely at odds with the spirit of collaboration. Moreover, this climate guarantees that their leadership will deserve to be called dysfunctional.

# REFERENCES

Ackoff, R. (1986), *Management in Small Doses*, New York: John Wiley & Sons.

Anderson, D. (1967), 'Socrates' concept of piety', *Journal of the History of Philosophy*, **5** (1), 1–13.

Argyres, N. and V. Mui (2000), 'Rules of engagement, informal leaders, and the political economy of organizational dissent', unpublished paper presented to the International Society of New Institutional Economics Conference, Tübingen, 22–24 September.

Axelrod, R. (2008), 'Advice and dissent', in A. Marturano and J. Gosling (eds), *Leadership: The Key Concepts*, New York: Routledge, pp. 3–5.

Banks, S. (ed) (2008) *Dissent and the Failure of Leadership*, Cheltenham, UK, and Northampton, MA, USA: Edward Elgar.

Belasco, J. and R. Stayer (1993), *Flight of the Buffalo: Soaring to Excellence, Learning to Let Employees Lead*, New York: Warner Books.

Bennis, W. (1989), *On Becoming a Leader*, New York: Addison-Wesley Publishing Company.

Benson, H. (ed) (1992) 'Editor's introduction', in *Essays on the Philosophy of Socrates*, New York: Oxford University Press, pp. 3–13.

Burns, J.M. (1978), *Leadership*, New York: Harper Torchbooks.

Ciulla, J. (1998), *Ethics: The Heart of Leadership*, Westport, CT: Quorum Books.

Davis, S. (1996), *Leadership in Conflict: The Lessons of History*, New York: St. Martin's Press.

de Bono, E. (1994), *de Bono's Thinking Course* (revised edn), New York: Facts on File, Inc.

Drath, W. (2001), *The Deep Blue Sea: Rethinking the Source of Leadership*, San Francisco, CA: Jossey-Bass.

Dvir, T. and B. Shamir (2003), 'Follower developmental characteristics as predicting transformational leadership: a longitudinal field study', *The Leadership Quarterly*, **14** (3), 327–44.

Esteban, R. and J. Collier (2003) 'Building moral competence in organizations: the difficult transition from hierarchical control to participative leadership', in H. Von Weltzien Hoivik (eds), *Moral Leadership in Action: Building and Sustaining Moral Competence in European Organizations*, Cheltenham, UK, and Northampton, MA, USA: Edward Elgar, pp. 159–73.

Graham, J.W. (1991), 'Servant-leadership in organizations: inspirational and moral', *The Leadership Quarterly*, **2** (2), 105–19.

Heidegger, M. (2002), *The Essence of Truth: On Plato's Cave Allegory and Theaetetus,* translated by T. Sadler, New York: Continuum.

Jaeger, W. (1943), *Paideia: The Ideals of Greek Culture* (vol. II), translated by G. Highet, New York: Oxford University Press.

Johnson, P. (1996), 'Antipodes: Plato, Nietzsche, and the moral dimension of leadership', Chapter 2 in P. Temes (ed.), *Teaching Leadership: Essays in Theory and Practice*, New York: Peter Lang.

Kellerman, B. (2004), *Bad Leadership: What It Is, How It Happens, Why It Matters*, Boston, MA: Harvard Business School Press.

Larson, E. and J. King (1996), 'The systemic distortion of information: an ongoing challenge to management', *Organizational Dynamics*, **24** (3), 49–61.

Martin, R. (2007), *The Opposable Mind: How Successful Leaders Win through Integrative Thinking*, Boston, MA: Harvard Business School Press.

Moore, B.N. and R. Parker (2009), *Critical Thinking*, 9th edn, New York: McGraw-Hill.

Moss, S.A., N. Dowling and J. Callanan (2009), 'Towards an integrated model of leadership and self regulation', *The Leadership Quarterly*, **20** (2), 162–76.

Oksenberg, M. (1998), 'Confronting a classic dilemma', *Journal of Democracy*, **9** (1), 27–34.

Pangle, T. (1987), *The Roots of Political Philosophy: Ten Forgotten Socratic Dialogues*, Ithaca, NY: Cornell University Press.

Patočka, J. (2002), *Plato and Europe*, translated by P. Lom, Stanford, CA: Stanford University Press.

Paul, R. (1995), 'The critical thinking movement in historical perspective', in R. Paul *Critical Thinking: How to Prepare Students for a Rapidly Changing World*, Santa Rosa, CA: Foundation for Critical Thinking, pp. 37–46.

Plato (1960), *Gorgias*, translated by W. Hamilton, New York: Penguin.

Plato (1968), *The Republic of Plato*, translated by A. Bloom, New York: Basic Books.

Plato (1984), 'Apology of Socrates', in Plato and Aristophanes, *Four Texts on Socrates: Plato's Euthyphro, Apology, and Crito and Aristophanes' Clouds*, translated by T. West and G. West, Ithaca, NY: Cornell University Press, pp. 63–97.

Price, T. (2008), *Leadership Ethics: An Introduction*, Cambridge: Cambridge University Press.

Reeve, C.D.C. (1989), *Socrates in the Apology: An Essay on Plato's Apology of Socrates*, Indianapolis, IN: Hackett.

Rhode, D. (2006), 'Moral counseling', *Fordham Law Review*, **75** (3), 1317–38.

Ricketts, J. (2005), 'The relationship between leadership development and critical thinking skills', *Journal of Leadership Education*, **4** (2), 27–41.

Sashkin, M. and W.E. Rosenbach (1993), 'A new leadership paradigm', in W.E. Rosenbach and R.L. Taylor (eds), *Contemporary Issues in Leadership*, San Francisco, CA: Westview Press, pp. 87–108.

Simon, H. (1983), *Reason in Human Affairs*, Stanford, CA: Stanford University Press.

Takala, T. (1998), 'Plato on leadership', *Journal of Business Ethics*, **17** (7), 785–98.

Taylor, A.E. (1953), *Socrates: The Man and His Thought*, Garden City, NJ: Anchor Books.

Versényi, L. (1963), *Socratic Humanism*, translated by L. Conversi, New Haven, CT: Yale University Press.

Weick, K. (2001), 'Leadership as the legitimation of doubt', in W. Bennis, G. Spreitzer and T. Cummings (eds), *The Future of Leadership: Today's Top Leadership Thinkers Speak to Tomorrow's Leaders*, San Francisco, CA: Jossey-Bass, pp. 91–102.

Wheatley, M. (2002), 'Restoring hope to the future through critical education of leaders', in C. Cherrey and L.R. Matusak (eds), *Building Leadership Bridges 2002*, College Park, MD: International Leadership Association, pp. 1–6.

Woodruff, P. (2005), 'The shape of freedom: democratic leadership in the ancient world', Chapter 1 in J. Ciulla, T. Price and S. Murphy (eds), *The Quest for Moral Leaders: Essays on Leadership Ethics*, Cheltenham, UK, and Northampton, MA, USA: Edward Elgar.

# 10. Leadership studies: out of business

## Sverre Spoelstra

## INTRODUCTION

Popular management books often stress that leadership is not a function:
Leaders are leaders because they have followers, not because of their
formal position in an organization. This is also one of the central ideas in
Robin Sharma's (2010) recent business bestseller *The Leader Who Had
No Title*. In the book, Blake Davis, the protagonist of the story, meets a
mysterious leader whose business card simply identifies him as 'human
being'. The mysterious man happens to know all the secrets of leadership, which he shares with Blake. At the end of the story Blake himself
has also become a leader and he gets a Porsche in reward.

That leadership is not to be equated with a formal function in an
organizational hierarchy is not surprising, but it is perhaps less obvious to
say that leadership may not be understood as existing for functional
purposes. This, however, is precisely how leadership is generally understood within popular books on the subject. Leaders are not supposed to
think functionally, for instance, in terms of inputs and outputs. A
calculating leader is not considered to be a 'real' leader. Sharma's book
also makes this point, and it summarizes the nonfunctional nature of
leadership as follows:

> Leadership has nothing to do with what you get [return on investment] or
> where you sit [formal position]. Leadership's a lot more about how brilliantly
> you work and how masterfully you behave [leadership as a good in itself].
> (2010, p. 18)

Of course, this is not where the story ends (if this was the end of the
story, we could no longer qualify the book as a *business* book: business
requires by definition a return on investment). The paradoxical importance of not being functional in leadership, that is not to think in terms of
inputs and outputs, is precisely that it brings functional benefits. Indeed,
according to Sharma (2010, p. 2), not thinking about 'what you get' or

'where you sit' will have tremendous pay-offs such as a successful career, idolizing followers, lots of money, happy relationships, a fulfilling life, and – in the case of Blake – a Porsche. The paradoxical message is that having a business mindset is deemed to be detrimental for business success. Success in business, the book suggests, can only be attained by focusing on more important things in life than business: things that can only be found *outside* of business. The book, for example, bluntly states that 'spectacularly caring [for other people]' as an end in itself will be followed by great financial rewards: 'Take care of people and the money will take care of itself' (Sharma 2010, p. 153). Further into the book we find an exceptionally clear formulation of the central paradox that guides the story: '*if your focus is on making money, it's off doing great work –* the very thing that will make you more money' (Sharma, 2010, p. 165, emphasis in original).

It is easy to find similar ideas in other leadership and business books, especially those that border on the self-help genre. Self-help books in business are meant to inspire its audience, and good news stories of the kind 'get rich by being yourself' do a wonderful job in this regard. However, my interest in this chapter is the academic discipline of leadership studies, which is traditionally not meant to inspire managers with good news fables. Yet, I will argue in this chapter that the same paradox (business is better business when you step out of business) informs most of what happens within the field of leadership studies. To be precise, I will suggest that leadership studies has offered different variations of this paradox since the 1980s, when concepts such as transformational leadership, charismatic leadership and servant leadership started to gain academic popularity. These concepts, as well as later leadership concepts such as authentic leadership, spiritual leadership and responsible leadership, are all characterized by a move away from business for the purpose of business. Put differently, these leadership concepts all make a claim for 'the usefulness of uselessness' (Taylor 2002, p. 62): a thing that is seen as a good or end in itself (and for that reason not designed for use) becomes part of a larger function that promises superior business performance.

This argument will be made by drawing upon the concept of the gift as the outside of business, and by looking at some examples of popular leadership concepts that offer versions of this gift. Then, I continue by suggesting that this move away from business, towards givenness, marks a transition from the scientific towards the religious. I conclude by asking why leadership studies have become so interested in the outside of business, and suggest an epistemological and a historical reason.

# OUT OF BUSINESS

What is it that can be found outside of business? If business is about exchange, about profit and rent, or about a return on investment, the best concept to describe the outside of business is the concept of the gift. After all, a gift is only a gift if it is not returned. When I speak in this chapter of a gift I refer to the term in the sense of Derrida's (1992) understanding of the gift: as something that by definition is outside of exchange relations. As soon as a gift is returned, it has become an exchange and therefore no longer a gift. I argue that leadership scholars construct leadership as a pure gift, which is the most radical way of disassociating leadership from business. People like Mother Teresa and Nelson Mandela become role models for leadership in business, precisely because they are outside of business. It will become apparent, however, that it is not so straightforward to leave business behind, and one could suspect that fantasies of pure gifts are themselves prone to be included in exchange relations (Dunne and Spoelstra 2010). Furthermore, Jacques Derrida (1992), in his reading of Marcel Mauss' *The Gift* (1990), argued how this opposition between gift and exchange makes it impossible to recognize the gift as such. To put it more precisely, it is the recognition of a gift as gift that turns the gift into an exchange. For example, as soon as you recognize that you have given something, you cannot help feeling good about yourself, which turns the gift into an exchange. This complex play between gift and exchange also manifests itself in leadership studies.

The concept of self-sacrifice, which has gained some popularity in leadership studies since the late 1990s (for example, Choi and Mai-Dalton 1999; De Cremer and Knippenberg 2004) may serve as an initial example. A fairly representative definition of self-sacrifice is offered by Choi and Mai-Dalton (1999: 399): 'self-sacrifice in organizational set-tings is defined as the total/partial abandonment, and/or permanent/temporary postponement of personal interests, privileges, or welfare in the (1) division of labour, (2) distribution of rewards, and (3) exercise of power'. Self-sacrificial leaders do not sacrifice in order to get something in return; they do so out of their good or ego-less character. In other words, from the perspective of the leader his or her self-sacrifice is a true gift (with no expectation of a return). Research undertaken in leadership studies subsequently asks if these generous gift-giving practices consti-tute a superior business exchange. They conclude that they indeed do. For example, studies show that self-sacrifice is related to the attribution of charisma (De Cremer and Knippenberg 2004), the encouragement of follower reciprocity (Choi and Mai-Dalton 1999), and an increase in organizational commitment and team efficiency (De Cremer et al. 2004). It is believed that all of these effects eventually contribute to the bottom line. In this example the leader gives something (up) for no apparent reason. Their sacrifice is a pure gift (it has nothing to do with business) and because of this purity business paradoxically prospers.

A more influential example is the concept of transformational leadership, which has dominated leadership studies since Bass' (1985) *Leadership and performance beyond expectations*. Bass and others defined the concept of transformational leadership precisely in opposition to exchange: the transformational leader is said to selflessly lift followers up to higher grounds, in opposition to the transactional leader who has a business mindset (getting maximum output for minimum input). The numerous quantitative studies on transformational leadership tend to show that the gift mindset of the transformational leader is better for business than the exchange mindset of the transactional leader (Bass 1999).

The concept of authentic leadership, which has possibly become the most influential concept within leadership studies since the rise of transformational leadership, is a third example of the turn towards givenness in leadership studies. Authenticity is yet another concept that cannot be explained in terms of exchange. Ideologically one is oneself for one's own sake, not to receive anything in return. Authenticity, like the gift of self-sacrifice, is only to be found outside of business relations because authenticity can never take the form of an exchange. Studies of authentic leadership report similar results to those conducted on the topic of self-sacrifice and transformational leadership: authenticity among leaders has been related to good business in the form of for example job satisfaction, employee motivation and organizational performance (for example, Gardner et al. 2011; Walumbwa et al. 2008).

In addition, when we zoom in on the elements of authentic leadership, we see the same paradox. For example, relational transparency, which has been identified as one of the four elements of authentic leadership, refers to 'presenting one's authentic self (as opposed to a fake or distorted self) to others' (Walumbwa et al. 2008, p. 95), what is normally referred to as sincerity. Sincerity (or similar notions such as honesty and transparency) is seen as an essential element of authentic leadership, and the advice to practitioners that follows from this insight is straightforward: 'So what should we do? It is simple, just do what is the right thing in your judgement and be completely transparent about why you are doing it' (Avolio 2005, p. 131). The leader is portrayed as being sincere and transparent because this is conceived as a worthy goal in its own right, not because it benefits the organization, which would make it a calculated form of sincerity (and thereby insincere). Pure sincerity, that is without any intent to make a profit, becomes the best way to make a profit.

Self-sacrificial leadership, transformational leadership and authentic leadership are only three examples of a turn away from exchange, towards a pure gift. I could also have mentioned the selflessness of the servant leader, the 'gift of grace' of the charismatic leader, or the Spirit embodied by the spiritual leader. All these concepts appeal to a gift outside of business that is, paradoxically, reported to be good for business.

However, more profitable business is not the only promise that leadership studies offer by means of these leadership concepts. Precisely because leadership is located outside of business, it can intervene in business from above. In this manner leadership is not only said to make business more profitable, it is also said to redeem business from itself. The basic idea is that leadership makes business ethical despite its unethical (or instrumental) nature. For example, Bass and Steidlmeier (1999) argue that transformational leaders transform their followers into ethical beings and their organizations into ethical entities because they are rooted in moral values that have nothing to do with the means-end logic of business. Authentic leadership, Avolio and Gardner (2005) argue, is even to be seen as 'the root of all positive forms of leadership', which is diametrically opposed to faith in business that professes money and exchange as the root of all good, as famously professed in Ayn Rand's (2007) *Atlas Shrugged*.

Most of the concepts that are discussed in leadership studies today have a religious origin (for example, spiritual leadership, servant leader-ship, charismatic leadership, visionary leadership), or they have religious connotations (such as transformational leadership, with connotations of a religious conversion). This is also true for the concept of sacrifice: to sacrifice means to make sacred, and to make sacred is to cut something off its worldly environment so that it gets a divine status. A relation between self-sacrifice and the attribution of charisma is therefore not surprising: once a person gets a sacred status, he or she will be considered to have some kind of 'gift of grace' (that is, charisma). These religious terms are not merely of metaphorical significance for leadership studies: it is precisely by making the leader sacred that leadership studies manage to move away from business (see Grint 2010; Sliwa et al. 2012). Once leadership is separated from business, leaders can intervene from the outside and purify business from its evils.

Even though the studies on transformational leadership and self-sacrifice in leadership are perhaps not as entertaining to read as Sharma's

*The Leader Who Had No Title*, we are left with a picture that is equally uplifting: business is no longer in need of business. The sooner we get rid of business, the better business we will have.

## BACK TO BUSINESS

As ten Bos (2011, p. 289) observes, the reason why 'we feel so disgusted by business managers when they claim that business ethics is good for profit' is because 'we sense that morality cannot be subjected in this way to a regimen of means and ends'. In other words, any claim from the business world that the outside of business is good for business is likely to result in contempt. Why is it then that leadership studies can make such an argument without producing similar feelings? The reason, I think, is because it is an academic discipline. The discipline implicitly defends itself, as if it were saying: 'It is not our fault that being outside of business happens to be good for business: our tests simply show that this is the case'.

However, there are good reasons to be sceptical of this conclusion, and it is not difficult to problematize many of the research designs that have underpinned leadership studies in the past 30 years or so. Ever since the (re-)discovery of the religious dimension of leadership, marked by the transition from exchange to gift, leadership studies have mixed the empirical and the ideal, or the descriptive and the normative. In many cases the ideal (the pure gift that redeems business) is validated empirically, despite the fact that it never shows itself empirically. For example, leadership scholars claim that, say, transformational leaders and authentic leaders are really existing people in business organizations, but the empirical tests are only concerned with appearances of these ideals in the heads of followers. Studies in authentic leadership show that the appearance of authenticity is good for business but do not show, and cannot possibly show, that authenticity is indeed the cause of this appearance.

The ideal is always bound to collapse in the empirical, where self-sacrifice, sincerity, and authenticity do exist, but only in impure expressions that are embedded in all kinds of business exchanges. When leadership scholars become too empirical, they quickly get entangled in contradictory logics. Here is one example:

> We also believe authentic leaders will be relatively transparent in expressing their true emotions and feelings to followers, while simultaneously *regulating such emotions to minimize displays of inappropriate or potentially damaging emotions*. That is, as authentic leaders come to know and accept themselves,

they will display higher levels of trustworthiness, openness, and willingness to share (*when appropriate*) their thoughts and feelings in close relationships. (Gardner et al. 2005: 358, emphasis added)

In this passage, the authors introduce a concept that is normally (wisely) avoided in discussions around authenticity and sincerity: politeness. Politeness, together with lying, may be seen as the opposite of sincerity because it results in a distorted picture of one's 'real' or 'authentic' self (if you are polite, you are by definition not sincere). Any form of politeness inscribes the gift back into a logic of exchange. However given that the authors understand that there is no business without politeness, they still attempt to condition authenticity upon a business logic that it is foreign to itself, to such an extent that it violates their ideal. As the liberal thinker Benjamin Constant observed, to be sincere only when it is socially appropriate is not to be sincere: 'Always to strive to be sincere [is] designed to appeal to an audience that would applaud such virtuous behaviour, and as such could paradoxically be a sign of a deeper insincerity' (Constant, paraphrased in Jay 2010, p. 67).

In short, the gifts that leadership scholars have found outside of business cannot be objectified in research. For example, authenticity is something that refuses any form of measurement or objectification: we never really know if, or to what extent, someone is authentic (even when we agree upon what this means) just like one cannot know if leaders truly sacrifice themselves (without a secret desire to turn sacrifice into exchange). All that a researcher can do is to ask other members of an organization if a person appears as authentic, and then test if authentic appearances have positive effects on various indicators of organizational performance. This is the direction that most research on authentic leadership has taken (Gardner et al. 2011). The idea that pure gifts are causing these appearances can only be motivated by faith. This is why leadership studies are ultimately a religious rather than a scientific enterprise: they are motivated by a faith that business can be redeemed through leadership interventions from above.

Why, then, are leadership studies so interested in the outside of business? Why do so many leadership scholars refuse to accept the obvious fact that business is – in most cases – very good for business, and that all those beautiful things that happen outside of business, tend to be rather bad for business? And why do leadership studies insist on measuring and objectifying phenomena that are immeasurable and non-objective?

# WHY ARE LEADERSHIP STUDIES OUT OF BUSINESS?

So far I have suggested that the underlying premise of leadership studies is the function of things that do not have a function, or the use of uselessness. This paradox is best understood through the concepts of exchange and gift. 'Business' refers to exchange: the very nature of business is unthinkable without exchange, and a true gift – a gift that is not returned – is by definition bad business. 'Leadership', in leadership studies, has come to refer to that which transcends exchange relations; it gives meaning and common purpose to business that is foreign to exchange relations.

This turn to the usefulness of uselessness (or negatively formulated: the discovery that business is bad for business) is fairly recent. Earlier studies of leadership, most explicitly leader–member exchange (LMX) theory (Graen and Uhl-Bien 1995) departed from the economic model of doing social science, which only grants reality to the stable components in exchange relations (subjects and objects). More recent theories of leadership start on the opposite end: they side with non-transactional concepts, such as spirituality, authenticity or charisma, all of which are attributed a higher reality than the exchange relations that are tradition-ally associated with business. Before the 1980s one rarely sees versions of the usefulness of uselessness, whereas since the 1980s it seems to have become the norm. Although a full exposition of this turn would require a more careful study, I will conclude by suggesting two possible reasons for this transformation: the first epistemological, and the second histori-cal.

The first, epistemological, reason could be the gradual realization that the most popular, predominantly religious, associations with the term 'leadership' – such as vision, charisma, inspiration and sacrifice – refuse to be captured in exchange relations. A vision of a better future, for example, carries its own reward; charisma, literally 'gift of grace', is thought to befall upon certain extraordinary individuals for no apparent merit; and the ultimate self-sacrifice is to give one's life without receiving anything in return. As soon as one deals with the word 'leadership', one sooner or later has to face these religious connotations, which means entering a sphere that cannot be dealt with scientifically. It is impossible to study leadership objectively for the simple reason that leadership shows itself to the faithful only. Leaders are perhaps best understood as ghosts, in the sense of 'a matter which has a spirit or spirit which has a matter' (Macherey 1999, p. 21), rather than as objects or subjects. Objects and subjects show themselves to the gaze of the researcher, but a ghost escapes all objectifying attempts as it is 'no longer anything purely material and/or purely spiritual, but only something invisible visible, insensible sensible, or incorporated' (Macherey 1999, p. 20). This wavering nature of leadership is well captured by research in spiritual leadership. Kanungo and Mendonça (1994), for example, see the leader as a (material) being that cannot do without a spirit, to the extent that it is difficult to separate the material from the spiritual.

If leaders are indeed best understood as ghosts, the methodological possibilities for leadership researchers are limited to the celebration of ghosts, the exorcism of ghosts (critical leadership studies), and a study of ghosts: any text on leadership is by definition a ghost story. While this may be seen as a provocative way of making the point, I am increasingly convinced that leadership studies has itself made the discovery that leadership is essentially something that cannot be objectified or measured (though it may not show much awareness of having made this discovery). Most leadership scholars would concede, for example, that there is not much value in measuring objective traits of real people who we call leaders. Little of interest will be found this way, as is well-known since the poor results of so-called trait research in leadership.

But why does business need to be redeemed through religion? I think this is where we also encounter a historical reason for the move away from business in leadership studies: the shattered faith in business following accounting scandals, the financial crisis, the climate crisis, and so on. Business is no longer considered to offer redemptive powers in its own right. Faith in the capitalist entrepreneur is shattered; business now needs the help of metaphysical friends such as deontology, virtue ethics, religion, or new age spirituality to legitimate itself (Sørensen and Spoelstra 2013). The religious connotations of leadership are very attractive in this context. Where 'normal' management scholars need to invent new concepts, such as corporate responsibility or social entre- preneurship, leadership scholars have started to re-mobilize the connota- tions of leadership that the term has captured for centuries, but which were not considered scientific or measurable enough in the times that leadership studies established itself as a scholarly discipline (roughly from the 1940s onwards).

This reinvention of religion in management studies in general, and leadership studies in particular, is, perhaps unsurprisingly, double-edged: on the one hand, scholars are genuinely looking for a better way of living together, to promote community over individuality, altruism over greed, and so on. On the other hand, the appeal to religious connotations and ideals can also slip in wishful thinking, which may prevent a critical investigation of business practices. Both are discernible in a concept such as transformational leadership: there is little reason to question if Bernard M. Bass (the most prominent transformational leadership scholar in business) was genuine when he said that he has always wanted leaders/ managers to wear the 'white hats of heroes', rather than the 'black hats of villains' (Bass and Steidlmeier 1999, p. 187). It is less clear, however, if the transformational leadership concept promotes these white hats: its attractive image may rather provide leaders, or participants in leadership development programmes, with a false sense of moral superiority (see Alvesson 2011).

However my greatest worry is not the effect that leadership studies have on managers and other practitioners. My biggest worry is that leadership studies have sacrificed the academic virtues of sincerity and truthfulness in its attempts to redeem business from itself. As a consequence, it may have moved too far into the direction of a deep insincerity that immediately hits you when you read a book such as Sharma's *The Leader Who Has No Title*:

> The powerful lessons I'll reveal will be given gently, carefully and with sincere encouragement. (...) The principles and tools you'll discover will automatically cause your career to fly, your happiness to soar, and your absolute best to fully express itself. But above all else, I promise you, I will be honest. I owe you that respect. (Sharma, 2010, p. 1–2, emphasis removed)

I fear that this type of insincerity (an insincere promise followed by the insincere assurance that it is sincere) has come to dominate leadership studies. Its false promise is the promise that business can do without itself. Contrary to Sharma, this promise does not need to be covered up by means of another false promise (of sincerity or truthfulness) for the simple reason that academic research already provides this promise by its very nature. If truthfulness is indeed sacrificed to pave the way for new business gospels (as noble as these may be), the real sacrifice may be the study of leadership itself.

## ACKNOWLEDGEMENTS

Many thanks to Helen Nicholson, Nick Butler, Stefan Tramer and the editors of this volume for their helpful comments on earlier versions of this chapter.

# REFERENCES

Alvesson, M. (2011), 'Leaders as saints: leadership through moral peak performance', in M. Alvesson and A. Spicer (eds), *Metaphors We Lead By: Understanding Leadership in the Real World*, London: Routledge, pp. 51–75.

Avolio, B.J. (2005), *Leadership Development in Balance: Made/Born*, Mahwah, NJ: Lawrence Erlbaum.

Avolio, B.J. and W.L. Gardner (2005), 'Authentic leadership development: getting to the root of positive forms of leadership', *Leadership Quarterly*, **16** (3), 315–38.

Bass, B.M. (1985), *Leadership and Performance Beyond Expectation*, New York: Free Press.

Bass, B.M. (1999), 'Two decades of research and development in transformational leadership', *European Journal for Work and Organizational Psychology*, **8** (1), 9–32.

Bass, B.M. and P. Steidlmeier (1999), 'Ethics, character, and authentic transformational leadership behavior', *Leadership Quarterly*, **10** (2), 181–217.

Choi, Y. and R.R. Mai-Dalton (1999), 'The model of followers' responses to self-sacrificial leadership: an empirical test', *Leadership Quarterly*, **10** (3), 397–421.

De Cremer, D., M. van Dijke and A. Bos (2004), 'Distributive justice moderating the effects of self-sacrificial leadership', *Leadership and Organization Development Journal*, **25** (5), 466–75.

De Cremer, D. and D. van Knippenberg (2004), 'How do leaders promote cooperation? The effects of charisma and procedural fairness', *Journal of Applied Psychology*, **87** (5), 858–66.

Derrida, J. (1992), *Given Time: Counterfeit Money*, Chicago, IL: University of Chicago Press.

Dunne, S. and S. Spoelstra (2010), 'The gift of leadership', *Philosophy Today*, **54** (1), 66–77.

Gardner, W.L., B.J. Avolio, F. Luthans, D.R. May and F.O. Walumbwa (2005). '"Can you see the real me?" A self-based model of authentic leader and follower development', *Leadership Quarterly*, **16** (3), 343–72.

Gardner, W.L., C.C. Cogliser, K.M. Davis and M.P. Dickens (2011), 'Authentic leadership: a review of the literature and research agenda', *Leadership Quarterly*, **22** (6), 1120–45.

Graen, G.B. and M. Uhl-Bien (1995), 'Relationship-based approach to leadership: development of leader–member exchange (LMX) theory of leadership over 25 years: applying a multi-level multi-domain perspective', *Leadership Quarterly*, **6** (2), 219–47.

Grint, K. (2010), 'The sacred in leadership: separation, sacrifice and leadership', *Organization Studies*, **31** (1), 89–107.

Jay, M. (2010), *The Virtues of Mendacity: On Lying in Politics*, London: University of Virginia Press.

Kanungo, R.N. and M. Mendonça (1994), 'What leaders cannot do without: the spiritual dimensions of leadership', in J.A. Conger (eds), *Spirit at Work: Discovering the Spirituality in Leadership*, San Francisco, CA: Jossey-Bass.

Macherey, P. (1999), 'Marx dematerialized, or the spirit of Derrida', in M. Sprinkler (ed.), *Ghostly Demarcations*, London: Verso.

Mauss, M. (1990), *The Gift: The Form and Reason for Exchange in Archaic Societies*, London: Routledge.

Rand, A. (2007), *Atlas Shrugged*, London: Penguin.

Sharma, R. (2010), *The Leader Who Had No Title: A Modern Fable on Real Success in Business and Life*, London: Simon & Schuster.

Sliwa, M., S. Spoelstra, B.M. Sørensen and C. Land (2012), 'Profaning the sacred in leadership studies: a reading of Murakami's *A Wild Sheep Chase*', *Organization*, reproduced on internet, scheduled for print publication.

Sørensen, B.M. and S. Spoelstra (2013), 'Faith', in C. Luetge (eds), *Handbook of the Philosophical Foundations and Business Ethics*, Heidelberg, Germany: Springer.

Taylor, M.C. (2002), 'Capitalizing (on) gifting', in E. Wyschogrod, J.J. Goux and E. Boynton (eds), *The Enigma of Gift and Sacrifice*, New York: Fordham University Press.

Ten Bos, R. (2011), 'The moral significance of gestures', *Business Ethics: A European Review*, **20** (3), 280–91.

Walumbwa, F.O., B.J. Avolio, W.L. Gardner, T.S. Wernsing and S.J. Peterson (2008), Authentic leadership: development and validation of a theory-based measure, *Journal of Management*, **34** (1), 89–126.

# 11. Does leadership create stupidity?

## Mats Alvesson and André Spicer

## INTRODUCTION

Leadership is typically associated with strong cognitive capacities. We assume that leaders are smart and according to conventional theories, 'modern business leaders are knowledge workers of the highest order' (McKenna et al. 2009, p. 183). This means leaders have high IQs and have the ability to work with complex bodies or knowledge. It also means that leaders should have the practical wisdom, which allows them to negotiate particular complex situations (Grint 2007). Leaders are thought to possess superior wisdom insofar as they are able to set a vision for their followers, using their superior intelligence to convince followers and engage in other intellectually demanding tasks. They are also wise enough to seek to harness the wisdom of their followers. To raise the capacity of followers is a key task for leaders. They do this by being humble, listening to their subordinates and even encouraging employees to find their inner smartness to lead themselves. In short, 'Wise leaders lead others to lead themselves' (Manz 1998, p. 99). They do this through the use of reason and superior observation, by allowing for non-rational aspects, valuing humane outcomes, being practically oriented and valuing aesthetic dimensions (McKenna et al. 2009).

While we think intelligence and wisdom are certainly desirable, it is not necessarily a dominant capacity in the world of leadership. Leaders sometimes engage in extremely irrational and stupid courses of action – and convince their followers to do the same (Kets de Vries 1980; Tourish and Pinnington 2002; Tourish and Vatcha 2005). Commentators have pointed out that many ideas about leadership, which are enthusiastically spouted by (want-to-be) leaders, often rest on very poor reasoning and pseudo-scientific or even mystical claims (Spoelstra 2010). Critics have noted that leadership relies upon an element of systematic stupification of followers. This is because leadership calls for an inclination of 'non-leaders' to be led and give significant space for the leader to do most of the thinking (Gemmill and Oakley 1992). Even if leadership is 'distributed' and less hierarchical, followers work within parameters that have been decided by leaders (Huzzard and Spoelstra 2011). This involves subordinates refraining from being particularly reflexive, thinking in wider ways or from engaging with the ambiguities. This is all seen as responsibilities of the leader. Being a follower, one should be disinclined from thinking independently and deviating from the ideas of the leader. Instead one should be prepared to accept that the leader is doing most of the difficult cognitive tasks. The job of a follower is to follow the visions, objectives, definitions of the situation and direct instructions set out by leaders. This, far from being about wisdom, the reality of leadership is often about the exercise of influence in a way which renders followers disinclined to use the range of intellectual resources at their disposal.

In this chapter, we want to challenge the widespread assumption that leadership primarily involves the mobilization of intelligence, rationality and wisdom. To do this, we argue that a crucial component of leadership is stupidity. There are many well-known cases of pure stupidity in leadership where leaders commit grand mistakes resulting in disastrous consequences. However, and of more interest for this chapter, even more widespread are instances where leaders and their followers systematically refrain from thinking too much, asking broader questions and engaging in deeper reflection with more ambiguous consequences for organizational functioning. We think that a central, if under-recognized, aspect of leadership entails systematically reducing and narrowing cognitive capacities with at least partly, positive organizational consequences for social relations and discipline. We refer to this as 'functional stupidity' (Alvesson and Spicer 2012). It entails a systematically supported curtailing of substantive reasoning, reflexivity and justification. Functional stupidity is supported by active stupidity management on the part of leaders as well as meta-stupidity management on the part of various idea-entrepreneurs who promote leadership fads and fashions. Such deliberate dampening of thinking creates followers who systematically seek to self-constrain their reflective capacities and play up those of the leader. This can create enthusiastic commitment to ideas of leadership, which in turn gives rise to functional outcomes such as smooth organizational functioning and the facilitation of individual careers. However, it can also give rise to more problematic outcomes including disillusionment as well as an increased risk of mistakes and shortcomings. These are not necessarily clearly recognized, but people may develop a feeling or suspicion that things could work much better.

To make this case, we proceed as follows. We begin by defining the concept of functional stupidity. We then consider how leadership involves the systematic cultivation of stupidity through active interventions by leaders and meta-stupidity management on the part of the leadership industry. We then look at the various forms of self-stupidity management this prompts on the part of followers and leaders themselves. Finally, we consider the potential outcomes of the deliberate dampening of cognitive abilities encouraged by leadership. We then conclude by drawing together the argument and suggesting the limits of leadership-induced stupidity.

## FUNCTIONAL STUPIDITY

In folk psychology stupidity is usually equated with some kind of mental deficiency. To be stupid is to suffer from what the more philosophical might call an 'epistemological lack'. This is not just to lack knowledge (as is ignorance) but also to lack the ability or willingness to use or *process* knowledge (Sternberg 2002). In recent years, cognitive psychologists have highlighted that there are many well-known cases where people who are apparently very smart do exceedingly stupid things. To put it another way, people with high IQs can engage in highly problematic thinking processes. Psychologists argue that this happens when intelligent people develop a fixation within problematic algorithms of thought or entertain a lack of willingness to question one's own deeply held beliefs (Stanovich 2002). For instance, professionals or experts frequently become highly attached to deeply held assumptions. They then seek information, which confirms these assumptions, and avoid other information, which contradicts it. This means that they artificially limit their cognitive abilities and seek to keep it within a very limited set of well-established assumptions and conventions.

Most psychological work on stupidity focuses on the individual in developing an explanation of how stupidity works. More recent inquiries into stupidity have pointed out that stupidity may actually be prompted by wide collective processes. For instance, Avital Ronell (2002) points out that stupidity is prompted by modern (post) enlightenment cultures of knowledge. She argues that the increasing emphasis on mastery of the world through intelligence prompts a widespread paranoia with avoiding stupidity. The increased emphasis on knowledge brings with it a widespread preoccupation with rooting out stupidity in others, and oneself. In this sense, stupidity becomes the focus on intense work. This point is taken further by Rene ten Bos (2007) who has argued that these attempts to root out stupidity through casting the light of reason on our activities can often result in a reinforcement of stupidity. Using the example of the widespread attachment to management knowledge, ten Bos argues, can lead to uninterrogated attachment to stupid courses of action. The central point here is that stupidity is not just an individual problem. It is a collective cognitive deficit. It entails a socially prompted limitation on the use of people's cognitive capacities.

In a recent article (Alvesson and Spicer 2012), we have asked what role organizations play in limiting the full use of people's cognitive resources. We argued that far from being hot-beds of smartness, many organizations actively encourage stupidity. For sure there are some extreme cases of organizations, which encourage pure stupidity and create extreme organizational dysfunctionality. However, more wide-spread are instances of organizations, which encourage stupidity that actually help organizations to function. We refer to this as *functional stupidity*. It is characterized by a lack of three aspects, which are central to the full use of cognitive capacities: reflexivity, justification and substantive reason giving. Lack or *minimization of reflexivity* involves an inability or unwillingness to question knowledge claims and norms, but be caught by a specific perspective or line of reasoning (Alvesson and Sköldberg 2009). This happens when members of an organization do not call into question dominant beliefs and expectations that they encounter in organizational life. What exists is thought to be given, natural and good (or unproblematic or inevitable and therefore not worth thinking about in terms of possible badness). For instance, members of a bureaucracy may not consider or question organizational (im)morality because 'what is right in the corporation is what the guy above you wants from you' (Jackall 1988, p. 6). Such a lack of doubt involves the repression of organizational members' capacity to use reason, to scruti-nize and critically assess knowledge claims.

The second aspect of functional stupidity is a lack of *justification*. This happens when actors do not provide, or demand, reasons and explanation (see Boltanski and Thévenot 2006; Habermas 1981). By not asking for justification, individuals are disinclined to engage in dialogue or ask for rationales. This often means assuming that an account of the reasons for a decision or action is not required. Not requiring justifications allows practices to be accepted without any significant critical scrutiny or robust process of reason giving. For instance, organizations will often adopt new practices with few robust reasons beyond the fact that it makes the company 'look good' (Alvesson 2013; Zbaracki 1998). One example of such a lack of reflexivity, substantive considerations and justifications in contemporary organizations is the obsession with the image-enhancing aspects of organizations. This involves a focus on idealized, good-looking practices and arrangements which boost status, image and identity of an organization (Alvesson 2013). Leadership in many contemporary organizations involves efforts to make employees buy into these good-looking images. It also helps to ensure they are communicated internally and externally with good faith and limited scepticism. It is often facilitated by a manager being an uncritical believer in image claims of an organization and discouraging subordinates from asking for justification of these messages.

The third aspect of functional stupidity is a lack of *substantive reasoning*. This happens when cognitive resources are concentrated and the thinking circles around a small set of concerns, which are defined by a specific organizational, professional or work logic. It entails the myopic application of instrumental rationality focused on the efficient achievement of a given end and the ignorance of broader substantive questions about what those ends actually are (Alvesson and Willmott 2012). For instance, an accountant may compress a broad range of issues into recordable numbers, thereby ignoring many of the more substantive debates around what exactly those numbers represent and the moral implications associated with using these numbers in decision-making (Dillard and Ruchala 2005). This is a form of stupidity because it halts a reasoned investigation and consideration of the possible links and implications of one's action. Instead it frames questions in a highly narrow and focused sense.

Functional stupidity entails a very low degree of reflection, justification and substantive reasoning. It is often encouraged by a widely shared culture of grandiosity, which builds an obsession with the development of fine images in place of substantive practices (Alvesson 2013). This often sustains a focus on superficial indicators (such as brands, certification, titles, etc.) in place of more substantive aspects. In addition, fashion-following and pressure to imitate others are key elements here. Within the context of organizations, it makes sense to talk about forms of active stupidity management. Central here are interventions on the part of various actors (managers, peers etc.) aimed at limiting processes of reasoning, justification and reflexivity in organizations. In addition, there are forms of meta-stupidity management, which involve a more systematic discouragement of broader critical thinking. Agents who are external to organizations such as consultants, gurus and management ideologists play a vital role here. Direct stupidity management and more indirect forms of stupidity meta-management prompt self-stupidity management by subordinates. They monitor themselves to ensure they do not get too carried away in reflexive thinking, demanding justifications or asking broader substantive questions. Organizational members remind themselves not to ask too many troubling questions least they make life difficult for themselves and those around them. Through this self-monitored stupidity, employees can produce some significantly positive outcomes for themselves. They can ensure a relatively steady progress through the organization and avoid troubling and anxiety-inducing questions. This in turn can build commitment to the organization and facilitate relatively smooth collective action around shared meanings around key issues. However, artificially cutting short broader thinking can also have more troubling consequences. At an individual level, it can create a sense of disillusionment. At the organizational level, the nurturing of stupidity can result in an increasing likelihood of mistakes. We will now flesh out this argument below.

## LEADERSHIP AS A SOURCE OF STUPIDITY

There are a variety of ways functional stupidity is prompted in organizations. For example propagating a fervent belief in organizational structures as a guarantor of orderliness and fairness is a way of prompting functional stupidity (Alvesson and Kärreman 2007). Cultivating enthusiasm for institutionalized practices is often used by organizations to make themselves look good, rather than to create any significant productive benefits (Meyer and Rowan 1977). Focusing on being action-oriented over careful analysis and consideration is yet another way functional stupidity is seeded (Brunsson 1985). However, one particularly powerful way functional stupidity is prompted in organizations is through a collective obsession with leadership.

It may sound strange to claim that leadership creates stupidity. The usual image we have of a leader is someone with a pensive but determined gaze. We often assume that leaders encourage the capacity or interest in thinking in their followers. Good leadership is sometimes defined as involving intellectual stimulation and stimulating learning and some would argue that leadership is about competence improvement and the opposite of stupidity-creation. Although this assumption may capture some of the more savoury aspects of leadership, we think it misses a central aspect of many forms of leadership: leadership often involves the active cultivation of stupidity. The history of many organizations is littered with such grand exercises of stupidity. Examples include Ford under the control of the ageing Henry Ford who insisted on the continued manufacturing of model T even when it was clear the customers found it obsolete and FBI under J. Edgar Hoover which focused more on spying on leftist academics than the Mafia (Kets de Vries 1980). While these are rather grand examples of stupidity, what is more frequent are subtle forms of *functional* stupidity prompted by leadership. This happens when leaders seek to reduce the capacity of their followers to think outside a predefined domain. It often involves cutting short complication by encouraging followers to avoid thinking, reflecting or asking for justifications. Instead followers are asked to buy into narrow assumptions and not ask too many questions. By doing this leaders limit how followers define, think, value and act in particular situations. By corralling followers' cognitive capacities, it is possible to create a degree of predictability, compliance and order. In this sense, encouraging stupidity through leadership can actually create functional outcomes. After all, organizations can be seen as based on shared meanings, partly taken for granted, and these shared meanings partly depend on organizational members not insisting on thinking independently and creating too much friction and uncertainty. In this sense, limiting free and varied thinking is a key element of the functioning of an organization. Somewhere this means a strong dose of functional stupidity.

## LEADERS AS STUPIDITY MANAGERS

How does leadership produce stupidity? Perhaps the most obvious way leadership works to manufacture stupidity is through the activities of leaders themselves. Leaders may demand absolute compliance from followers (Spicer 2011). In some organizations such as certain parts of the military, a commanding style of leadership is deeply institutionalized and followers systematically learn compliance and stupidity (Dixon 1994). Similar processes occur in organizations with 'strong' cultures and 'cultish' features (Tourish and Pinnington 2002). Here there are strong expectations and pressures on followers to be disciplined and obedient. The leader is to be respected and orders are to be followed. Inclination to question or engage in independent thinking is to be systematically avoided. Such authoritarian organizations are built on a strong differentiation between a leader and followers. Those in subordinate positions should refrain from critical thinking, reflectivity and asking for justification. They should assume that the leader knows best. In this sense, followers are systematically stupified.

In most contemporary organizations strictly authoritarian forms of leadership are not very popular. Followers are not required to show absolute compliance with the views of a forceful leader. Virtually all organizations include some expectation of members using some degree of judgement rather than blind obedience. However, this does not mean that stupidity has disappeared as a crucial ingredient in contemporary leadership. Few organizations give priority to free, varied thinking and critical questioning. One of the ways that contemporary leaders seek to encourage stupidity in their followers is through transformational leadership (TFL). TFL is a way of doing leadership whereby 'leaders transform followers. That is, followers are changed from being self-centred individuals to being committed members of a group' (Sashkin 2004, p. 175). There are different views of what TFL includes, but typical ingredients are individualized consideration, intellectual stimulation, idealized influence (charisma) and inspirations. Advocates of TFL assume that the leader has significant influence on followers' self-confidence, enthusiasm, and identification with the group/organization and voluntary compliance. The literature is full of strong claims about the grandiose accomplishments of transformational leaders. These including 'connect-(ing) followers' self-concepts to the organization's mission and vision through idealized influence, inspirational motivation, intellectual stimulation and individualized consideration' (Hartnell and Walumbwa 2011, p. 232) and 'defining and inculcating in organization members the belief that they can effect, if not control, their environment, including government regulation, market competition, and technological change' (Sashkin 2004, p. 194).

The very idea of TFL means that leaders position themselves as superior figures who have a clear vision and can transform suboptimal followers into much better people (Tourish and Pinnington 2002; Tourish and Vatcha 2005). 'Visionary' leaders can make their followers less self-centred. This of course assumes that followers are mainly passive subjects who are to be improved by leaders' considerations, stimulations and inspirations. Furthermore, it assumes followers are happy to passively receive all the good things that flow from the leader. To insist on critical thinking, being reflective about the situation or asking for justifications appears to be counterproductive and it would make the leader's work of transforming followers quite difficult, if not impossible. Indeed, the task of a transformational leader is to encourage followers to put aside their independent thinking and commit themselves to the leader's vision and inspiring communication. This is often encouraged through high-pressure corporate cultures, which strictly circumscribe the scope for broader processes of reasoning, calling for justification and reflexivity in favour of commitment, compliance and enthusiasm. In this sense, employees are cajoled to suspend their reason in favour of visions and compliance. The more subordinates can be convinced to adapt a transformation-responsive attitude, the easier the TFL project becomes.

Transformational leadership has certainly proved popular. However, the folly of this kind of transformational leadership has been recognized by even some of its most ardent supporters (for example, Bass and Steidlmeier 1999). One upshot of this has been the rise of more 'democratic', 'authentic', 'distributed' or 'facilitative' forms of leadership (Alvesson and Spicer 2011). These forms of leadership tend to portray the leader as a humble figure who seeks to have a positive impact on followers without the heroism of commander and transformer models. These leaders seek to facilitate the growth and activity of their followers – often giving them significant space to take the lead and engage in activity. One of the many new labels for (positive) leadership is 'the Superleader'. This is a person who 'focuses primarily on the empowering roles of helping, encouraging and supporting followers in the development of personal responsibility, individual initiative, self-confidence, self-goal setting, self-problem solving, opportunity thinking, self-leadership and psychological ownership over their tasks and duties' (Houghton et al. 2003, p. 133). They do this through encouraging learning from mistakes, avoiding punishment, listening more, talking less, creating independence and interdependence, and avoiding dependence. The accent is upon providing, supporting and coaching rather than propagating a strong vision and direction.

It is widely assumed that the adoption of facilitative forms of leadership means that followers are developed to become more competent or wiser people. In this context, leadership is seen as anti-stupidity work. Followers enter organizations as immature and moderately smart, are targeted for development by the Superleader and are then lifted to a higher level of ability. Of course, this can happen. After all, in many contexts, leaders are more senior, well-educated, experienced and informed than their followers. This can mean leaders can give the 'right' instructions, get people to adapt 'appropriate' values as well as facilitate learning and competence development. Still the idea is that all significant people-improving, direction and development come from a leader. This indicates an (assumed) passivity and weakness on the behalf of followers. Such a position may be relevant in cases where followers are inexperienced. In many other cases, it may encourage a certain form of attachment to the leader which is not actually required or motivated by followers' various capacities and resources. Through playing their facilitation role, leaders may actually create a kind of space where followers are assumed to need support, coaching, counselling and so on from the leader (in most cases from their manager). By representing themselves as figures who help followers to grow, leaders can reinforce the passivity and dependence of followers in order to build up a sense of self-esteem and usefulness (Huzzard and Spoelstra 2011). When leaders and leadership are emphasized, followers become much focused and potentially dependent on leaders exercising a monopoly of the input on follower growth. Other sources of inspiration, support and learning become less important. This is not to deny that followers may benefit strongly from inspiration and the support from others. There is also a range of alternative options to be considered here, such as for example reading books and articles, participating in courses and conferences, learning from peers, drawing upon professional and social networks. The idea that leaders are the key people who make followers function better assumes that employees are relatively passive, not particularly capable of taking initiative, and cannot use resources outside the leader–follower relationship. This set of assumptions reinforces a form of functional stupidity.

## THE LEADERSHIP INDUSTRY AS META-STUPIDITY MANAGERS

Stupidity is not created by leaders alone. The leadership industry is also to blame. The leadership industry is made up of a broad group of people whose job is promoting ideas of leadership. They include gurus, consultants, journalists, policy makers, coaches and leadership educators. Through encouraging a wider enthusiasm for and belief in ideas of leadership, the leadership industry encourages leaders, aspiring leaders and followers to adopt what are often very questionable ideas. Moreover, targets of leadership knowledge are subtly discouraged from thinking more broadly or deeply about many of the (often superficial) ideas about leadership. In this respect, purveyors of leadership ideologies (such as Gurus, educational institutions and so on) are important meta-stupidity managers.

One way that the leadership industry does meta-stupidity management is by placing an extraordinary significance on the person (presumed) to be doing leadership, creating the expectation that the contemporary organizational world circle around leaders doing leadership. Some make outlandish claims that all global problems including wars, ecological disasters and economic turmoil are due to poor leadership (Greenleaf 1977). Others are more measured in their enthusiasm for leadership. For instance, Heifetz and Laurie (1997) point out that 'a leader is responsible for direction, protection, orientation, managing conflict and shaping norms' (p. 127). This may sound uncontroversial, but this seemingly pedestrian statement implies that followers are *not* responsible for these basic aspects of organizational life. It simply makes them into people who implement the leaders' direction, receive their protection, whose conflicts are managed and who are the target of norm manipulation activities. Non-leaders are reduced to being recipients of leaders' impressive acts. With this follows a disinclination to use the full range of cognitive capacities. In other words, encoded in the concept of leadership is the assumption that followers need to be led. They are people who might not be able to think for themselves, let alone direct, protect, orient, manage conflict and shape norms. So, the greater the emphasis on leadership, the more followership and subordination is emphasized. This marginalizes the use of critical reflection. In other words, influential leadership means a degree of stupidity on behalf of the subordinate.

The leadership industry also plays an important role in mystifying the leader. This happens through leadership being frequently portrayed as an almost magic force that has a positive impact on followers (Spoelstra 2010). Leadership is elevated from a somewhat pedestrian and everyday activity into something, which can have miraculous and almost metaphysical impacts. For instance the figure of the leader is often attributed almost superhuman abilities. The idea of leadership is given significant scope to do all sorts of amazing things. This faith in the innate goodness of leadership and its transformative power often means people shy away from considering the more mundane mechanics of influencing people, getting the job done or even asking whether leadership is actually necessary. Rather, leadership propagators focus on the apparently miraculous achievements associated with notions of leadership. This seductive message that leadership involves superhuman acts encourages a lack of serious reflection on notions of leadership. The mundane realities of actually doing leadership are often ignored in favour of a highly positive discourse around the topic (Alvesson and Sveningsson 2003). Furthermore, because 'true' leadership is positioned as being innately beneficial, few, if any, substantive questions are often asked about leadership discourse. Finally, because of the reliance on fuzzy concepts such as 'vision', 'values' and 'authenticity', purveyors of leadership discourse rarely stray into more elaborate and substantive justifications. As well as being represented as being miraculous, leadership is promoted in a highly idealized ethical form by the leadership industry. This often involves projecting a sense of moral goodness onto the figure of the leader (Alvesson 2011). Put in the crudest form, it is assumed that a real leader is good. If he or she is bad then he or she is not a leader (or perhaps an inauthentic one) (Bass and Steidlmeier 1999). This seems to indicate that people are eager to preserve some idealized notion of the leader. By doing so, they preserve this category from critical reflection. Even though a lot of leadership literature is more reflective and acknowledges the complexities of the real world, all too often a naïve faith in good leadership is present. This invites strong suspicions about the stupidity of leadership. Of course, as we cannot be sure that our 'leaders' are really good (authentic, transformational, Super or whatever) some scrutiny seems appropriate. However, if our would-be leader appears to be of the right stuff, then enthusiastically following the leader is the right thing to do. No need to think critically here.

Of course, far from everybody takes the messages of the leadership industry seriously. Often the pronouncements of leadership gurus are a source of mirth and ridicule. Notwithstanding these reactions, there is a strong undertone of stupidity reinforcement. This happens in terms of naive expectations of what leadership means and what leaders can be expected to do, and in the construction of non-leaders as leader-dependent followers with small possibilities of taking initiative.

## LEADERSHIP AND SELF-STUPIFICATION

Direct acts of stupidity management coupled with more subtle forms of meta-stupidity management can cut short people's mobilization of wisdom, intelligence and other cognitive resources. Followers are encouraged to narrow their intellectual horizons and buy into leadership acts as well as broader ideas about leadership. At the same time, leaders (or aspiring leaders) are encouraged to think about themselves in often idealistic, mystical and even fantastic ways. The result is that some thinking (and fantasizing) about leadership is encouraged. But at the same time, broader thinking which goes beyond leadership or perhaps even against leadership is discouraged. The result can be an irrational attachment to the benefits and importance of leadership – sometimes beyond any reasonable doubt or evidence to the contrary. So, why is it that both actual and potential leaders as well as followers often are so willing to be seduced by ideas of leadership?

Perhaps one of the main ways that ideas about leadership are so enthusiastically embraced is because it promises leaders and leader wannabees a reinforced sense of identity and self-esteem (Alvesson and Sveningsson 2003). Discourses of leadership are infused with identity scripts, which give people identity material they can work with in their on-going struggle to fashion an appealing and attractive sense of self. This is particularly desirable in settings where other occupational and administrative identities (such as manager, administrator, bureaucratic, officer worker, etc.) are marked in increasingly negative ways. By positioning oneself as a leader (or at least a person aspiring to lead) significantly positive identity affects are promised: one has access to an attractive script, which is generally valued. To position oneself as a follower is much less appealing. But some versions of leadership – particularly focusing transformational or facilitative ideas, indicate that subordinates are able to access an attractive stock of identity crafting material. They can see themselves not as mundane workers carrying out boring administrative or operational tasks. Rather humdrum activities become about carrying out a 'mission' or are an opportunity to engage in profound psychological development: a leader who 'sees' and confirms followers. The result is that ideas of leadership and associated material get incorporated into the internal narratives of both many leaders and some followers, attributing strong development, confirmation and climate creating powers to the leader. Because these ideas become so closely connected with narratives of oneself and/or hero-worshipping, they are often jealously guarded by both followers and leaders alike. They do so in a way that internal conversation in many cases becomes infused with themes of leadership. The result is that stories about themselves (and their identity projects) are moulded in a way that marginalizes troubling or difficult questions. If these difficult questions are occasionally asked, it is within rather constrained boundaries.

Leadership (or followership) self-talk is typically bolstered by other cognitive processes. One of the most important aspects here are processes of attribution. This entails a tendency to over-attribute either positive or negative results to leaders. They are thought to be responsible for significant outcomes, which often go far beyond the reasonable remit. This relies on a number of well-known biases of attribution. One is the fundamental attribution error – whereby we are more likely to over-value the importance of internal characteristics (rather than situational charac-teristics) on behaviour. In addition, cultural attribution biases interfere so that people from individualistic cultures such as North America or Europe are more likely to look for individual causes. This means the characteristics of leaders are often the focus of much attribution in the west. Finally, there are self-serving biases whereby individuals are more likely to attribute their own successes to individual factors. The result is that leaders are often likely to reinforce the importance of their own leadership in organizational success (instead of more situational factors including characteristics of the market, organizational structures and so on). Followers also are likely to locate successes (as well as failures) in the figure of the leader, while they ignore more complex conditions and relations. By focusing on leadership as the key causal factor, both leaders and followers are able to short-cut much of the difficult thinking and ambiguous information which is often required to make more accurate or realistic attributions (Calder 1977; Meindl 1995).

As well as an overenthusiasm for attributing positive (and negative) outcomes to the internal characteristics of a leadership, there is also a well-known tendency of individuals to focus on consistencies around ideas of leadership and to avoid any contradictions or ambiguities. Theories of cognitive dissonance point out that it is often difficult and uncomfortable for individuals to hold conflicting beliefs. This is because the existence of conflicting beliefs can create a tension, which individuals seek to reduce (often through changing an aspect of their beliefs). For instance, individuals who were part of religious cults who believed that the end of the world was coming, and then were faced with evidence that the world had indeed not ended, often adjusted their beliefs to create some degree of consistency. They might claim that they had been saved in order to spread the word (Festinger 1957). We see similar dynamics at play in the case of leadership – people who are encouraged to buy into ideas of leadership are often faced with contradictory information about the benefits and potential negative outcomes of leadership. They may be faced with evidence that despite being deemed as 'very important', leadership actually produces few results or may even create negative outcomes. Such conflicting information often does not lead people to abandon their belief in the ideals or broad importance of leadership. Rather, they disregard contrary evidence and focus on information, which confirms, or at least does not actively contradict, their ideas about leadership. In this sense, broader thinking about leadership (and its potential contradictions) is avoided. This means that individuals can side-step the resulting discomfort which so often results from cognitive contradictions. However, more than this, people develop consistent yet simplified understandings of leadership and how it works. The result is that all good things are assumed to go together and leadership is thought to be naturally connected with positive characteristics and outcomes.

## OUTCOMES

So far we have argued that leadership acts coupled with the efforts of the leadership industry result in employees curtailing independent and broader critical thinking. These entreatments to buy into ideas of leadership are often enthusiastically taken up by managers wanting to see themselves and be seen as leaders. They can often enthusiastically cling to these ideas because it provides them with a valued and meaningful sense of self (often in the face of boring or meaningless work), a sense of simple internal attribution (in the face of confusing patterns of causality) and a sense of cognitive consistency (in the face of ambiguity). But what are the results of the cognitive narrowing encouraged by discourses of leadership?

We have already highlighted many of the significant affective and cognitive benefits, which come from uncritically buying into ideas of leadership. These include bolstering self-esteem, enabling simplistic patterns of attribution and reducing cognitive dissonance. Taken together, these aspects can help individuals to reduce experiences of ambiguity and anxiety, which are often endemic in many complex organizations. By doing this, individuals can put their doubts aside and focus on developing commitment to a course of action. As well as saving themselves from doubt and cognitive tensions, individuals can garner more material benefits. This happens when individuals are able to nurture an image of themselves as committed individuals who buy into valued visions articulated by leaders and the leadership industry more generally. To appear – in talk, dress and manner – as a leader, without any signs on doubt and hesitation about one's leadership, facilitates success. To show ambivalence and doubt about whether leadership may be a career-stopper or at least a source of uncertainty and distraction, lowering confidence and work commitment. Such (apparent) commitment can help individuals to make their way through the organization by showing fuzzy 'leadership competences which now seems to be necessary in constructing a career.

In addition to helping individuals to make their way in their careers, buying into notions of leadership can also help the organization as a whole to function. This is because individuals are encouraged to put aside what can often be disruptive and difficult criticism of individual leaders or ideas of leadership more generally. This can help to get individuals to invest in ideas of leadership or visions of the leader, and build commitment to a course of action. Although the premises of this action may prove to be problematic, even irrational at times, at least notions of leadership help to organize activity. In this sense, commitment to leadership can help to facilitate an action orientation and smooth organizational functioning.

The active encouragement of leadership-induced stupidity may have some beneficial outcomes for individuals as well as the organization as a whole. But it can have a negative side as well. For individuals an irrational commitment to leadership can result in a sense of nagging disappointment. This opens up when the promises of leaders or the leadership industry become increasingly separated from the realities of managerial work in the real world. This gap between ideals and actual performances might be experienced clearly when an individual leader promises significant personal transformation to employees and followers then receive something far less lustrous. Frustrations may also follow when an individual has invested heavily in notions of leadership, which eventually appear as problematic and even self-defeating. Often this disappointment becomes more severe as an individual makes greater psychic investment in the ideas of leadership. Thus a powerful suspension of critical questioning can produce an equally powerful rebound effect. The result is jilted leadership junkies. Some seek to solve the problem by simply moving on to the next fad or fashion offered by the leadership industry. This happened when many true believers transitioned from investing in ideas of transformational leadership to notions of 'distributed', 'authentic' or 'facilitative' leadership. Others might become bitter, yet passive, cynics who simply find it hard to buy into any ideas about leadership at all – even when leadership may actually be needed for some particular pressing issue. A third group may become virulent anti-leadership activists who actively resist any attempts to create and exercise forms of leadership.

As well as creating negative outcomes for individuals, thoughtless commitment to leadership can also potentially create negative collective outcomes. By buying into ideas of leadership, organizations can become overcommitted to ideas which may prove useful in particular contexts but may prove to be lame or even destructive in other contexts. This happens when organizations cut short broader reflection and discussion about when leadership is useful, how much leadership is needed and what kind of leadership may be needed. The emphasis on leadership means that many members of an organization are relegated to being followers, who might be good at following the prompts of a leader, but are less able in independent thinking and taking initiative outside what is being envisioned by the manager. By avoiding these kinds of broader discussions that move beyond leader-driven agendas organizations often become vulnerable to the imperfections of those seen as leaders. This in turn can create highly destructive outcomes such as the loss of autonomy, the pursuit of questionable goals and the misrecognition of major issues in the organization or environment. For instance, an overly enthusiastic commitment to charismatic forms of leadership in many organizations has created a kind of 'corporate cultism' (Tourish and Pinnington 2002). Equally, an untrammeled attachment to 'facilitative' ideas of leadership which emphasize coaching and sharing of leadership responsibilities can mean organizations devote significant amounts of their resources and times to quasi-therapeutic rituals and become unable to respond sufficiently to pressing emergencies. Finally, an overriding belief in the importance of leadership (in whatever form it might appear) can lead to followers in organizations ignoring the many other forms of co-ordination, which can take the place of leadership (ranging from bureaucracy to self-managed teams to forms of professional co-ordination). This can create one-dimensional organizations where whatever the problem is leadership is seen as the answer.

## CONCLUSION

Leaders are superior to other mortals, intellectually and morally. At least this is a widely shared assumption in many discussions of leadership in both popular and academically focused literature. Leaders are thought to exercise not just cognitive prowess but also 'practical wisdom'. While we think this is certainly important, it does not capture the entire picture. In this chapter, we have argued that leadership often works through prompting stupidity in both followers as well as in leaders (or aspiring leaders). By this, we mean that leadership can cut short broader processes of independent thinking. Indeed, the very idea of leadership means a separation of people into leaders and followers and a creation or reinforcement of strongly asymmetrical relations, where the ideas, values, emotions and priorities of followers are supposed to be shaped by leaders possessing superior ideas, insights and knowledge as well as personal attributes.

We have argued that leadership can work through encouraging followers and leaders alike to refrain from complicating things with their own ideas, arguments, doubts or independent thinking, but adapt and follow a leadership formula. Thus, far from being a negative thing, the stupification prompted by leadership can actually prove to be functional. By reducing independent thinking and reflection, it may lead to positive outcomes such as common thinking, shared values and smooth operations. Individuals may be spared the anxieties of thinking for themselves or experiencing ambiguity and ambivalence about their work or career. Buying into ideas of leadership can help them craft a smooth path through their organizations and working life without too much taxing reflection, doubt, ambivalence and confusion.

We might assume that functional stupidity is largely limited to authoritarian leadership found in many cultish organizations where any hints of independent thought are strictly frowned upon. However, we have argued that the rise of transformational and facilitative modes of leadership does not necessarily result in a decline in functional stupidity. It is based on the assumption that leaders are morally, spiritually or socially superior to their followers. Followers are still encouraged to put

clear constraints on independent and critical thinking and orient themselves to responsiveness to leaders. A true follower relies heavily on the
leader to do the thinking and decision-making about the key issues, such
as visions, strategies, values, morality and identities. Subordinates are
expected to take a follower position and passively accept the broader
messages of the leader. More democratic forms of 'shared leadership' are
also not immune to such criticisms. We have argued that these forms of
leadership often result in a kind of leadership attachment whereby the
leader becomes the figure who is supposed to directly or indirectly
organize the inputs and framing of what makes a person improve. The
follower retreats from exercising critical judgment, particularly about
their leader and the basic values the leader preaches. So the more
emphasis there is on leadership, the more there are elements of followership and subordination. This marginalizes the use of critical reflection
about the activities one is being led to accomplish. In this sense,
functional stupidity is a key element of the idea of leadership and
leadership can therefore be viewed as stupidity management.

While functional stupidity may take hold through practices of leadership – there is another side of the story. Sometimes acts of leadership and
broader discourses of leadership may not be as powerful as many
assume. Instead of being taken on by individuals in organizations, ideas
about leadership are often simply grandiose talk, which the audience
treats with a mixture of mild amusement, distain and boredom. Consider
a quintessential leadership act – 'communicating a vision'. The leader is
engaged in developing and communicating the 'vision' while followers
receive the visions and are transformed by it. But in many organizations,
subordinates are not so interested, impressed or responsive. Some may be
actively hostile towards attempts to create a vision and view it as
'corporate bullshit'. Others may find the vision to be a mild distraction or
even irrelevant to the more mundane details of their day-to-day work.
Still others might entirely miss the vision. After all, organizations are full
of communications and influence processes in many directions and fuzzy
visions can easily get lost in such a morass of communication.

The crucial point here is that attempts to do leadership do not always
have the intended impact on followers. Rarely can (aspiring) leaders fully
exercise the recipes for leadership espoused by the leadership industry.
For this reason, the real stupidity may be the belief that leadership has
the large impact on organizational life we are led to believe it does. The
extent of stupification by leadership discourses probably is very different
between different organizations and people, including between managers,
professionals and other non-managerial staff. It does seem to vary less
among most representatives of the leadership industry. Perhaps leadership

talk actually stupifies the people that are most committed to it – that is members of the large and expanding leadership industry.

## REFERENCES

Alvesson, M. (2011), 'Leader as saints: leadership through moral peak performance', in M. Alvesson and A. Spicer (eds), *Metaphors we Lead by: Understanding Leadership in the Real World*, London: Routledge, pp. 51–75.

Alvesson, M. (2013) *The Triumph of Emptiness*, Oxford: Oxford University Press.

Alvesson, M. and D. Kärreman (2007), 'Unraveling HRM: identity, ceremony, and control in a management consultancy firm', *Organization Science*, **18** (4), 711–23.

Alvesson, M. and K. Sköldberg (2009), *Reflexive Methodology*, London: Sage.

Alvesson, M. and A. Spicer (eds) (2011), *Metaphors We Lead By: Understanding Leadership in the Real World*, London: Routledge.

Alvesson, M. and A. Spicer (2012), 'A stupidity-based theory of organizations', *Journal of Management Studies*, **49** (7), 1194–220.

Alvesson M and S. Sveningsson (2003), 'Good visions, bad micro-management and ugly ambiguity: contradictions of (non) leadership in knowledge-intensive organization', *Organization Studies*, **24** (6), 961–88.

Alvesson, M. and H. Willmott (2012), *Making Sense of Management*, London: Sage.

Bass, B.M. and P. Steidlmeier (1999), 'Ethics, character and authentic transformational leadership behaviour', *Leadership Quarterly*, **10** (2), 181–218.

Boltanski, L. and L. Thévenot (2006), *On Justification*, Princeton, NJ: Princeton University Press.

Brunsson, N. (1982), 'The irrationality of action and action rationality: decisions, ideologies and organizational actions', *Journal of Management Studies*, **19** (1), 29–44.

Brunsson, N. (1985), *The Irrational Organization*, Chichester: Wiley.

Calder B. (1977), 'An attribution theory of leadership', in B.M. Staw and G.R. Salanick (eds), *New Directions in Organizational Behaviour*, Chicago, IL: St Clair.

Dillard, J.F. and L. Ruchala (2005), 'The rules are no game: from instrumental rationality to administrative evil', *Accounting, Auditing and Accountability Journal*, **18** (5), 608–30.

Dixon, J.F. (1994), *On the Psychology of Military Incompetence*, London: Pimlico.

Festinger, L. (1957), *A Theory of Cognitive Dissonance*, Stanford, CA: Sanford University Press.

Gemmill, G. and J. Oakley (1992), 'Leadership: an alienating social myth', *Human Relations*, **45 (2)**, 113–29.

Greenleaf, R.K. (1977), *Servant Leadership: A Journey in Legitimate Power and Greatness*, Mahwah, NJ: Paulist Press.

Grint K. (2005b), 'Problems, problems, problems: the social construction of "leadership"', *Human Relations*, **58** (11), 1467–94.

Habermas, J. (1984), *The Theory of Communicative Action, Vol. 1*, London: Heinemann.

Hartnell C. and F. Walumbwa (2011), 'Transformational leadership and organizational culture', in N. Ashkanasy, C. Wilderon and M. Peterson (eds), *The Handbook of Organizational Culture and Climate*, 2nd edn, Thousand Oaks, CA: SAGE, pp. 225–48.

Heifetz, R.A. and D.L. Laurie (1997), 'The work of leadership', *Harvard Business Review*, **75** (1), 124–34.

Houghton, J.P., C.P. Neck and C.C. Manz (2003), 'Self leadership and super leadership: the art and heart of creating shared leadership in teams', in C.L. Pearce and J.A. Conger, Shared Leadership: *Reframing the Hows and Whys of Leadership*, Thousand Oaks, CA: Sage, pp. 123–140.

Huzzard, T. and S. Spoelstra (2011), 'Leaders as gardeners: leadership through facilitating growth', in M. Alvesson and A. Spicer (eds) *Metaphors We Lead By: Understanding Leadership in the Real World*, London: Routledge, pp. 76–95.

Jackall R. (1988), *Moral Mazes: Bureaucracy and Managerial World*, Oxford: Oxford University Press.

Kets de Vries, M. (1980), *The Irrational Organization*, London: Tavistock.

Manz, C.C. (1998), *The Leadership Wisdom of Jesus: Practical Lessons for Today*, San Francisco, CA: Berret-Koelher.

McKenna, B., D. Rooney and K.B. Roal (2009), 'Wisdom principles as a meta-theoretical basis for evaluating leadership', *Leadership Quarterly*, **20** (2), 177–90.

Meindl J. (1995), 'The romance of leadership as a follower-centric theory: a social constructionist approach', *Leadership Quarterly*, **6** (3), 329–41.

Meyer, J.W. and B. Rowan (1977), 'Institutionalized organizations: formal structure as myth and ceremony', *American Journal of Sociology*, **83** (2), 340–63.

Ronell, A. (2002), *Stupidity*, Chicago, IL: University of Illinois Press.

Sashkin M. (2004), 'Transformational leadership approaches: a review and synthesis', in J. Antonakis, A.T. Cianciolo and R.J. Sternberg (eds), *The Nature of Leadership*, Thousand Oaks, CA: SAGE, pp. 171–96.

Spicer, A. (2011), 'Leaders as commanders: leadership through creating clear direction', in M. Alvesson and A. Spicer (eds), *Metaphors We Lead By: Understanding Leadership in the Real World*, London: Routledge, pp. 118–37.

Spoelstra, S. (2010), 'Business miracles', *Culture and Organizations*, **16** (1), 87–101.

Stanovich, K.E. (2002), 'Rationality, intelligence and levels of analysis in cognitive science: is dysrationalia possible?', in R.J. Sternberg (ed.), *Why Smart People Can Be So Stupid*, New Haven, CT: Yale University Press, pp. 124–58.

Sternberg, R.J. (eds) (2002), *Why Smart People Can Be So Stupid*, New Haven, CT: Yale University Press.

ten Bos, R. (2007), 'The vitality of stupidity', *Social Epistemology*, **21** (2), 139–50.

Tourish D. and A. Pinnington (2002), 'Transformational leadership, corporate cultism and the spirituality paradigm: an unholy trinity in the workplace?', *Human Relations*, **55** (2), 147–52.

Tourish, D. and N. Vatcha (2005), 'Charismatic leadership and corporate cultism at Enron: The elimination of dissent, the promotion of conformity an organizational collapse', *Leadership*, **1** (4), 455–80.

Zbaracki, M. (1998), 'The rhetoric and reality of total quality management', *Administrative Science Quarterly*, **43** (3), 602–36.

# 12. Vain and vainglorious leaders?

## Alf Rehn

## INTRODUCTION

Vanity of vanities, saith the Preacher, vanity of vanities; all is vanity.
What profit hath a man of all his labor which he taketh under the sun?

Ecclesiastes

Is leadership a vanity? Or, more to the point, is there a connection between leadership and vanity, and if so, what is this connection? Leaders are of course supposed to be above such petty things – particularly if we subscribe to the notion that the term leadership refers to the manner in which special individuals can influence and enlist others into achieving something grander than what is possible for an individual. If leadership is a process of social influence where those who succeed will be charismatic, wise and emotionally intelligent (see, for example, Goleman et al. 2002), then vanity would seem to be of no use to understanding it, except as an example of barriers to leadership and what not to do. Still, most of us have come across people in a leadership position who are nothing if not vain and vainglorious – although leadership scholars tend to quickly dismiss these as 'mere managers' and not really examples of leadership at all (see Bass and Bass 2008).

On the other hand, vanity is connected to striving for excellence and to pride, both aspects of business life that can be exceptionally important for leadership. While only very few would see constant primping and attention to one's looks (for instance, vanity towards one's own image) as a desirable treat in a leader, just as many would probably agree that a leader who does not particularly care about the end-result of a project (for instance, pride in one's accomplishments) is not really a leader. In this manner – where leaders are expected to look good, but not be too obsessed with being good-looking, vanity may well be connected to instances of great leadership, at least if this vanity is focused in the right way. For instance, the near-beatification of Steve Jobs has often talked in adulatory tones about his attention to detail and his monomaniacal pursuit of getting products 'just so'. One instance of this can be seen in Jobs' insistence that when the iPhone was first introduced at a WWDC (such as the Apple Worldwide Developers Conference) keynote, the accompanying image on his slide-deck had to portray the phone with the time set to 9:42 AM, which was the exact time it was unveiled. In other words, Jobs did not want to stand on stage with an image of a phone with the clock set to the wrong time. This, in the mythology of Apple, is often presented as proof of an attention to detail and a desire for excellence. However, could this not also be seen as a case of vanity, of not wanting to look anything less than 'perfect'?

Vanity, or vainglory, is commonly understood as a preoccupation with the self, most particularly with the presentation of the self (Woodforde 1995). It can also be understood as an excessive belief in one's own capacities, and is through this connected to pride and even hubris (Dyson 2006). In both cases, the person afflicted by vanity will strive to carefully manage his/her image, appearance and also hold a very high opinion of the same – and his/her abilities. In popular culture, and thus popular discourse, vanity is often represented through the character of the vain woman, one who needs to continuously look her best, even to the point of comedy or moral flaw. The vain woman is one who would not help a person in need if this might damage her manicure or her haute couture outfit, or one who is so preoccupied with fixing her makeup that she does not notice she is stepping into a puddle or in front of a car. As such, vanity is in popular culture and media connected to both a moral flaw and a comic ludicrousness. This is further heightened if the vain person in question is a man, as female vanity is often seen as a normal feminine trait somewhat exaggerated, the vain man is seen as much more of an aberration. Egoistical, prone to hubris and at the same time comically focused on his own looks, the vain man is a stock character in popular culture, and always as either a villain or a foil (Toplin 1993).

Through such iconic representations, vanity has in modern culture become both a moral flaw and a somewhat silly affectation. The vain person is either unethical due to his or her solipsistic worldview, or a frivolous character not to be taken seriously. In both cases, vanity represents something of an antithesis to leadership. Whereas the latter is serious, the former is frivolous. Where leadership is about seeing the big picture and involving people, vanity is about focusing solely on the self, at the cost of everything else. However, the usual manner in which this is discussed – or assumed – is still a far cry from how the sin of vanity was originally brought into the discussions of human capacity and humanity's capacity for frailty.

# THE THEOLOGY OF VAINGLORY

Vainglory. The seventh struggle facing us is that with the spirit of vainglory – this multifaceted, deceitful and subtle passion, which often is very difficult to notice and recognize, and to protect yourself from. Other passions are plain and unvaried, but this one is multifaceted and attacks the warrior of Christ from all sides: during his struggle and even after he has achieved victory. Vainglory attempts to wound the warrior through all manner of ways: his clothing, and his physical build, and walk, and voice, and being well read, and his work, and his vigilance, and fasting, and praying, and solitary life, and his knowledge, and education, and silence, and submissiveness, and humility, and benevolence. It is akin to a dangerous rock hiding below the waves, which inflicts a sudden disastrous wreck to the seafarers when they least expect it. (St. John Cassian, The Institutes of the Cenobia and the Remedies for the Eight Principal Vices)

I will in this chapter argue that vanity, which at times has been known as vainglory, is a concept and a notion that has a long intellectual and leadership history, but which has transmuted in late capitalism. Where it was once seen as a sin and a warning not to elevate oneself above ones position, today it has almost the opposite meaning – although it is rarely referred to as vanity any longer. What was once the sin of vanity might today be the necessity of cultivating a personal brand ...

In theology, particularly within Christian thought, vanity is no mere character flaw, but instead a sin of the highest order. In the original list of eight 'evil thoughts' listed by Evagrius Ponticus, κενοδοξία (boasting) was listed, and as this was translated into Latin – greatly thanks to St John Cassian – it was recast as *vanagloria*. In Pope Gregory I's later, more well-known list of seven deadly sins, vanity was positioned as one aspect of pride – the most dangerous sin of them all, as it is seen as the root of the others. Pride and vanity is also tied to the figure of the fallen angel Lucifer – the light-bringer, the morning star – who saw himself as equal to God. Through this, vanity (and pride) is connected to the demonic, the antithesis of the life divine. In Orthodox thought, on the other hand, vanity is on the list of the eight main passions. Here too the potential demonic character of vanity is emphasized, as these passions are at times referred to as being both sinful and diabolical.

The sin of vanity, then, is connected to rebelling against God, and to forget one's place in the order of things. A person driven by the passion of vainglory will not heed the fact that they are a humble, trivial agglomeration of mortal matter, no more than a speck of dust in the grand scheme of things. To think of oneself as something more is to think that Man can ascend without God, and is thus a dangerous heresy – as nothing is possible without God. Through vanity, and pride, Man can then give in to the other sins. Why not be gluttonous, haven't you deserved it? Sloth makes sense, for why work harder when one is already so great? And so on.

Medieval thought was terrified of vanity as it unleashed the possibility of unbridled individualism, rather than prostrating yourself before the divine mystery; not only when it came to the acts and beliefs of the great unwashed, but also when it came to the leaders of men. In medieval texts – all of which were more or less religious texts – the necessity of leaders staying humble in the face of God and the Church is a constant motif. Interestingly, this occurs around the time that trade, and the organizational and managerial processes this engenders, starts to develop greatly in Europe. In many ways, business – a process through which value is often created out of what seems to be thin air – would have been seen as a challenge to the ordered system of the Church. Where one saw value as springing from merely one fount, that of the Godhead, the other started to subtly indicate that value might also be brought through something as pedestrian as clever management of risk and resources (see Langholm 1992).

Looking at the notion in the 21st century, the theological notions of vanity might seem somewhat outdated and irrelevant. However, it is important to note that vanity has been part of the discussion of what it means to be a good person, or a good leader, for a very long time. The story of king Cnut the Great (Knútr inn ríki, 985–1035), who took his throne to the seaside in order to command back the waves, has been told and retold either as proof of the vanity of kings or a cunning display of modesty in the face of vain courtiers for a very long time. Similarly, warnings against the sin of vanity and pride play a major role in the literary tradition of *specula principum*, works of instruction for rulers and princes-to-be. While we might no longer subscribe to the notion that a vain leader is an abomination unto God, the fact that the vanity of leaders has been a topic for discussion for a long time cannot be denied.

## THE VAIN LEADER

The key argument, then, of this chapter is that vanity is neither absent from modern leadership nor just a pathology within the same. Rather than arguing the fairly trivial point that leaders, by and large, should be above such human frailties, I will argue that we can say something about what it means to be a leader in a media-infused, post-industrial age by observing leadership through the concept of vanity. Where the theological and the historical approach to this issue was to warn people away from a (potentially deadly) sin, I will argue that the modern case is more complex, with vanity being both a problem and a proposed solution.

Within the scope of this volume, it is important to note that I do not claim that vanity is an emotion per se, but rather an example of what I previously have referred to as socio-moral feelings (see Rehn and Lindahl 2011). Whereas you would not normally say you feel vain in the same manner you would say you feel happy or angry, except perhaps in a self-depreciating way, you can feel exceptionally proud, worried about how you appear and so on, which emphasizes the relational nature of vanity. We often feel as if we can recognize foibles such as vanity and pride in others. Vanity might thus be seen as an emotional response to specific social figurations (see Elias 1969), in part as a learned response to the pressures of establishing a social role. If, for instance, a leader is socialized into a culture where expectations are to keep up a perfect exterior at all times, this can create a pattern of focusing on appearance, coupled with an emotional response when this appearance is threatened or potentially questioned. Such behaviours may then be interpreted in their surroundings as vanity. This somewhat circumspect definition is to note that vanity – as a nexus of social behaviours and emotional responses – is irreducibly social and relational. Whereas it is of course possible to be happy or stupid (see Chapter 11) in isolation, vanity demands at least an imagined audience, an imagined social context.

Within the scope of leadership, this context comes quite naturally. Managers (who I here assume will often at least strive towards being seen as leaders) are in most organizations in a position where they are continuously under the gaze of those they manage/lead. When it comes to chief executives, managing directors and CEOs, this is enhanced further. With the increasing mediatization of society in general and business in particular (Lundby 2009), the manager/leader is not only subjected to the gaze of his or her own organization, but caught in the eye of media and thus the general public. In such a situation, appearing slovenly or unkempt will cause comments in media and may even affect stock prices (see Chen and Meindl 1991; Sinha et al. 2012), and may also be looked upon unfavourably by the organization. For managers at somewhat lower rungs of the corporate ladder, the focus may be less intense, but at the same time the pressures may be greater. Although it is exceptionally difficult to measure this with any rigour, there is ample evidence that physical image plays a role in how managers are viewed, and can be assumed to at least affect organizational matters such as career progression (see for example Heilman and Saruwatari 1979).

There is thus some pressure on managers to manage their image, even when we are talking about such superficial matters as looks – something that I am here taking as extending to, for example, presentation materials and media appearance. It is also important to note that this does not necessarily mean that such attention and management is a bad thing – quite the contrary. Whereas one can question whether physical beauty should be noticed or cared about as an aspect of leadership, the skilful handling of, for example, media and the capacity to make a convincing presentation are obviously something more than mere affectations.

The leader paying close attention to, for example, the typography on her PowerPoint-deck could thus be seen both as vain – stressing above everything else the presentation of the self, even through something like type – and as exhibiting a critical management skill in a mediatized age. Whereas a manager in the 1950s might have been expected to live up to a certain image (for example, polished shoes, conservative suit and subdued tie), the contemporary manager is placed in a much more complex position when it comes to the presentation of the self. Image work, which in the age of 'organization man' (Whyte 1956) was a question of following a set of well-established rules regarding dress and decorum, is today both more complex and more externalized. The modern leader is not only expected to carry herself in a manner befitting someone who may at any point in time become the subject of a media piece, she is further expected to maintain a professional image in the materials she uses, and even present herself in for example social media in a manner befitting a leader. The umbrella term for all this, and for image work in post-industrial society, is 'a personal brand' and the cultivation of this is increasingly seen as critical for the leader who wishes to be taken seriously.

With this as a background, one could argue that vanity – of differing forms – is no longer merely a character flaw in leaders, but that a measure of the same is in fact expected from someone wishing to make a mark in an age of mediatized business discourse and ever-present personal brands. Vanity, then, would be something of a vice counted among leadership requirements, a sin that the contemporary leader needs to learn how to negotiate. Too little of it will make you seem old-fashioned, too much will again indicate an egoist at best and a sociopath at worst. In this manner, understanding the role of vanity in leadership is less a question of understanding how leaders can be vain, and more a question of understanding the image work that the contemporary leader is expected to engage in.

# ON PERSONAL BRANDING AND SELF-IDOLATRY

The sin of *vanagloria* was the sin of pride, and boasting, and creating an idol of oneself. Curiously, these are all aspects of image work that a modern leader is supposed not only to embody, but also to actively cultivate, at least if we believe the bevy of books on why the new leaders will be people who take charge of their own personal brand and leverage this into fame and fortune. As examples, consider the bestselling advice books of Gary Vaynerchuck, who argues we should all *Crush It!: Why NOW Is the Time to Cash In on Your Passion* (Vaynerchuck 2009), Seth Godin whose *Tribes* has the subtitle *We Need You to Lead Us* (Godin 2008), or Dan Schawbel's paean to success in an age of social media, *Me 2.0* (Schawbel 2010) – a title which could be seen as communicating the very essence of the contemporary vogue for personal branding. Leaders, in this context, are not just people who have managed to master the art of leading people, but also individuals who have recast themselves into a brand, into an idea, into a 2.0 version. This movement was started by the quintessential self-promoter Tom Peters, who in the August 1997 issue of *Fast Company* wrote an article by the name of 'The Brand Called You', which argued we should all become 'the CEO of Me Inc.'. Following from this, a number of gurus, many driven by the inexorable rise of social media, have argued that one exists only insofar as one is present in the never-ending new media cycle, and that success (of any kind) could be measured in click-throughs, retweets, 'likes' and the likes.

Through this, the notion of 'visibility' (or, even more disturbingly, 'virality' or 'shareability') has become a key element in how importance in a mediatized world is understood. If you are not followed, if you are not retweeted, if you are not interesting enough to have 'klout', you are not a true leader. Of particular interest here is the latter term – the Klout score. This is a commercial measurement, pioneered and controlled by the company behind klout.com, and is an increasingly popular way of measuring influence online, increasingly used in hiring processes – even for management positions. In May 2012, Seth Stevenson wrote an article in *Wired* with the title 'What Your Klout Score Really Means'. This article details – as part of its overall argument – the story of Sam Fiorella, who after being shortlisted for a VP position at a marketing agency is given short shrift after it comes out that his Klout score was a measly 34, and a person with the far more impressive 67 is hired instead.

In this manner, *vanagloria* is looking less like a sin and more like a demand – without a modicum of branding, bragging and braggadocio the contemporary leader can quickly be sidelined. As such, the modern leader may be caught in a particularly tricky dilemma. If you choose a path of modesty and being a listening, facilitating leader, or what in the leadership literature has at times been referred to as 'servant leadership' (Russell and Stone 2002), you may well receive accolades from those working closest with you, but at the same time your personal brand may suffer from not having assertively positioned yourself as a visible leader (such as you not having 'crushed it' in the frat-boy parlance of Gary Vaynerchuck, one of the gurus in the field). Still, if you choose to fully assert brand 'You', you may well lose the respect and followership of your closest collaborators. Vanity, then, has become something that needs to be carefully managed.

Were this merely a case of individually dealing with whether to engage with social media or not, the issue would not be particularly difficult, as this then would be a matter of platforms and where one wishes to engage. The problem emerges when the aforementioned mediatization of business positions strong personal brands as the *sine qua non* for the contemporary leader. Looking to the characters (sic) most often used in popular media as exemplars of leadership, we see a clear movement away from valorizing the industrialist – a traditionally minded leader with a long-term perspective – towards celebrating the media- and sound bite (such as Twitter)-friendly personal brand. Where an aspiring manager in the 1940s might have looked up to Alfred Sloan or Walt Disney, and his colleague in the 1970s might have idolized Thomas Watson Junior or Bill Hewlett, the contemporary careerist is more likely to revere people such as Richard Branson (who has studiously worked at his brand as a rebel and adventurer, penning several books that champion his self-image) or Oprah (who has named a magazine after herself and worked hard to make her first (almost only) name stand out as a key brand signifier); or perhaps, most obviously of all, Steve Jobs.

## THE STRANGE CASE OF STEVE JOBS

Looking at the points I have tried to make so far, the perhaps most telling case of them all would be that of one Steven Paul 'Steve' Jobs (1955–2011), and particularly the manner in which his image work has been interpreted and idolized in popular discourse – valorized in a plethora of books such as the mega-bestselling biography (Isacsson 2011), magazine articles and general punditry. Steve Jobs stands as perhaps the greatest personal brand in business at the moment of writing, with a fair chance of being seen as a historically great business leader. This stems mostly from the undeniable fact that he engineered and executed one of the most exceptional corporate turn-arounds ever, saving the beleaguered Apple Inc. from bankruptcy and making it one of the world's most valuable corporations, at least up until 2012.

While not a great believer in social media – he did not tweet, but if he had, his Klout would have been astronomical – Jobs was, however, a master of controlling the image of both his company and himself. In his later, more famous years, he was never photographed in anything else except his uniform of a black turtleneck sweater, jeans and sneakers (he favoured New Balance 991's). His insistence on controlling photographs of himself was legendary, as was his favourite image, Albert Watson's now iconic monochrome close-up (used both in Apple's marketing and as the cover of Isacsson's authorized biography). Jobs was also famous for being exceptionally details-focused when it came to product design and user experience, something that culminated in the closely choreographed 'Steve-notes' at the WWDCs (Apple Worldwide Developers Conferences).

These latter stage-shows deserve to be noted, as they in a sense embody the notion of the CEO embodying the corporation, and also stand as the acme of corporate κενοδοξία. Access to the keynotes at WWDC is closely monitored and controlled. It is widely understood that the keynote is the culmination of the conference, and also the stage for the big 'reveals' (such as the place where the newest gear will be introduced). Everything is geared towards a singular moment, and building up excitement towards this. The Steve-note proper was often (but not always) opened by Jobs, after which other Apple personnel or close collaborators were given stage-time, but the key presentations and the most important introductions were always handled by Jobs himself. The keynotes were accompanied by highly polished graphics and demonstrations, all designed to convey a feeling of awe towards Apple's products. The Steve-notes were also steeped in ritual. For instance, one of the highlights was the feigned end of the keynote interrupted by Jobs intoning 'One more thing … ' in order to reveal a particularly impressive product, a moment most of the faithful waited breathlessly for.

The Steve-notes are of course not the only instances of Jobs's work at Apple that could be interpreted as vanity. As the company worked on finishing the first version of OS X, Jobs was overseeing the design with what might best be described as monomaniacal attention (Isacsson 2011), insisting that every aspect had to be perfect. One telling instance of this was insisting that the buttons (such as interface elements that the user interacts with when for example saving a document) should be more beautiful than anyone else's. In fact, when presenting Aqua, the user interface in question, he stated: 'We made the buttons on the screen look so good you'll want to lick them' (quoted in *Fortune*, 24 January, 2000). Vic Gundotra, senior VP (engineering) at Google, retells the following about being called up on Sunday by Jobs:

> 'So Vic, we have an urgent issue, one that I need addressed right away. I've already assigned someone from my team to help you, and I hope you can fix this tomorrow' said Steve.

> 'I've been looking at the Google logo on the iPhone and I'm not happy with the icon. The second O in Google doesn't have the right yellow gradient. It's just wrong and I'm going to have Greg fix it tomorrow. Is that okay with you?' Vic Gundotra, posted on Google+, 25 August 2011

Many have taken examples such as these as proof positive of Steve Jobs being an exceptional CEO, with an almost supernatural feel for user experience and a similarly superhuman attention to detail. In the context of this chapter, I would argue that these examples also point to something we might call productive vanity (such as a case of being obsessed with presenting a perfect façade and managing to channel this into a dynamic engagement with product development). Rather than condemning Steve Jobs for being vain (although he may well have been), I suggest that his attention to the presentation of the self – as suggested by his adoption of a specific uniform, choreographing his public appearances and micro-managing photographers – also extended to wanting the corporation he led to exhibit a perfect outward face as well. This, then, extended to the look of the products as well – to a point that at times beggars belief. According to the authorized biography by Walter Isacsson (2011), things that Jobs insisted on being perfect included:

1. The shade of grey used on the restroom signs at the Apple Stores.
2. The aesthetics of the circuit-board of the Mac-computers, something a user would rarely if ever see due to them being inside the casing.
3. The kind of wood used on the display tables inside Apple Stores.
4. And, disturbingly, the masks for oxygen he had to use while in terminal care, and which he initially refused to use as they were too ugly.[/nl]

What the case of Steve Jobs, and the near-beatification of him, tells is a tale of vanity and pride being something that may have gone from a sin, to a tacit demand on managers, to an increasingly open positive characteristic for leaders. Seeing as how Steve Jobs is by now almost routinely presented as an icon to follow and/or emulate, the notion that leaders should not be vain needs to be revisited – or critiqued. However, herein also lies the shadow of what happens when vanity – individual or ascribed – is elevated to a normal, even necessary state of affairs, when leaders are supposed to live out their self-image and craft stories of themselves in order to be seen as truly great.

## THE CULT OF PERSONALITY

The perhaps most extreme form of vanity is the cult of personality, where the image of the leader becomes idealized to the point of worship – effectively realizing the worst fears of medieval theology. Such cults can be created by leaders themselves, cast upon them by followers or formed through media images and public discourse. For instance, while it is undoubtedly true that the bloodline of Kim Il-sung, Kim Jong-il and Kim Jong-un built a cult of personality for themselves, the strange case of the idolization of Steve Jobs seems to be more a media construction than anything else, and it is not entirely clear whether it should be understood in this fashion. This said, understanding cults of personality give us a point of reference as to what can happen at the extremes of vanity in leadership.

An exceptional case, perhaps the most exceptional case in modern times, of this kind of extreme and institutionalized vanity is that of Saparmurat Niyazov (1940–2006), leader of Turkmenistan between 1990 and 2006. As this former Chairman of the Supreme Soviet of the Turkmen Soviet Socialist Republic engineered the declaration of independence for the country, he started styling himself as 'Türkmenbaşy', which stands for 'leader of the Turkmens', although his fuller title was 'His Excellency Saparmurat Türkmenbaşy, President of Turkmenistan and Chairman of the Cabinet of Ministers'. As Türkmenbasy he went on to forming the new state in the image he felt most correct, combining traditional notions with a generous helping of self-worship. A key element here was the writing and later large-scale adoption of the Ruhnama as a key text for the nation. The book, which combines poetry (not all of which was written by Niyazov), aphorisms and aggressively rewritten histories of Turkmenistan and Niyazov, was originally meant as 'merely' guidance for Turkmen youth, but eventually turned up in everything from job interviews and driving tests. Its teaching also started phasing out things such as algebra and science in schools.

Interestingly, this is not even close to the most bizarre move of Niyazov. Arguably, this title should go to his renaming of the months and the days of the week. The latter's renaming might be seen as somewhat odd – with for example Tuesday becoming 'young day' (Ýaşgün) and Thursday 'justice day' (Sogapgün) – but it was the renaming of the months that was more telling. September was renamed Ruhnama, for the 'holy book', and December became Bitaraplyk (Independence). April was clearly an important month, as it now became Gurbansoltan, named after Niyazov's mother. In addition, cities were renamed – Krasnovodsk became Türkmenbaşy – schools and airports, which often got the names of close family members of Niyazov.

One of the more exceptional vanities created in this vein is a 12-metre high gold-plated statue of Saparmurat Niyazov himself. The status, which was placed on top of the Neutrality Arch in Ashgabat (now dismantled and moved), was designed to rotate 360° so that it would always face the sun. As the Arch was one of the highest buildings in the area, this meant that the golden idol of the leader was continuously towering over the city, basking in the sun. A similar statue was built for the Ruhnama, which opened its cover every night at eight, and play out a recorded message with teachings. No wonder, really, as Niyazov in 2006 stated that he would converse with God/Allah and that he could now ratify that a person who has read the book three times would be ensured a place in heaven.

It would be easy to see all this as merely insanity, or to laugh at it as a case of leadership pathologies. However, another way to see this would be as a logical if extreme continuation of the notion that a leader should build a 'brand' of themselves, or that a leader should engage in storytelling that enables them to transcend individual achievement. While I by this do not wish to argue that charismatic leadership (Yukl 1999) will lead to cults of personality, nor that notions of storytelling in leadership (Denning 2005) can be implicated in cases of such cults, it is important to note the extreme points while trying to understand how notions of contemporary leadership spread.

## LEADERSHIP AT VANITY FAIR

Almost five thousand years ago, there were pilgrims walking to the Celestial City, as these two honest persons are: and Beelzebub, Apollyon, and Legion, with their companions, perceiving by the path that the pilgrims made, that their way to the city lay through this town of Vanity, they contrived here to set up a fair; a fair wherein, should be sold all sorts of vanity, and that it should last all the year long. Therefore at this fair are all such merchandise sold, as houses, lands, trades, places, honours, preferments, titles, countries, kingdoms, lusts, pleasures, and delights of all sorts, as whores, bawds, wives, husbands, children, masters, servants, lives, blood, bodies, souls, silver, gold, pearls, precious stones, and what not.

And, moreover, at this fair there is at all times to be seen juggling cheats, games, plays, fools, apes, knaves, and rogues, and that of every kind.

(John Bunyan, *The Pilgrim's Progress*)

What I have tried to indicate in this chapter and through the vignettes is that vanity needs to be reassessed in an age of mediatized business, and that many phenomena that are today highlighted as part of the modern leaders toolkit (for example, social media, personal branding and story-telling) need to be analysed from the perspective of vanity as well. This is not in order to ridicule or belittle, but rather to form a fuller picture. My aim in this chapter has not been to claim that vanity is bad and should be excised from leadership, but rather than the contemporary leader (and possibly the historical one as well) needs to balance the productive and the pathological aspects of the same.

In my earlier work, I have discussed how matters we often see as pure moral goods, such as the case of reflectivity in research, can in fact be seen as cases of vanity (Rehn 2009). Here, I am in a sense turning this argument around, stating that at least partial attention to vanities such as for example Klout-scores and the presentation of the self can be positive and even necessary in a modern leadership context.

While I ended in a case of personality cults, this is not to suggest that the attention paid to for example Steve Jobs would end in such, but rather to indicate that issues such as storytelling and paying attention to the aesthetics of presentation can lead us down a number of paths, and that both blanket denials and overeager boosting of 'productive vanity' will, in all likelihood, lead us astray.

In Bunyan's *The Pilgrim's Progress*, a Christian allegory that is often seen as one of the most important works in English literature, Vanity Fair – not to be confused with Thackeray's satirical novel from 1848 – was the worldliest place of them all, a lethally dangerous place for those pure of heart (the hero Christian's companion Faithful was executed here). However, it was not without potential for salvation – Hopeful joins the progress in this very same place. Something similar may be said about the vanity fair that is contemporary business life. Vanity may be a sin, but it may also lead to a strange kind of beatification. Exhibit too little, and you are unprofessional. Exhibit too much, and you may still lead a country or the world's most successful company. Like it or not, the vain leader may have become a fellow traveller for leadership, a constant companion in an age of personal brands and mediatized business.

# REFERENCES

Bass, B.M. and R. Bass (2008), *The Bass Handbook of Leadership: Theory, Research, and Managerial Applications*, New York: Free Press.

Bunyan, J. (1678–79 [1965]), *The Pilgrim's Progress from This World to That Which Is to Come*, London: Penguin Books.

Cassian, St J. (420–429 [2000]), *The Institutes of the Cenobia and the Remedies for the Eight Principal Vices*, Mahwah, NJ: Newman Press of the Paulist Press.

Chen, C. and J. Meindl (1991), 'The construction of leadership images in the popular press: the case of Donald Burr and People Express', *Administrative Science Quarterly*, **36** (4), 521–51.

Denning, S. (2005), *The Leader's Guide to Storytelling: Mastering the Art and Discipline of Business Narrative*, San Francisco, CA: Jossey-Bass.

Dyson, M.E. (2006), *Pride*, Oxford: Oxford University Press.

Elias, N. (1969), *The Civilizing Process, Vol. I: The History of Manners*, Oxford: Blackwell.

Godin, S. (2008), *Tribes: We Need You To Lead Us*, New York: Penguin Books.

Goleman, D., R.E. Boyatzis and A. McKee (2002), *Primal Leadership: Realizing the Power of Emotional Intelligence*, Cambridge, MA: Harvard Business Press.

Heilman, M.E. and L.R. Saruwatari (1979), 'When beauty is beastly: the effects of appearance and sex on evaluations of job applicants for managerial and nonmanagerial jobs', *Organizational Behavior and Human Performance*, **23** (3), 360–72.

Isacsson, W. (2011), *Steve Jobs*, New York: Simon & Schuster.

Langholm, O. (1992), *Economics in the Medieval Schools. Wealth, Exchange, Value, Money and Usury according to the Paris Theological Tradition, 1200–1350*, Leiden, Netherlands: E.J. Brill.

Lundby, K. (2009), *Mediatization: Concept, Changes, Consequences*, New York: Peter Lang.

Peters, T. (1997), 'The brand called You', *Fast Company*, **10** (10), accessed at www.fastcompany.com/28905/brand-called-you.

Rehn, A. (2009), 'The false coin of reflection? Contributions, reflection and the economic logics of academia', *Tamara Journal for Critical Organization Inquiry*, **7** (3), 88–97.

Rehn, A. and M. Lindahl (2011), 'Leadership and the "right to respect": on honour and shame in emotionally charged management settings', *European Journal of International Management*, **5** (1), 62–79.

Russell, R. and A. Stone (2002), 'A review of servant leadership attributes: developing a practical model', *Leadership & Organization Development Journal*, **23** (3), 145–57.

Schawbel, D. (2010), *Me 2.0*, New York: Kaplan.

Sinha, P., K. Inkson and J. Barker (2012), 'Committed to a failing strategy: celebrity CEO, intermediaries, media and stakeholders in a co-created drama', *Organization Studies*, **33** (2), 223–45.

Stevenson, S. (2012), 'What your klout score really means', *Wired*, 20.05, accessed at www.wired.com/business/2012/04/ff_klout/all/1.

Toplin, R.B. (1993), *Hollywood as Mirror: Changing Views of Outsiders and Enemies in American Movies*, Westport, CT: Praeger.

Vaynerchuck, G. (2009), *Crush It!: Why NOW Is the Time to Cash In on Your Passion*, New York: HarperCollins.

*Wired* (2012), May, accessed at www.wired.com/business/2012/04/ff_klout/all/1.

Whyte, W. (1956), *The Organization Man*, New York: Simon & Schuster.

Woodforde, J. (1995), *The History of Vanity*, Stroud: Alan Sutton Publishing.

Yukl, G. (1999), 'An evaluation of conceptual weaknesses in transformational and charismatic leadership theories', *The Leadership Quarterly*, **10** (2), 285–305.

# Index